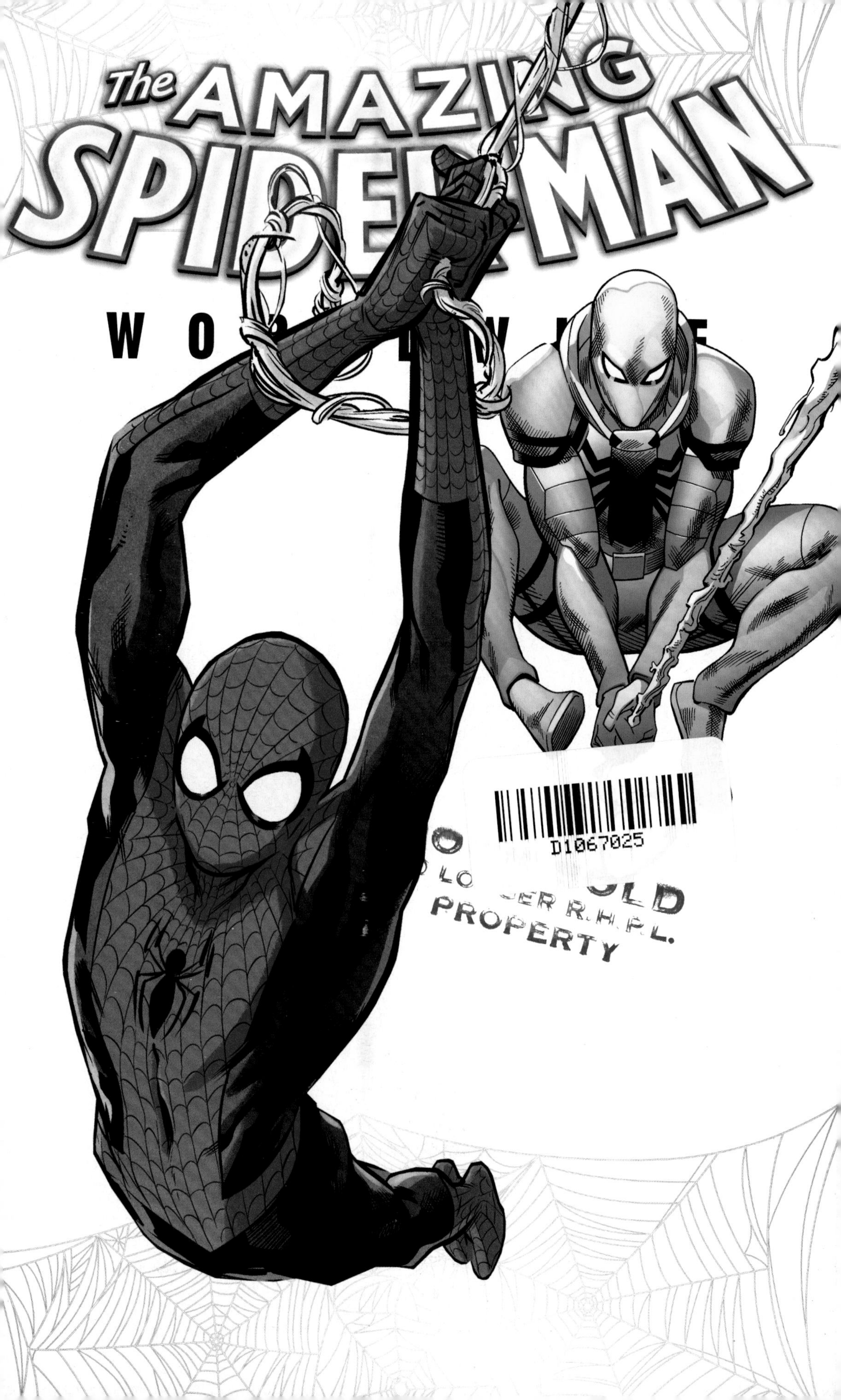
The AMAZING SPIDER-MAN

COLLECTION EDITOR: **JENNIFER GRÜNWALD**
ASSISTANT EDITOR: **CAITLIN O'CONNELL**
ASSOCIATE MANAGING EDITOR: **KATERI WOODY**
EDITOR, SPECIAL PROJECTS: **MARK D. BEAZLEY**

VP PRODUCTION & SPECIAL PROJECTS: **JEFF YOUNGQUIST**
SVP PRINT, SALES & MARKETING: **DAVID GABRIEL**
BOOK DESIGNER: **ADAM DEL RE**

EDITOR IN CHIEF: **C.B. CEBULSKI**
CHIEF CREATIVE OFFICER: **JOE QUESADA**
PRESIDENT: **DAN BUCKLEY**
EXECUTIVE PRODUCER: **ALAN FINE**

AMAZING SPIDER-MAN: WORLDWIDE VOL. 8. Contains material originally published in magazine form as AMAZING SPIDER-MAN #794-796 and ANNUAL #42, and AMAZING SPIDER-MAN #25. First printing 2018. ISBN 978-1-302-90759-4. Published by MARVEL WORLDWIDE, INC., a subsidiary of MARVEL ENTERTAINMENT, LLC. OFFICE OF PUBLICATION: 135 West 50th Street, New York, NY 10020. Copyright © 2018 MARVEL No similarity between any of the names, characters, persons, and/or institutions in this magazine with those of any living or dead person or institution is intended, and any such similarity which may exist is purely coincidental. **Printed in Canada.** DAN BUCKLEY, President, Marvel Entertainment; JOHN NEE, Publisher; JOE QUESADA, Chief Creative Officer; TOM BREVOORT, SVP of Publishing; DAVID BOGART, SVP of Business Affairs & Operations, Publishing & Partnership; DAVID GABRIEL, SVP of Sales & Marketing, Publishing; JEFF YOUNGQUIST, VP of Production & Special Projects; DAN CARR, Executive Director of Publishing Technology; ALEX MORALES, Director of Publishing Operations; DAN EDINGTON, Managing Editor; SUSAN CRESPI, Production Manager; STAN LEE, Chairman Emeritus. For information regarding advertising in Marvel Comics or on Marvel.com, please contact Vit DeBellis, Custom Solutions & Integrated Advertising Manager, at vdebellis@marvel.com. For ˙   ˙ctured between 4/27/2018 and 5/29/2018 by SOLISCO PRINTERS, SCOTT, QC, CANADA.

10 9 8 7 6 5 4 3 2 1

The AMAZING SPIDER-MAN

WORLDWIDE

AMAZING SPIDER-MAN ANNUAL #42

DAN SLOTT
WRITER

CORY SMITH
PENCILER

TERRY PALLOT
INKS & FINISHES

BRIAN REBER
COLOR ARTIST

VC's JOE CARAMAGNA
LETTERER

AMAZING SPIDER-MAN #794-796

DAN SLOTT & CHRISTOS GAGE
WRITERS

STUART IMMONEN (#794) &
MIKE HAWTHORNE (#795-796)
PENCILERS

WADE VON GRAWBADGER (#794) &
TERRY PALLOT (#795-796) WITH **CAM SMITH** (#796)
INKS & FINISHES

MARTE GRACIA (#794-795) & **ERICK ARCINIEGA** (#796)
COLOR ARTISTS

VC's JOE CARAMAGNA
LETTERER

"POLICE & THIEVES"

CHRISTOS GAGE
WRITER

TODD NAUCK
ARTIST

RACHELLE ROSENBERG
COLOR ARTIST

VC's TRAVIS LANHAM
LETTERER

"SPIDER-SENSE & SENSIBILITY"

DAVID HEIN
WRITER

MARCUS TO
ARTIST

IAN HERRING
COLOR ARTIST

VC's JOE CARAMAGNA
LETTERER

ALEX ROSS
COVER ART

ALLISON STOCK & TOM GRONEMAN
ASSISTANT EDITORS

DEVIN LEWIS
ASSOCIATE EDITOR

NICK LOWE
EDITOR

SPIDER-MAN CREATED BY
STAN LEE & STEVE DITKO

ANNUAL
42

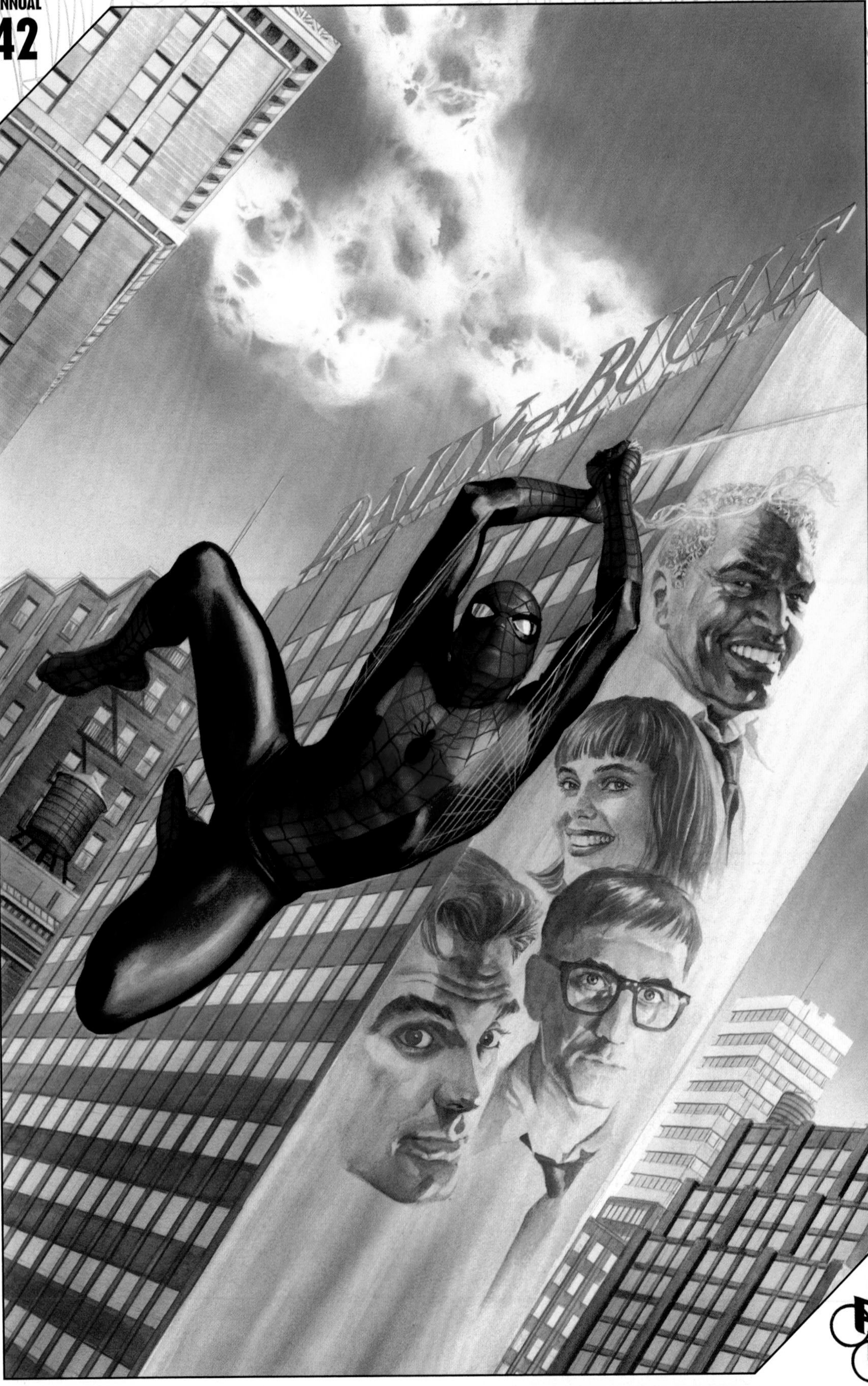
DAILY BUGLE

"BURY THE LEDES"

WHEN PETER PARKER WAS BITTEN BY A RADIOACTIVE SPIDER, HE GAINED THE PROPORTIONAL SPEED, STRENGTH AND AGILITY OF A SPIDER; ADHESIVE FINGERTIPS AND TOES; AND THE UNIQUE PRECOGNITIVE AWARENESS OF DANGER CALLED "SPIDER-SENSE"! AFTER LEARNING THAT WITH GREAT POWER THERE MUST ALSO COME GREAT RESPONSIBILITY, HE BECAME THE CRIME-FIGHTING SUPER HERO CALLED...

the AMAZING SPIDER-MAN

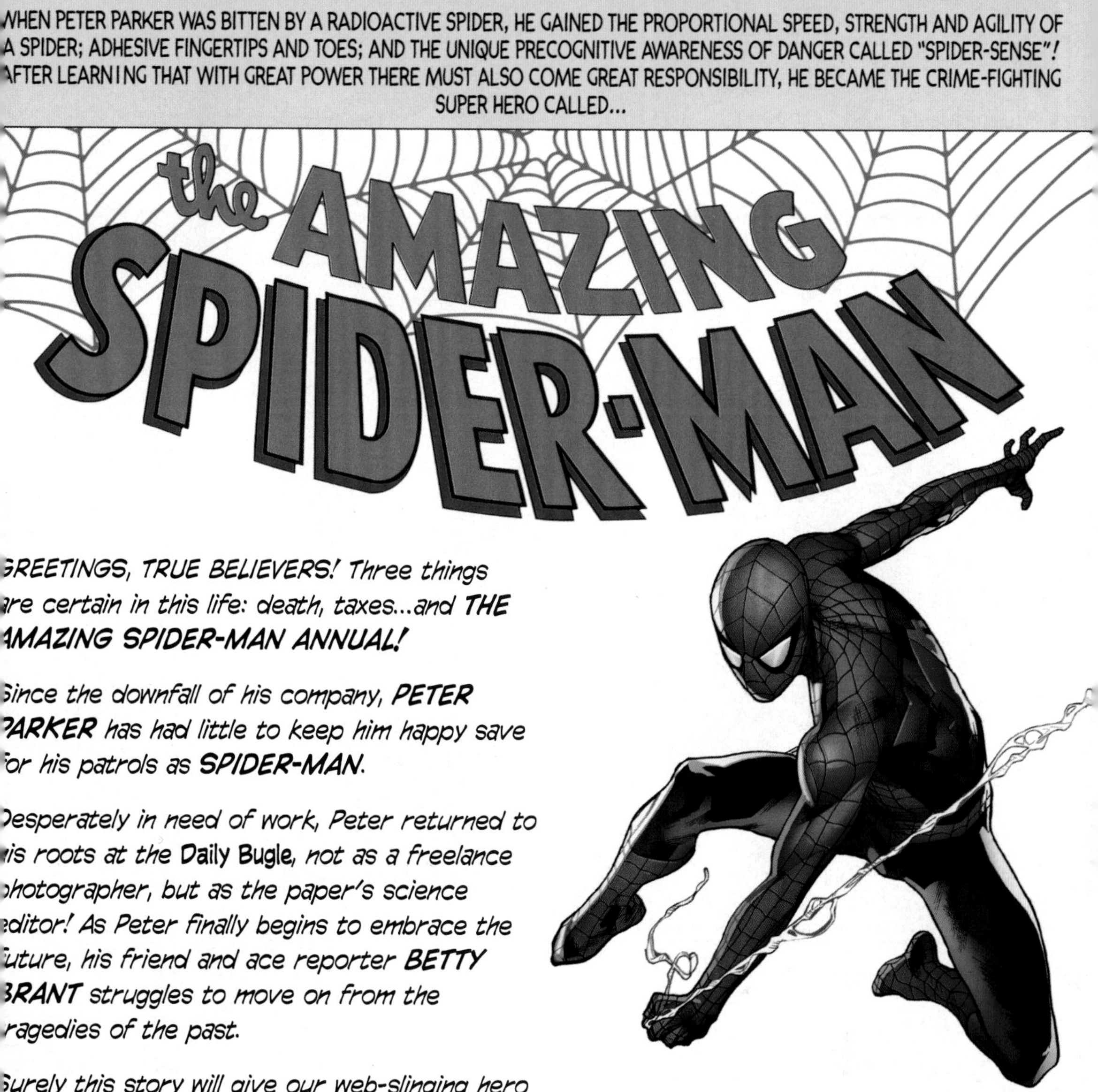

*GREETINGS, TRUE BELIEVERS! Three things are certain in this life: death, taxes...and **THE AMAZING SPIDER-MAN ANNUAL!***

*Since the downfall of his company, **PETER PARKER** has had little to keep him happy save for his patrols as **SPIDER-MAN**.*

Desperately in need of work, Peter returned to his roots at the Daily Bugle, *not as a freelance photographer, but as the paper's science editor! As Peter finally begins to embrace the future, his friend and ace reporter **BETTY BRANT** struggles to move on from the tragedies of the past.*

Surely this story will give our web-slinging hero a much-needed respite from the harrowing events of "THREAT LEVEL: RED." HA! Don't bet on it! Read on!

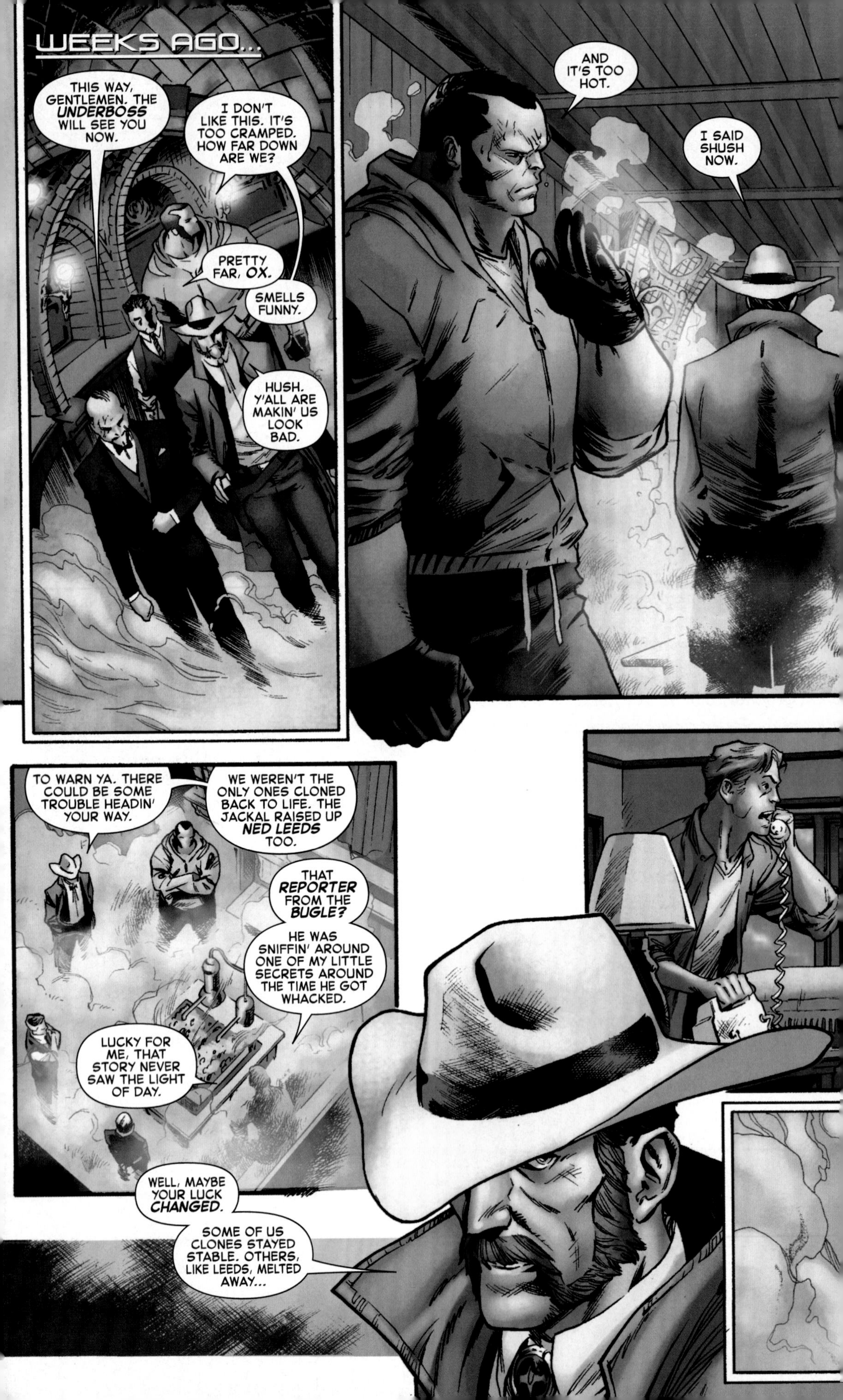

WEEKS AGO...
THIS WAY, GENTLEMEN. THE UNDERBOSS WILL SEE YOU NOW.
I DON'T LIKE THIS. IT'S TOO CRAMPED. HOW FAR DOWN ARE WE?
PRETTY FAR, OX.
SMELLS FUNNY.
HUSH. Y'ALL ARE MAKIN' US LOOK BAD.
AND IT'S TOO HOT.
I SAID SHUSH NOW.
TO WARN YA. THERE COULD BE SOME TROUBLE HEADIN' YOUR WAY.
WE WEREN'T THE ONLY ONES CLONED BACK TO LIFE. THE JACKAL RAISED UP NED LEEDS TOO.
THAT REPORTER FROM THE BUGLE?
HE WAS SNIFFIN' AROUND ONE OF MY LITTLE SECRETS AROUND THE TIME HE GOT WHACKED.
LUCKY FOR ME, THAT STORY NEVER SAW THE LIGHT OF DAY.
WELL, MAYBE YOUR LUCK CHANGED.
SOME OF US CLONES STAYED STABLE. OTHERS, LIKE LEEDS, MELTED AWAY...

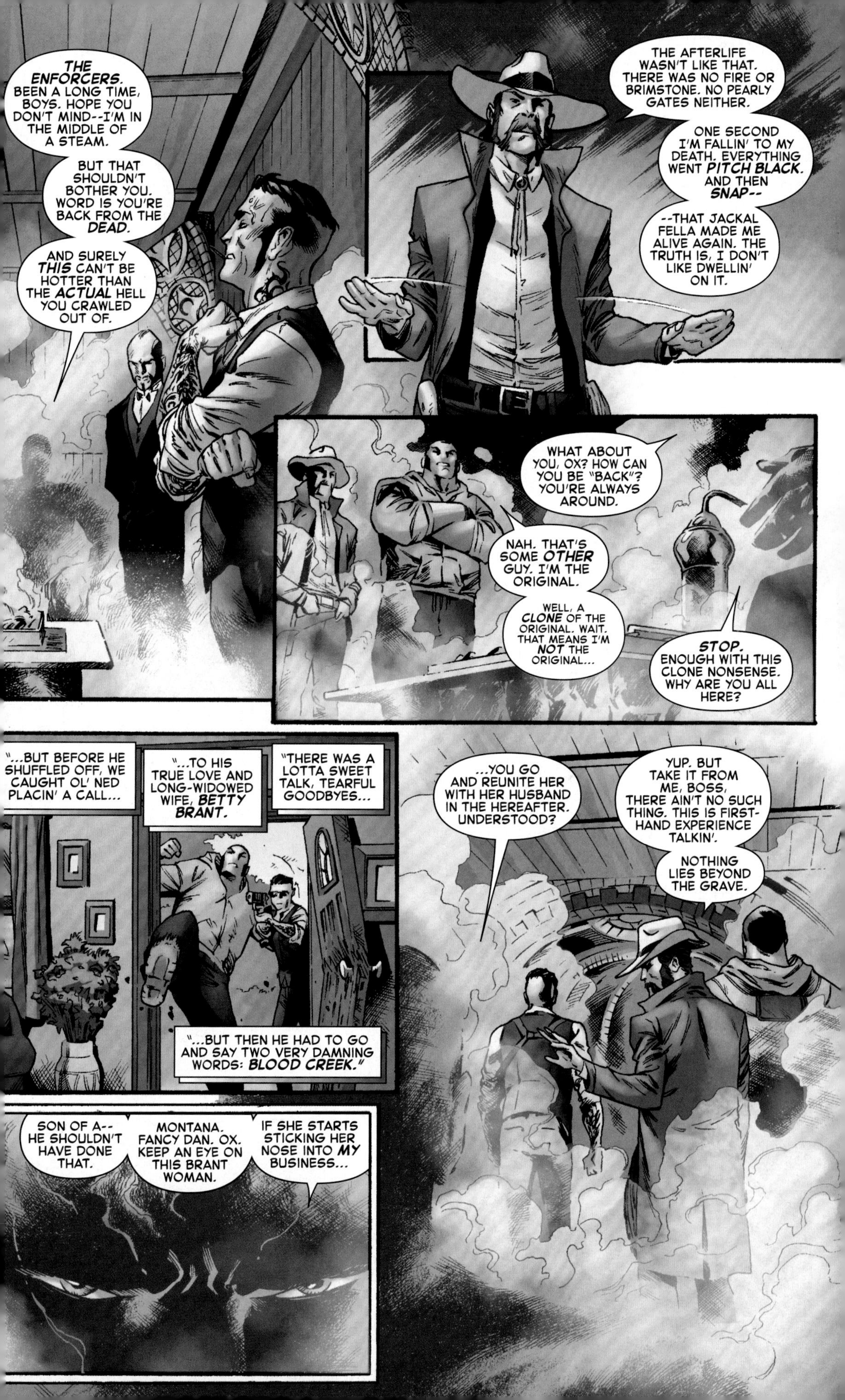
THE ENFORCERS. BEEN A LONG TIME, BOYS. HOPE YOU DON'T MIND--I'M IN THE MIDDLE OF A STEAM.
BUT THAT SHOULDN'T BOTHER YOU. WORD IS YOU'RE BACK FROM THE DEAD.
AND SURELY THIS CAN'T BE HOTTER THAN THE ACTUAL HELL YOU CRAWLED OUT OF.
THE AFTERLIFE WASN'T LIKE THAT. THERE WAS NO FIRE OR BRIMSTONE. NO PEARLY GATES NEITHER.
ONE SECOND I'M FALLIN' TO MY DEATH. EVERYTHING WENT PITCH BLACK. AND THEN SNAP--
--THAT JACKAL FELLA MADE ME ALIVE AGAIN. THE TRUTH IS, I DON'T LIKE DWELLIN' ON IT.
WHAT ABOUT YOU, OX? HOW CAN YOU BE "BACK"? YOU'RE ALWAYS AROUND.
NAH. THAT'S SOME OTHER GUY. I'M THE ORIGINAL.
WELL, A CLONE OF THE ORIGINAL. WAIT. THAT MEANS I'M NOT THE ORIGINAL...
STOP. ENOUGH WITH THIS CLONE NONSENSE. WHY ARE YOU ALL HERE?
"...BUT BEFORE HE SHUFFLED OFF, WE CAUGHT OL' NED PLACIN' A CALL...
"...TO HIS TRUE LOVE AND LONG-WIDOWED WIFE, BETTY BRANT.
"THERE WAS A LOTTA SWEET TALK, TEARFUL GOODBYES...
"...BUT THEN HE HAD TO GO AND SAY TWO VERY DAMNING WORDS: BLOOD CREEK."
SON OF A-- HE SHOULDN'T HAVE DONE THAT.
MONTANA. FANCY DAN. OX. KEEP AN EYE ON THIS BRANT WOMAN.
IF SHE STARTS STICKING HER NOSE INTO MY BUSINESS...
...YOU GO AND REUNITE HER WITH HER HUSBAND IN THE HEREAFTER. UNDERSTOOD?
YUP. BUT TAKE IT FROM ME, BOSS, THERE AIN'T NO SUCH THING. THIS IS FIRST-HAND EXPERIENCE TALKIN'.
NOTHING LIES BEYOND THE GRAVE.

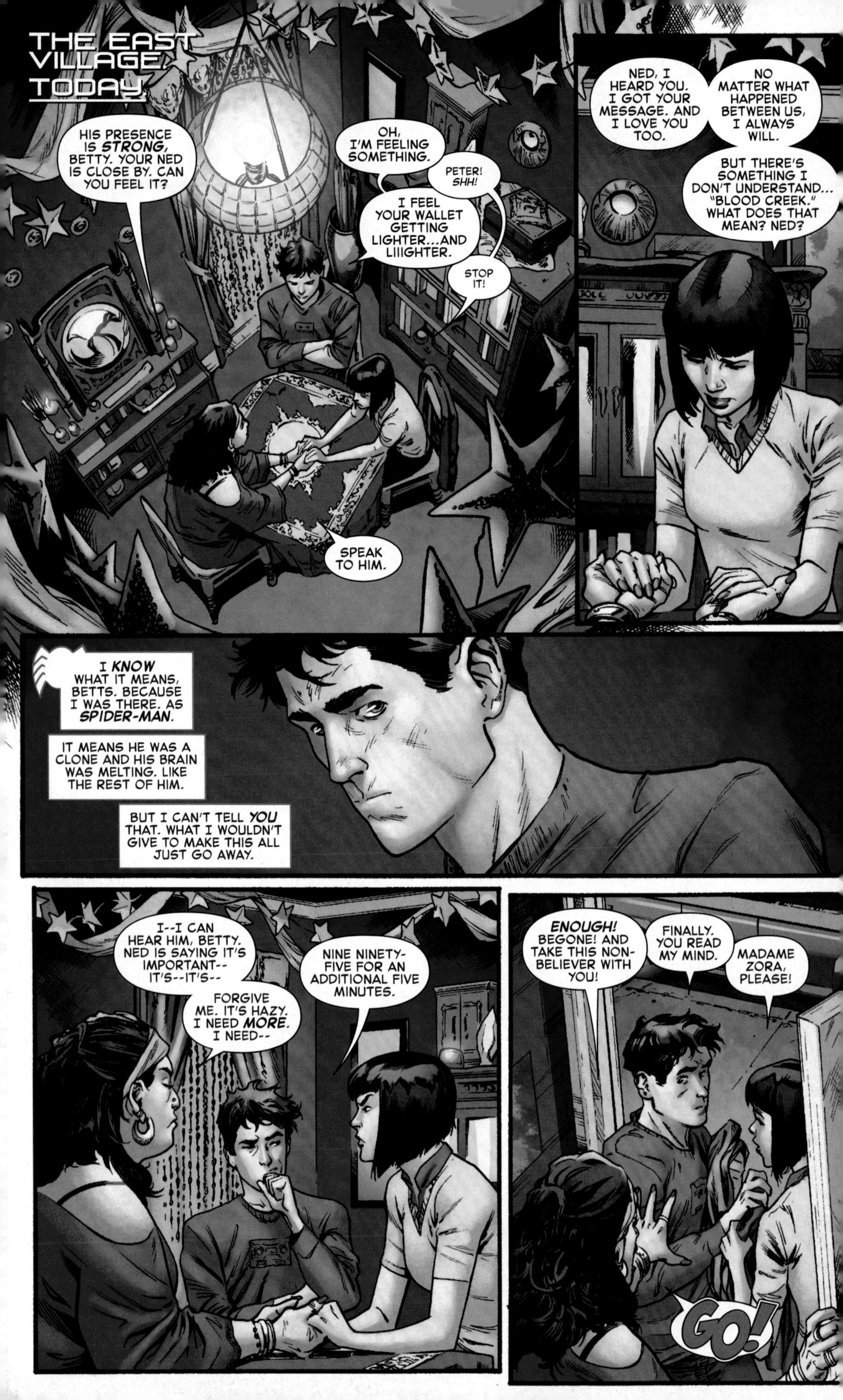

THE EAST VILLAGE. TODAY.
HIS PRESENCE IS **STRONG,** BETTY. YOUR NED IS CLOSE BY. CAN YOU FEEL IT?
OH, I'M FEELING SOMETHING.
I FEEL YOUR WALLET GETTING LIGHTER...AND LIIIGHTER.
PETER! *SHH!*
STOP IT!
SPEAK TO HIM.
NED, I HEARD YOU. I GOT YOUR MESSAGE. AND I LOVE YOU TOO.
NO MATTER WHAT HAPPENED BETWEEN US, I ALWAYS WILL.
BUT THERE'S SOMETHING I DON'T UNDERSTAND... "BLOOD CREEK." WHAT DOES THAT MEAN? NED?
I **KNOW** WHAT IT MEANS, BETTS. BECAUSE I WAS THERE. AS ***SPIDER-MAN.***
IT MEANS HE WAS A CLONE AND HIS BRAIN WAS MELTING. LIKE THE REST OF HIM.
BUT I CAN'T TELL ***YOU*** THAT. WHAT I WOULDN'T GIVE TO MAKE THIS ALL JUST GO AWAY.
I--I CAN HEAR HIM, BETTY. NED IS SAYING IT'S IMPORTANT-- IT'S--IT'S--
FORGIVE ME. IT'S HAZY. I NEED ***MORE.*** I NEED--
NINE NINETY-FIVE FOR AN ADDITIONAL FIVE MINUTES.
ENOUGH! BEGONE! AND TAKE THIS NON-BELIEVER WITH YOU!
FINALLY. YOU READ MY MIND.
MADAME ZORA, PLEASE!
GO!

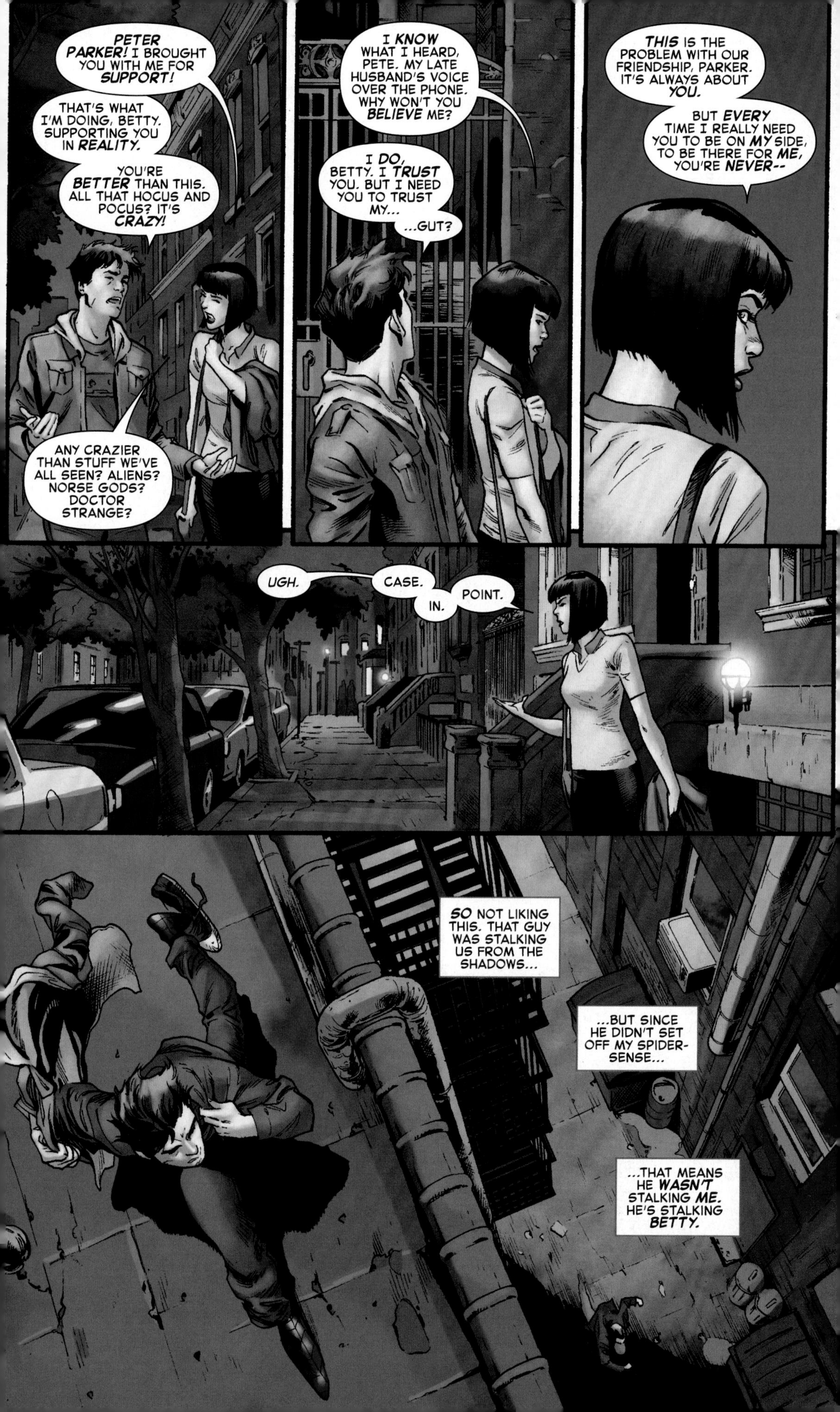
PETER PARKER! I BROUGHT YOU WITH ME FOR SUPPORT!
THAT'S WHAT I'M DOING, BETTY. SUPPORTING YOU IN REALITY.
YOU'RE BETTER THAN THIS. ALL THAT HOCUS AND POCUS? IT'S CRAZY!
ANY CRAZIER THAN STUFF WE'VE ALL SEEN? ALIENS? NORSE GODS? DOCTOR STRANGE?
I KNOW WHAT I HEARD, PETE. MY LATE HUSBAND'S VOICE OVER THE PHONE. WHY WON'T YOU BELIEVE ME?
I DO, BETTY. I TRUST YOU. BUT I NEED YOU TO TRUST MY...
...GUT?
THIS IS THE PROBLEM WITH OUR FRIENDSHIP, PARKER. IT'S ALWAYS ABOUT YOU.
BUT EVERY TIME I REALLY NEED YOU TO BE ON MY SIDE, TO BE THERE FOR ME, YOU'RE NEVER--
UGH.
CASE.
IN.
POINT.
SO NOT LIKING THIS. THAT GUY WAS STALKING US FROM THE SHADOWS...
...BUT SINCE HE DIDN'T SET OFF MY SPIDER-SENSE...
...THAT MEANS HE WASN'T STALKING ME. HE'S STALKING BETTY.

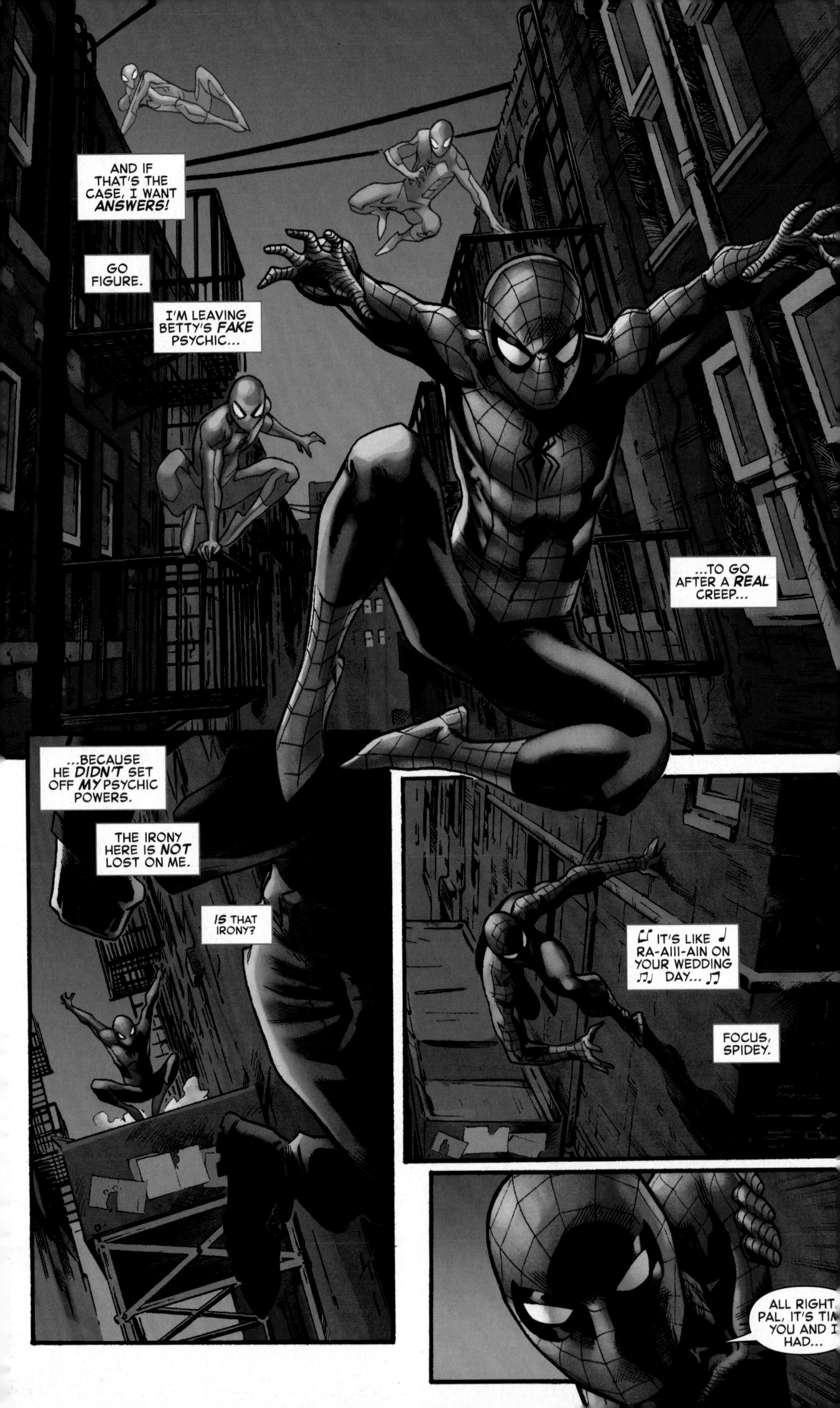

AND IF THAT'S THE CASE, I WANT ANSWERS!
GO FIGURE.
I'M LEAVING BETTY'S FAKE PSYCHIC...
...TO GO AFTER A REAL CREEP...
...BECAUSE HE DIDN'T SET OFF MY PSYCHIC POWERS.
THE IRONY HERE IS NOT LOST ON ME.
IS THAT IRONY?
♫ IT'S LIKE ♩ RA-AIII-AIN ON YOUR WEDDING ♫♩ DAY... ♫
FOCUS, SPIDEY.
ALL RIGHT, PAL, IT'S TIM YOU AND I HAD...

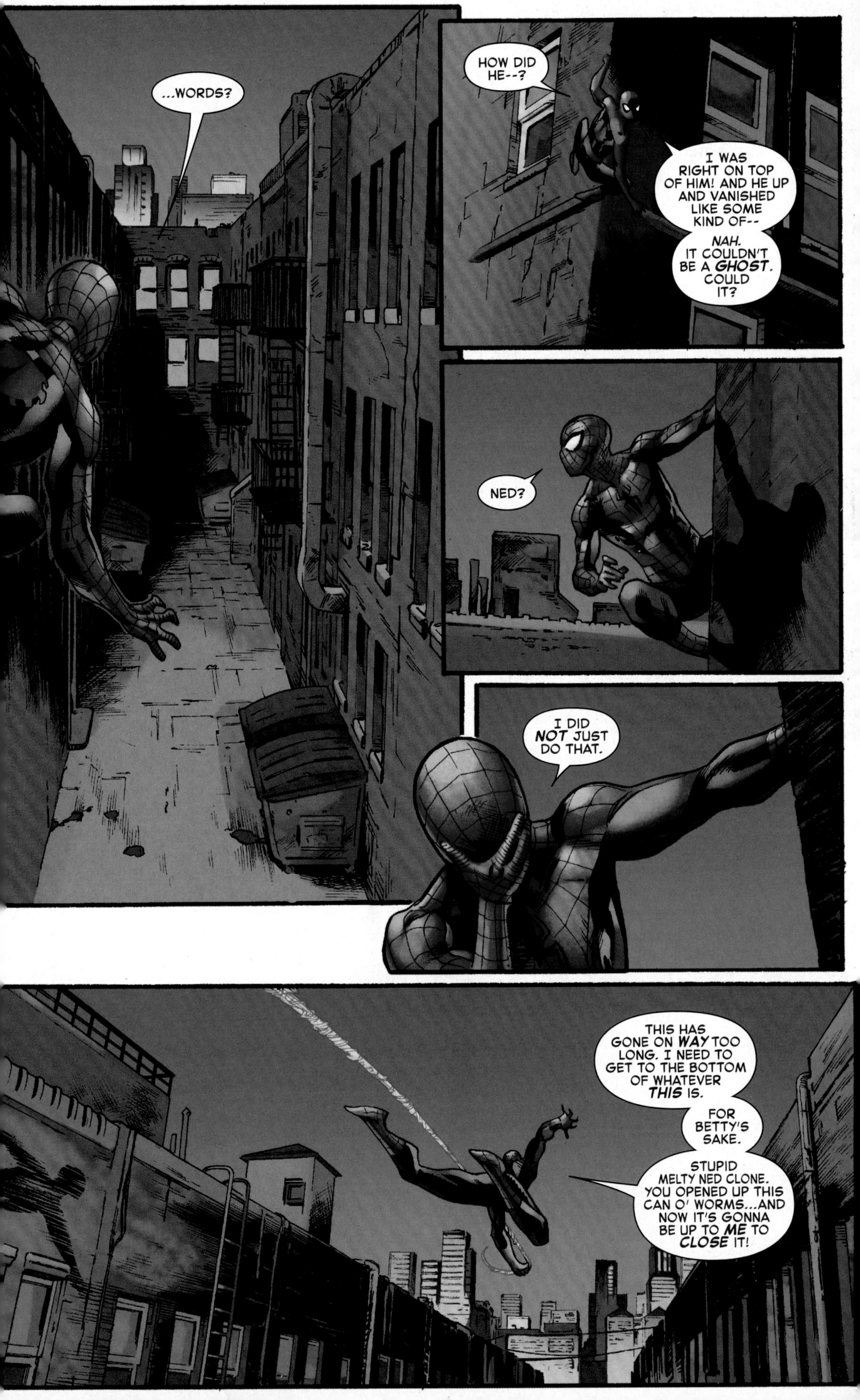

...WORDS?
HOW DID HE--?
I WAS RIGHT ON TOP OF HIM! AND HE UP AND VANISHED LIKE SOME KIND OF--
NAH. IT COULDN'T BE A GHOST. COULD IT?
NED?
I DID NOT JUST DO THAT.
THIS HAS GONE ON WAY TOO LONG. I NEED TO GET TO THE BOTTOM OF WHATEVER THIS IS.
FOR BETTY'S SAKE.
STUPID MELTY NED CLONE. YOU OPENED UP THIS CAN O' WORMS...AND NOW IT'S GONNA BE UP TO ME TO CLOSE IT!

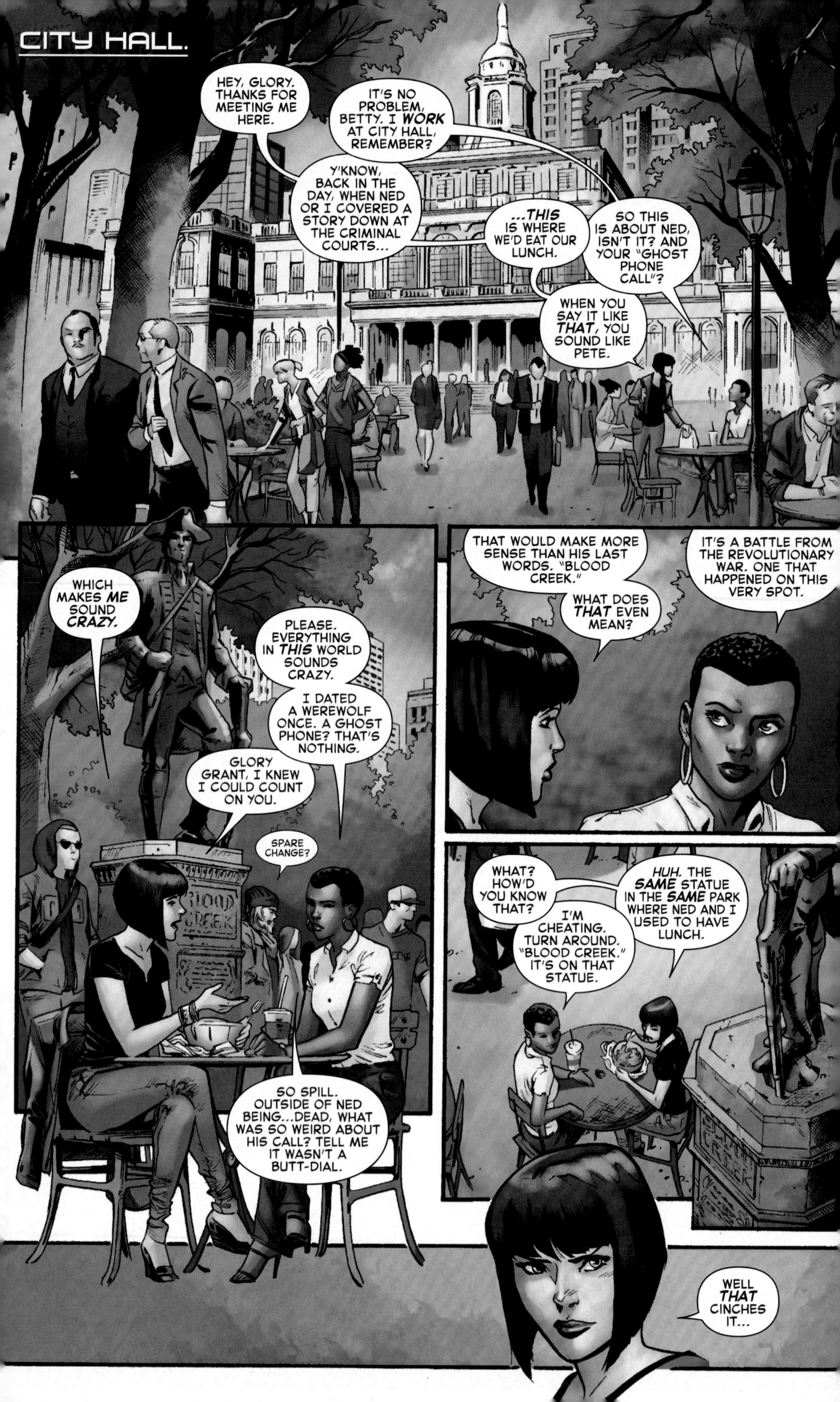
CITY HALL.
HEY, GLORY. THANKS FOR MEETING ME HERE.
IT'S NO PROBLEM, BETTY. I WORK AT CITY HALL, REMEMBER?
Y'KNOW, BACK IN THE DAY, WHEN NED OR I COVERED A STORY DOWN AT THE CRIMINAL COURTS...
...THIS IS WHERE WE'D EAT OUR LUNCH.
SO THIS IS ABOUT NED, ISN'T IT? AND YOUR "GHOST PHONE CALL"?
WHEN YOU SAY IT LIKE THAT, YOU SOUND LIKE PETE.
WHICH MAKES ME SOUND CRAZY.
PLEASE. EVERYTHING IN THIS WORLD SOUNDS CRAZY.
I DATED A WEREWOLF ONCE. A GHOST PHONE? THAT'S NOTHING.
GLORY GRANT, I KNEW I COULD COUNT ON YOU.
SPARE CHANGE?
SO SPILL. OUTSIDE OF NED BEING...DEAD, WHAT WAS SO WEIRD ABOUT HIS CALL? TELL ME IT WASN'T A BUTT-DIAL.
THAT WOULD MAKE MORE SENSE THAN HIS LAST WORDS. "BLOOD CREEK."
WHAT DOES THAT EVEN MEAN?
IT'S A BATTLE FROM THE REVOLUTIONARY WAR. ONE THAT HAPPENED ON THIS VERY SPOT.
WHAT? HOW'D YOU KNOW THAT?
I'M CHEATING. TURN AROUND. "BLOOD CREEK." IT'S ON THAT STATUE.
HUH. THE SAME STATUE IN THE SAME PARK WHERE NED AND I USED TO HAVE LUNCH.
WELL THAT CINCHES IT...

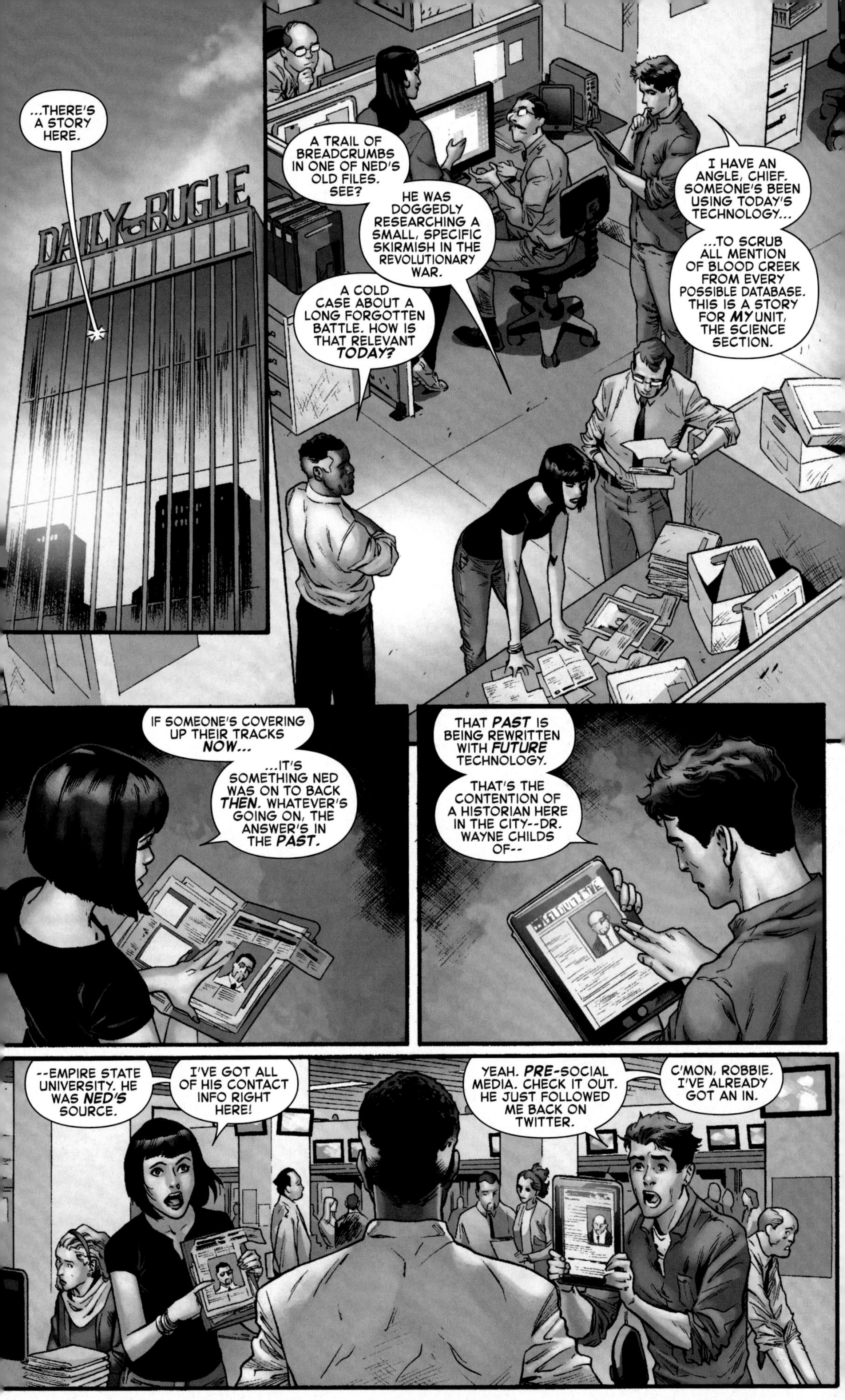
...THERE'S A STORY HERE.
DAILY BUGLE
A TRAIL OF BREADCRUMBS IN ONE OF NED'S OLD FILES. SEE?
HE WAS DOGGEDLY RESEARCHING A SMALL, SPECIFIC SKIRMISH IN THE REVOLUTIONARY WAR.
A COLD CASE ABOUT A LONG FORGOTTEN BATTLE. HOW IS THAT RELEVANT TODAY?
I HAVE AN ANGLE, CHIEF. SOMEONE'S BEEN USING TODAY'S TECHNOLOGY...
...TO SCRUB ALL MENTION OF BLOOD CREEK FROM EVERY POSSIBLE DATABASE. THIS IS A STORY FOR MY UNIT, THE SCIENCE SECTION.
IF SOMEONE'S COVERING UP THEIR TRACKS NOW...
...IT'S SOMETHING NED WAS ON TO BACK THEN. WHATEVER'S GOING ON, THE ANSWER'S IN THE PAST.
THAT PAST IS BEING REWRITTEN WITH FUTURE TECHNOLOGY.
THAT'S THE CONTENTION OF A HISTORIAN HERE IN THE CITY--DR. WAYNE CHILDS OF--
--EMPIRE STATE UNIVERSITY. HE WAS NED'S SOURCE.
I'VE GOT ALL OF HIS CONTACT INFO RIGHT HERE!
YEAH. PRE-SOCIAL MEDIA. CHECK IT OUT. HE JUST FOLLOWED ME BACK ON TWITTER.
C'MON, ROBBIE. I'VE ALREADY GOT AN IN.

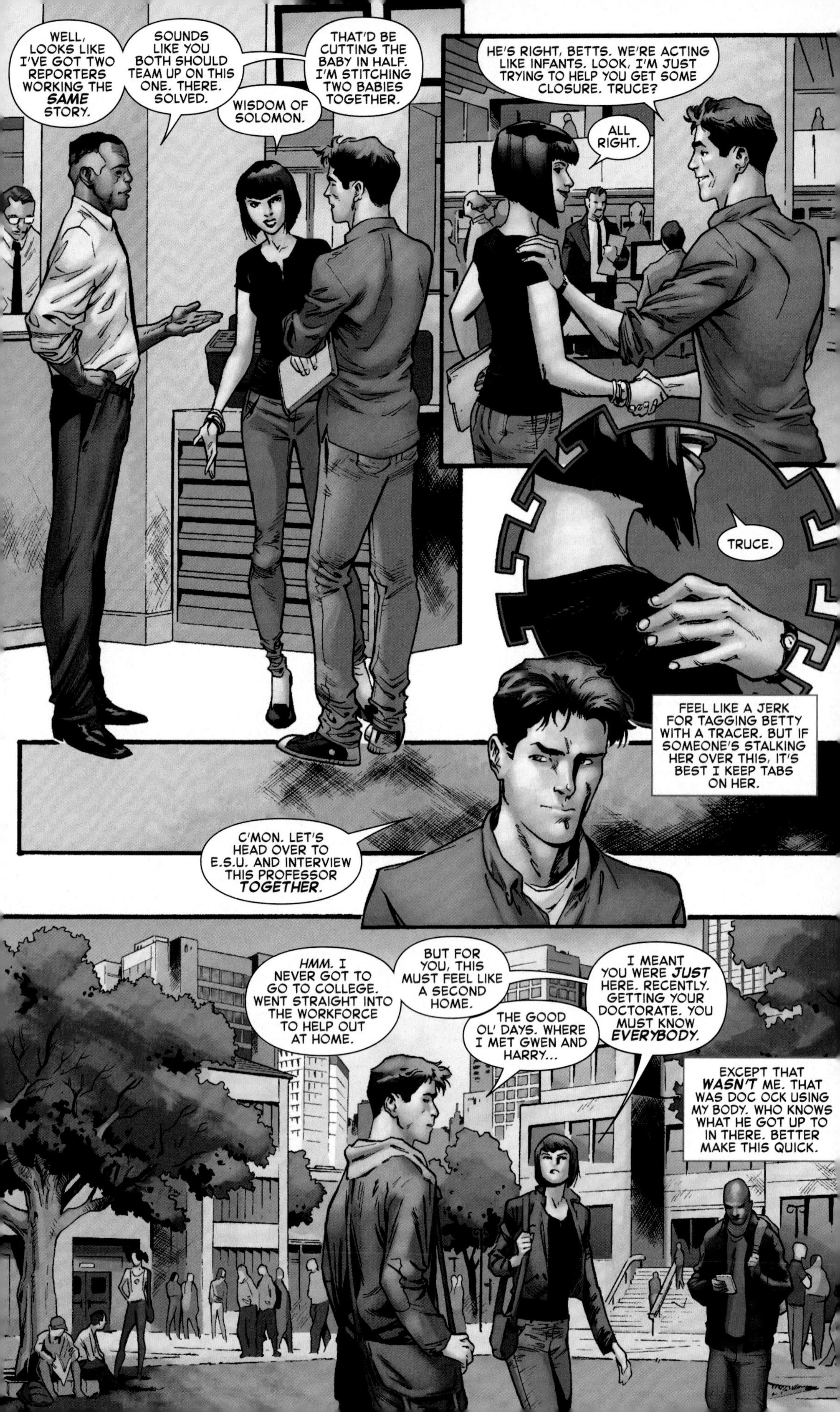
WELL, LOOKS LIKE I'VE GOT TWO REPORTERS WORKING THE SAME STORY.
SOUNDS LIKE YOU BOTH SHOULD TEAM UP ON THIS ONE. THERE. SOLVED.
THAT'D BE CUTTING THE BABY IN HALF. I'M STITCHING TWO BABIES TOGETHER.
WISDOM OF SOLOMON.
HE'S RIGHT, BETTS. WE'RE ACTING LIKE INFANTS. LOOK, I'M JUST TRYING TO HELP YOU GET SOME CLOSURE. TRUCE?
ALL RIGHT.
TRUCE.
FEEL LIKE A JERK FOR TAGGING BETTY WITH A TRACER. BUT IF SOMEONE'S STALKING HER OVER THIS, IT'S BEST I KEEP TABS ON HER.
C'MON. LET'S HEAD OVER TO E.S.U. AND INTERVIEW THIS PROFESSOR TOGETHER.
HMM. I NEVER GOT TO GO TO COLLEGE. WENT STRAIGHT INTO THE WORKFORCE TO HELP OUT AT HOME.
BUT FOR YOU, THIS MUST FEEL LIKE A SECOND HOME.
THE GOOD OL' DAYS. WHERE I MET GWEN AND HARRY...
I MEANT YOU WERE JUST HERE. RECENTLY. GETTING YOUR DOCTORATE. YOU MUST KNOW EVERYBODY.
EXCEPT THAT WASN'T ME. THAT WAS DOC OCK USING MY BODY. WHO KNOWS WHAT HE GOT UP TO IN THERE. BETTER MAKE THIS QUICK.

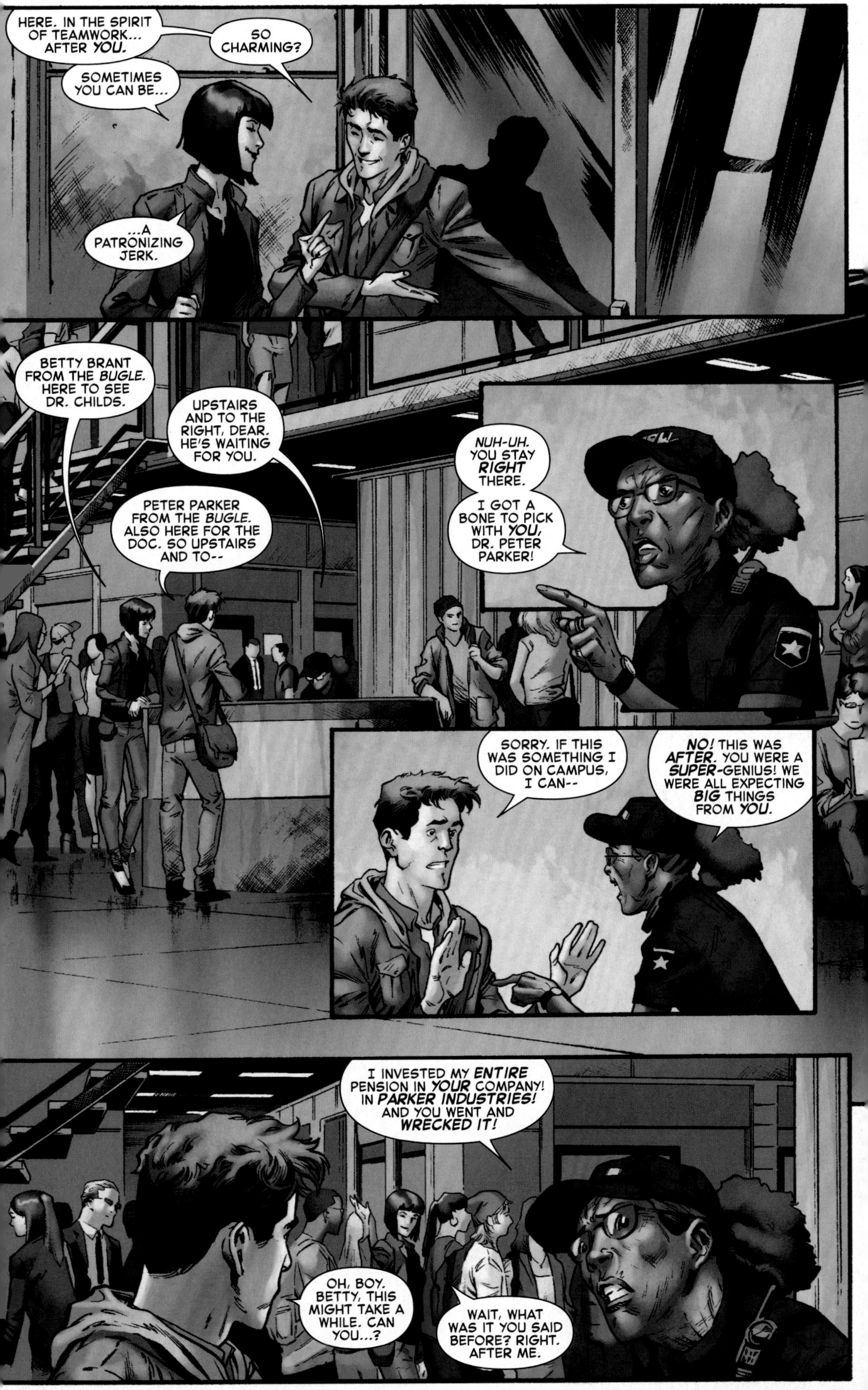
HERE. IN THE SPIRIT OF TEAMWORK... AFTER YOU.
SOMETIMES YOU CAN BE...
SO CHARMING?
...A PATRONIZING JERK.
BETTY BRANT FROM THE BUGLE. HERE TO SEE DR. CHILDS.
UPSTAIRS AND TO THE RIGHT, DEAR. HE'S WAITING FOR YOU.
PETER PARKER FROM THE BUGLE. ALSO HERE FOR THE DOC. SO UPSTAIRS AND TO--
NUH-UH. YOU STAY RIGHT THERE.
I GOT A BONE TO PICK WITH YOU, DR. PETER PARKER!
SORRY. IF THIS WAS SOMETHING I DID ON CAMPUS, I CAN--
NO! THIS WAS AFTER. YOU WERE A SUPER-GENIUS! WE WERE ALL EXPECTING BIG THINGS FROM YOU.
I INVESTED MY ENTIRE PENSION IN YOUR COMPANY! IN PARKER INDUSTRIES! AND YOU WENT AND WRECKED IT!
OH, BOY. BETTY, THIS MIGHT TAKE A WHILE. CAN YOU...?
WAIT, WHAT WAS IT YOU SAID BEFORE? RIGHT. AFTER ME.

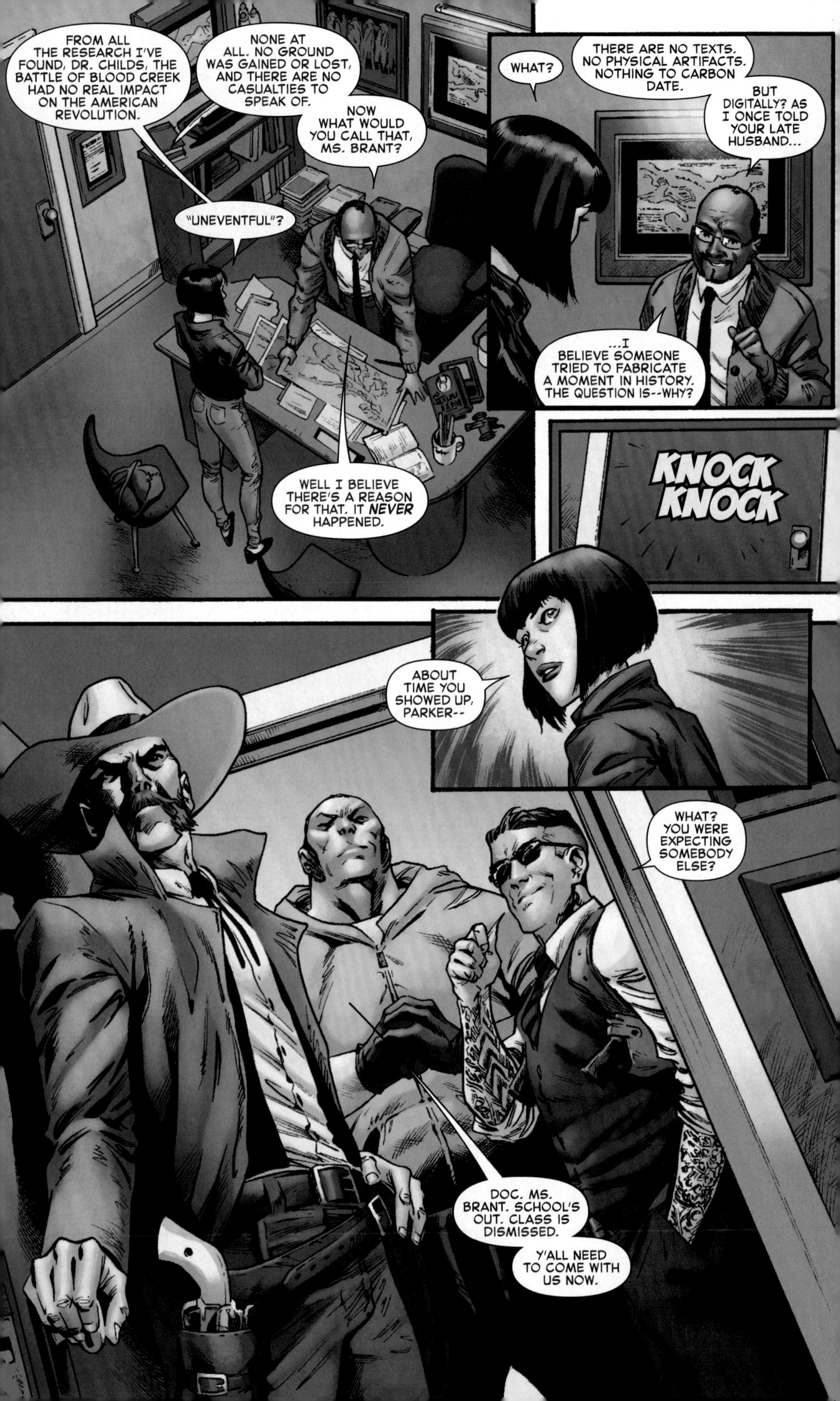
FROM ALL THE RESEARCH I'VE FOUND, DR. CHILDS, THE BATTLE OF BLOOD CREEK HAD NO REAL IMPACT ON THE AMERICAN REVOLUTION.
NONE AT ALL. NO GROUND WAS GAINED OR LOST, AND THERE ARE NO CASUALTIES TO SPEAK OF.
NOW WHAT WOULD YOU CALL THAT, MS. BRANT?
"UNEVENTFUL"?
WELL I BELIEVE THERE'S A REASON FOR THAT. IT NEVER HAPPENED.
WHAT?
THERE ARE NO TEXTS. NO PHYSICAL ARTIFACTS. NOTHING TO CARBON DATE.
BUT DIGITALLY? AS I ONCE TOLD YOUR LATE HUSBAND...
...I BELIEVE SOMEONE TRIED TO FABRICATE A MOMENT IN HISTORY. THE QUESTION IS--WHY?
KNOCK KNOCK
ABOUT TIME YOU SHOWED UP, PARKER--
WHAT? YOU WERE EXPECTING SOMEBODY ELSE?
DOC. MS. BRANT. SCHOOL'S OUT. CLASS IS DISMISSED.
Y'ALL NEED TO COME WITH US NOW.

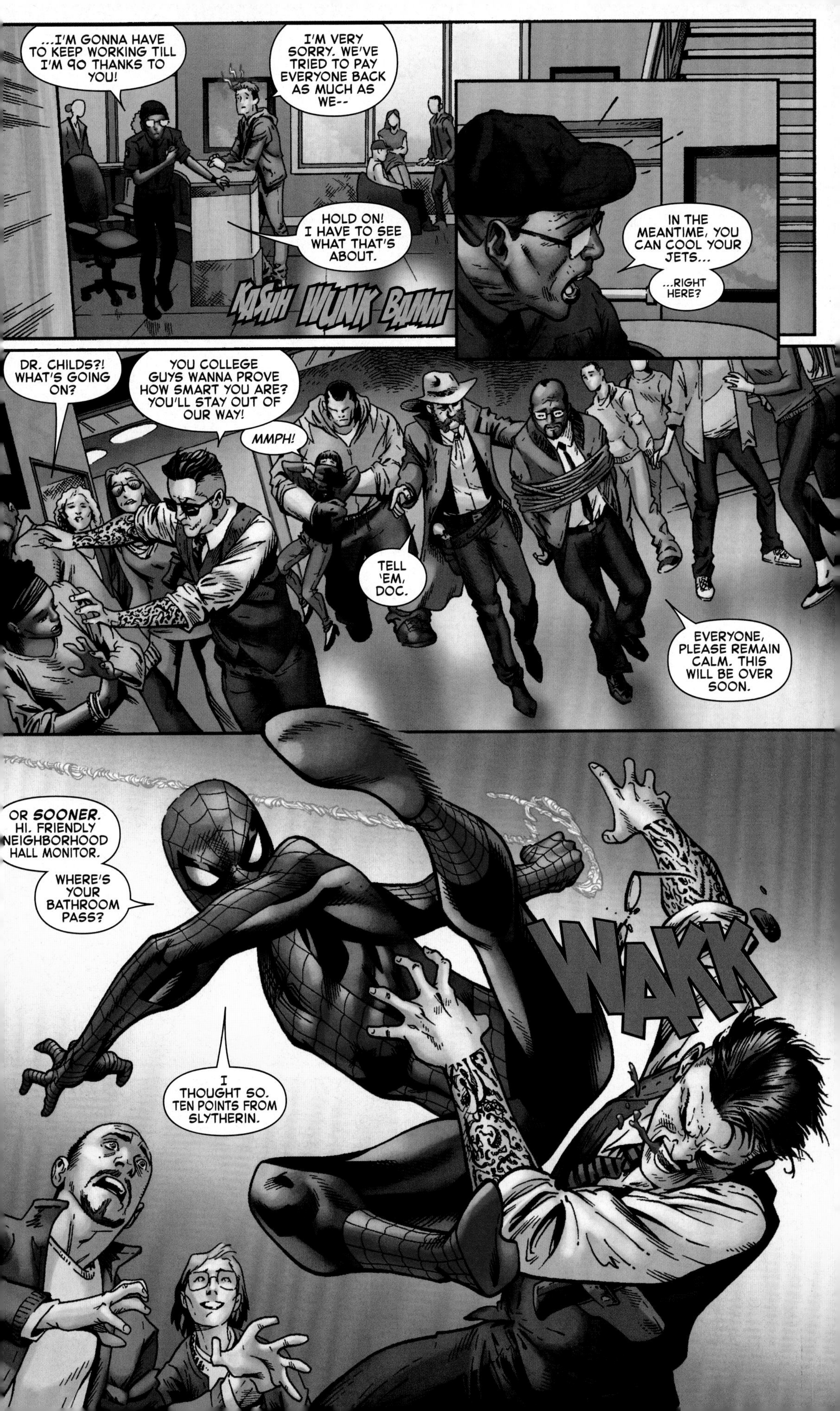
...I'M GONNA HAVE TO KEEP WORKING TILL I'M 90 THANKS TO YOU!
I'M VERY SORRY. WE'VE TRIED TO PAY EVERYONE BACK AS MUCH AS WE--
HOLD ON! I HAVE TO SEE WHAT THAT'S ABOUT.
KASHH WUNK BAMM
IN THE MEANTIME, YOU CAN COOL YOUR JETS...
...RIGHT HERE?
DR. CHILDS?! WHAT'S GOING ON?
YOU COLLEGE GUYS WANNA PROVE HOW SMART YOU ARE? YOU'LL STAY OUT OF OUR WAY!
MMPH!
TELL 'EM, DOC.
EVERYONE, PLEASE REMAIN CALM. THIS WILL BE OVER SOON.
OR SOONER. HI. FRIENDLY NEIGHBORHOOD HALL MONITOR.
WHERE'S YOUR BATHROOM PASS?
WAKK
I THOUGHT SO. TEN POINTS FROM SLYTHERIN.

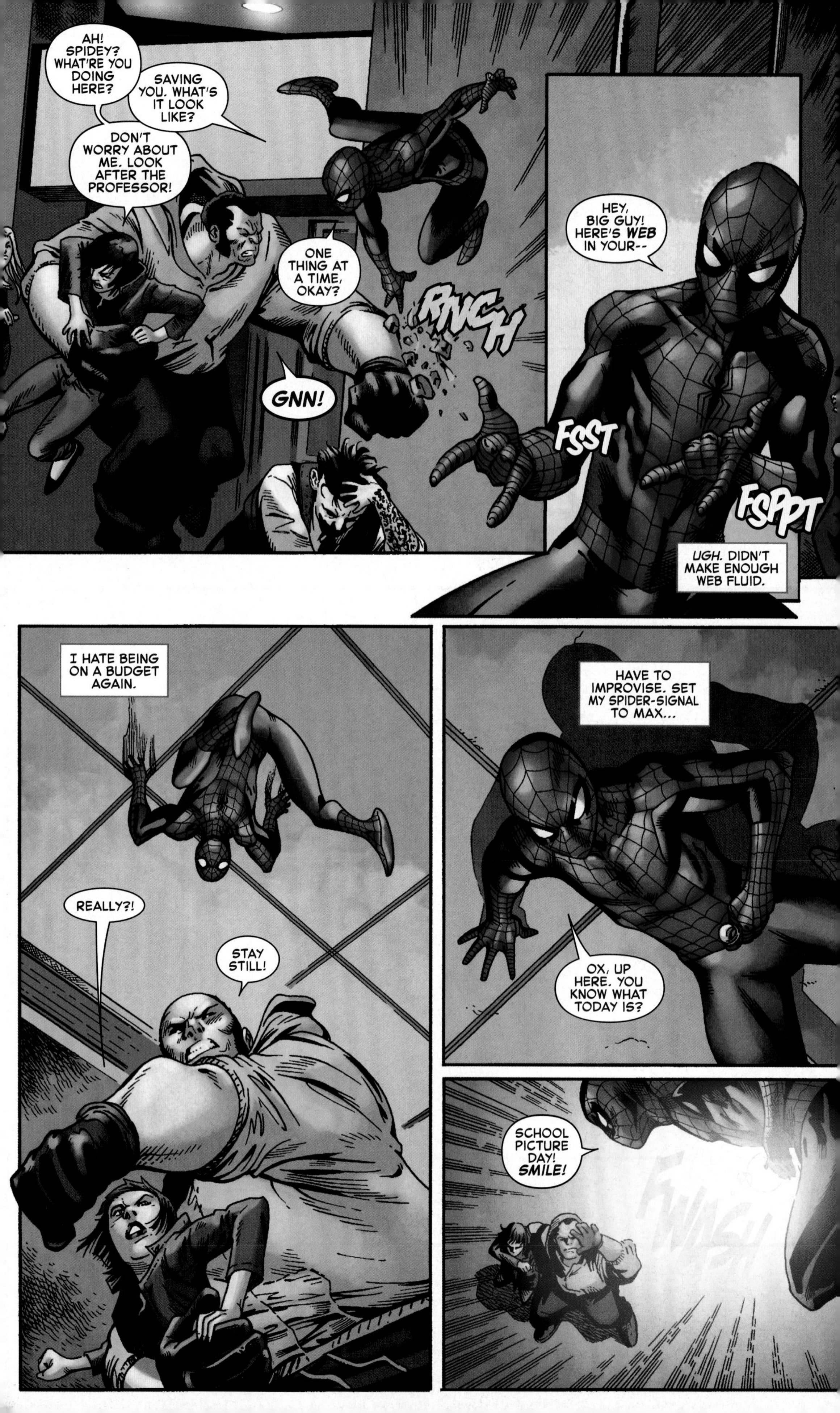
AH! SPIDEY? WHAT'RE YOU DOING HERE?
SAVING YOU. WHAT'S IT LOOK LIKE?
DON'T WORRY ABOUT ME. LOOK AFTER THE PROFESSOR!
ONE THING AT A TIME, OKAY?
RNCH
GNN!
HEY, BIG GUY! HERE'S *WEB* IN YOUR--
FSST
FSPPT
UGH. DIDN'T MAKE ENOUGH WEB FLUID.
I HATE BEING ON A BUDGET AGAIN.
REALLY?!
STAY STILL!
HAVE TO IMPROVISE. SET MY SPIDER-SIGNAL TO MAX...
OX, UP HERE. YOU KNOW WHAT TODAY IS?
SCHOOL PICTURE DAY! *SMILE!*
FWASH

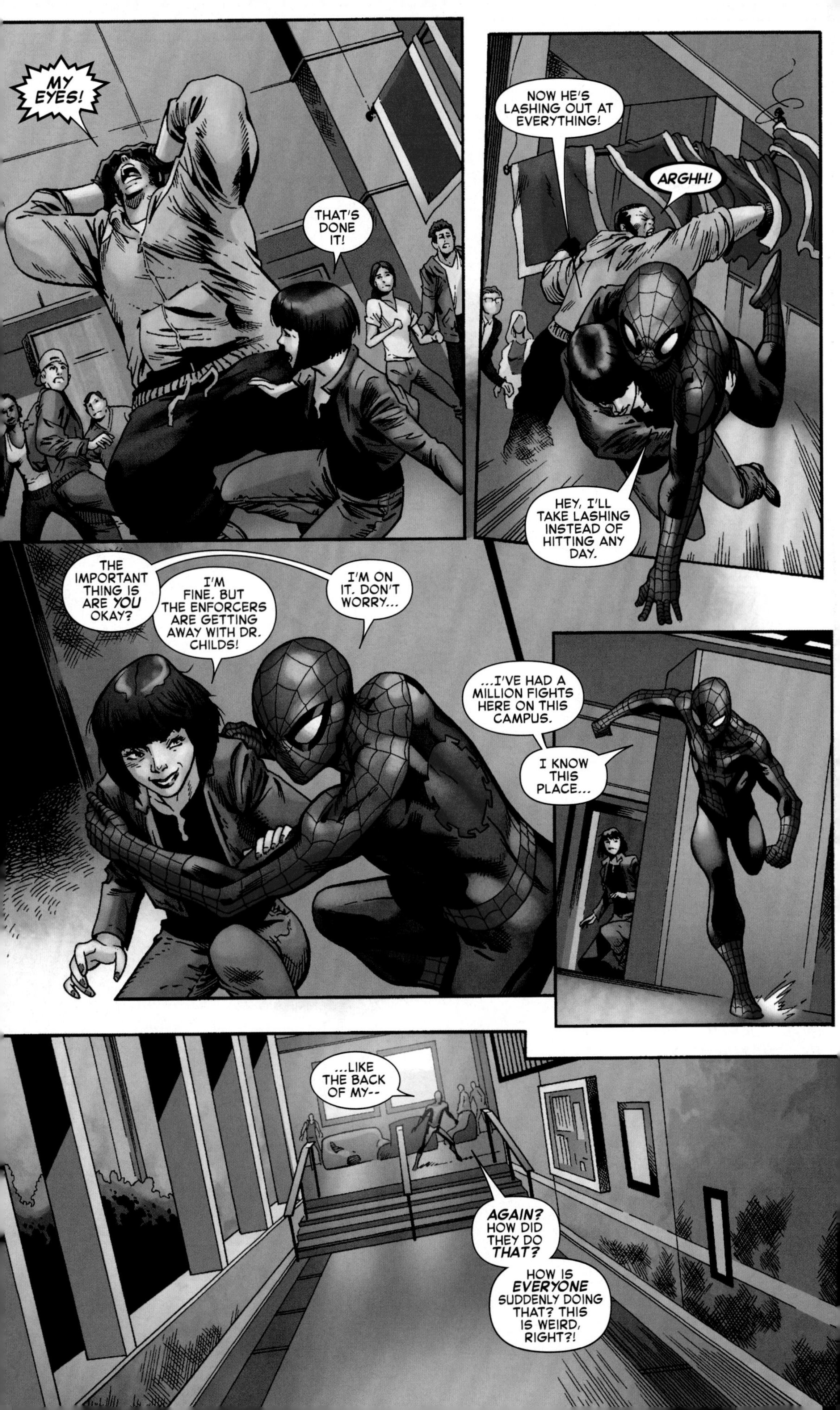
MY EYES!
THAT'S DONE IT!
NOW HE'S LASHING OUT AT EVERYTHING!
ARGHH!
HEY, I'LL TAKE LASHING INSTEAD OF HITTING ANY DAY.
THE IMPORTANT THING IS ARE *YOU* OKAY?
I'M FINE. BUT THE ENFORCERS ARE GETTING AWAY WITH DR. CHILDS!
I'M ON IT. DON'T WORRY...
...I'VE HAD A MILLION FIGHTS HERE ON THIS CAMPUS.
I KNOW THIS PLACE...
...LIKE THE BACK OF MY--
AGAIN? HOW DID THEY DO *THAT?*
HOW IS *EVERYONE* SUDDENLY DOING THAT? THIS IS WEIRD, RIGHT?!

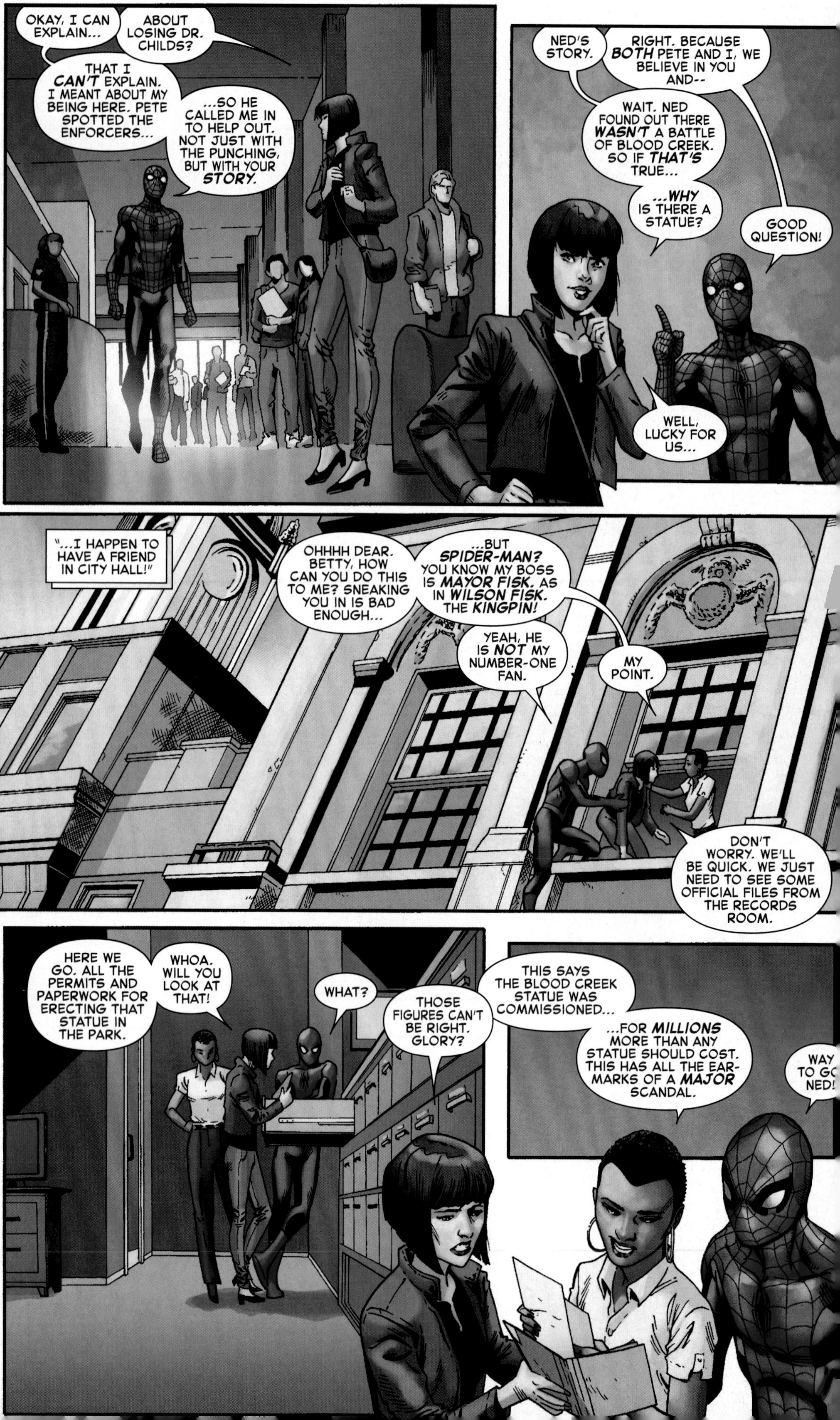
OKAY, I CAN EXPLAIN...
ABOUT LOSING DR. CHILDS?
THAT I CAN'T EXPLAIN. I MEANT ABOUT MY BEING HERE. PETE SPOTTED THE ENFORCERS...
...SO HE CALLED ME IN TO HELP OUT. NOT JUST WITH THE PUNCHING, BUT WITH YOUR STORY.
NED'S STORY.
RIGHT. BECAUSE BOTH PETE AND I, WE BELIEVE IN YOU AND--
WAIT. NED FOUND OUT THERE WASN'T A BATTLE OF BLOOD CREEK. SO IF THAT'S TRUE...
...WHY IS THERE A STATUE?
GOOD QUESTION!
WELL, LUCKY FOR US...
"...I HAPPEN TO HAVE A FRIEND IN CITY HALL!"
OHHHH DEAR. BETTY, HOW CAN YOU DO THIS TO ME? SNEAKING YOU IN IS BAD ENOUGH...
...BUT SPIDER-MAN? YOU KNOW MY BOSS IS MAYOR FISK. AS IN WILSON FISK. THE KINGPIN!
YEAH, HE IS NOT MY NUMBER-ONE FAN.
MY POINT.
DON'T WORRY. WE'LL BE QUICK. WE JUST NEED TO SEE SOME OFFICIAL FILES FROM THE RECORDS ROOM.
HERE WE GO. ALL THE PERMITS AND PAPERWORK FOR ERECTING THAT STATUE IN THE PARK.
WHOA. WILL YOU LOOK AT THAT!
WHAT?
THOSE FIGURES CAN'T BE RIGHT. GLORY?
THIS SAYS THE BLOOD CREEK STATUE WAS COMMISSIONED...
...FOR MILLIONS MORE THAN ANY STATUE SHOULD COST. THIS HAS ALL THE EAR-MARKS OF A MAJOR SCANDAL.

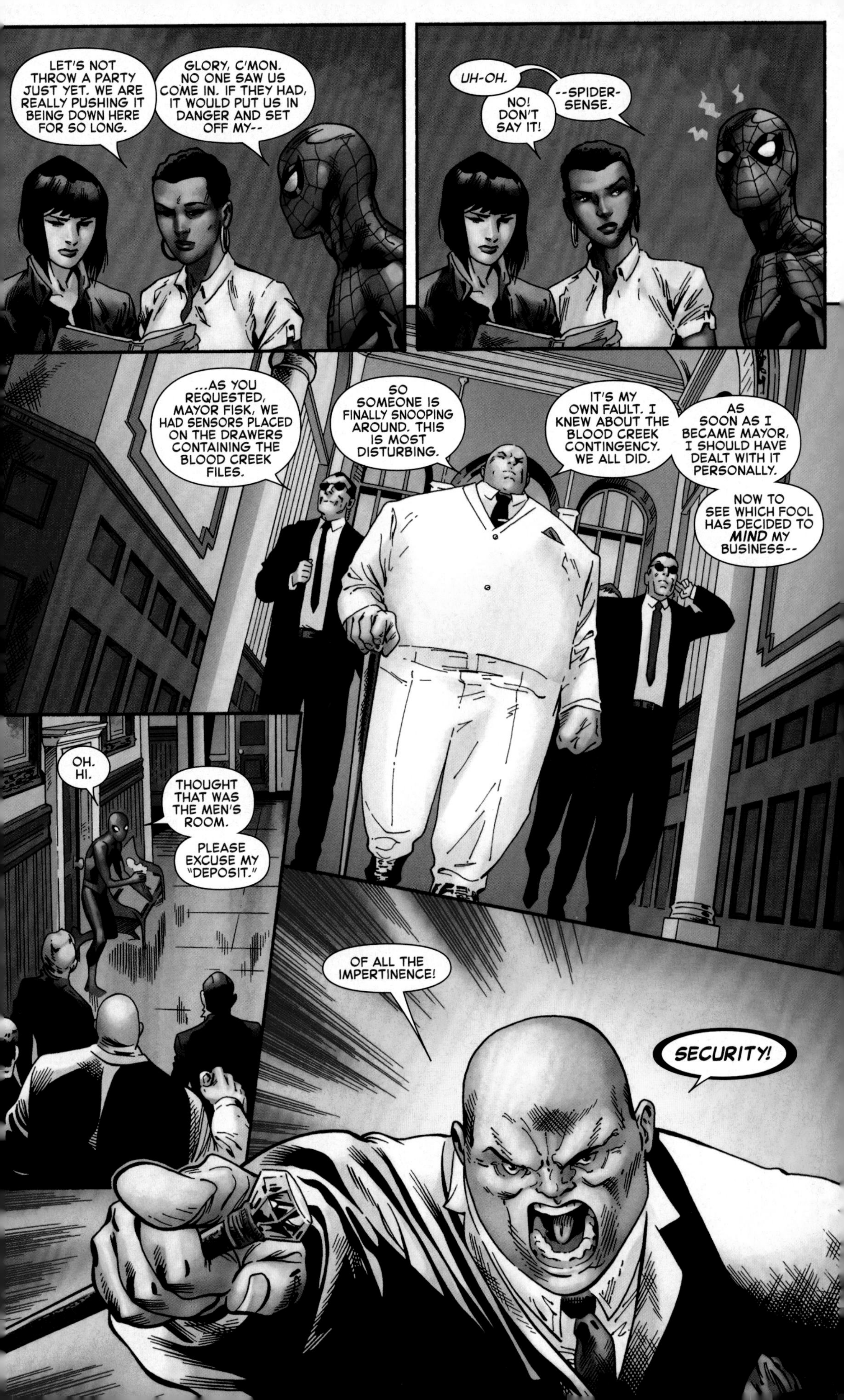
LET'S NOT THROW A PARTY JUST YET. WE ARE REALLY PUSHING IT BEING DOWN HERE FOR SO LONG.
GLORY, C'MON. NO ONE SAW US COME IN. IF THEY HAD, IT WOULD PUT US IN DANGER AND SET OFF MY--
UH-OH.
NO! DON'T SAY IT!
--SPIDER-SENSE.
...AS YOU REQUESTED, MAYOR FISK, WE HAD SENSORS PLACED ON THE DRAWERS CONTAINING THE BLOOD CREEK FILES.
SO SOMEONE IS FINALLY SNOOPING AROUND. THIS IS MOST DISTURBING.
IT'S MY OWN FAULT. I KNEW ABOUT THE BLOOD CREEK CONTINGENCY. WE ALL DID.
AS SOON AS I BECAME MAYOR, I SHOULD HAVE DEALT WITH IT PERSONALLY.
NOW TO SEE WHICH FOOL HAS DECIDED TO MIND MY BUSINESS--
OH. HI.
THOUGHT THAT WAS THE MEN'S ROOM.
PLEASE EXCUSE MY "DEPOSIT."
OF ALL THE IMPERTINENCE!
SECURITY!

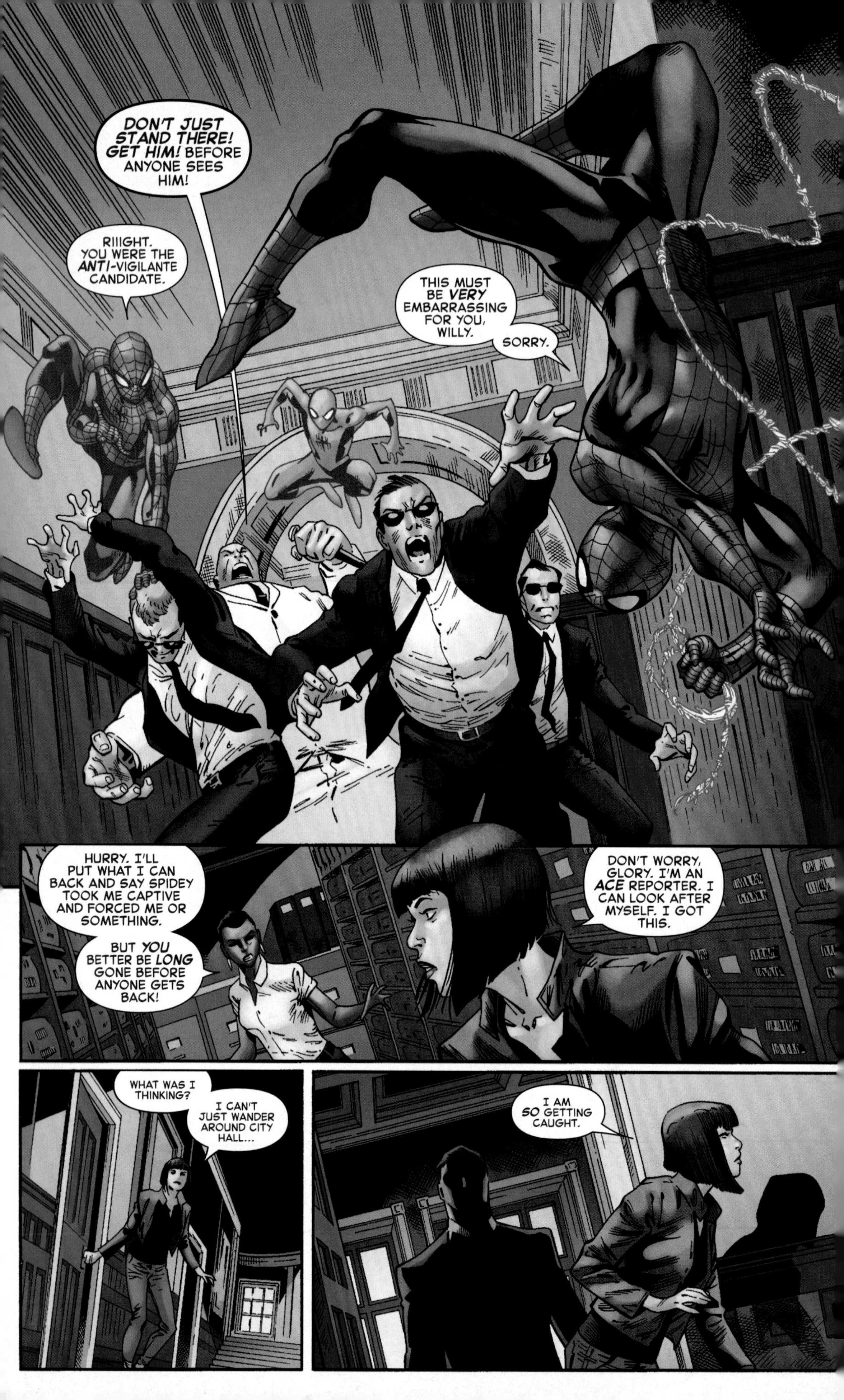
DON'T JUST STAND THERE! GET HIM! BEFORE ANYONE SEES HIM!
RIIIGHT. YOU WERE THE ANTI-VIGILANTE CANDIDATE.
THIS MUST BE VERY EMBARRASSING FOR YOU, WILLY.
SORRY.
HURRY. I'LL PUT WHAT I CAN BACK AND SAY SPIDEY TOOK ME CAPTIVE AND FORCED ME OR SOMETHING.
BUT YOU BETTER BE LONG GONE BEFORE ANYONE GETS BACK!
DON'T WORRY, GLORY. I'M AN ACE REPORTER. I CAN LOOK AFTER MYSELF. I GOT THIS.
WHAT WAS I THINKING?
I CAN'T JUST WANDER AROUND CITY HALL...
I AM SO GETTING CAUGHT.

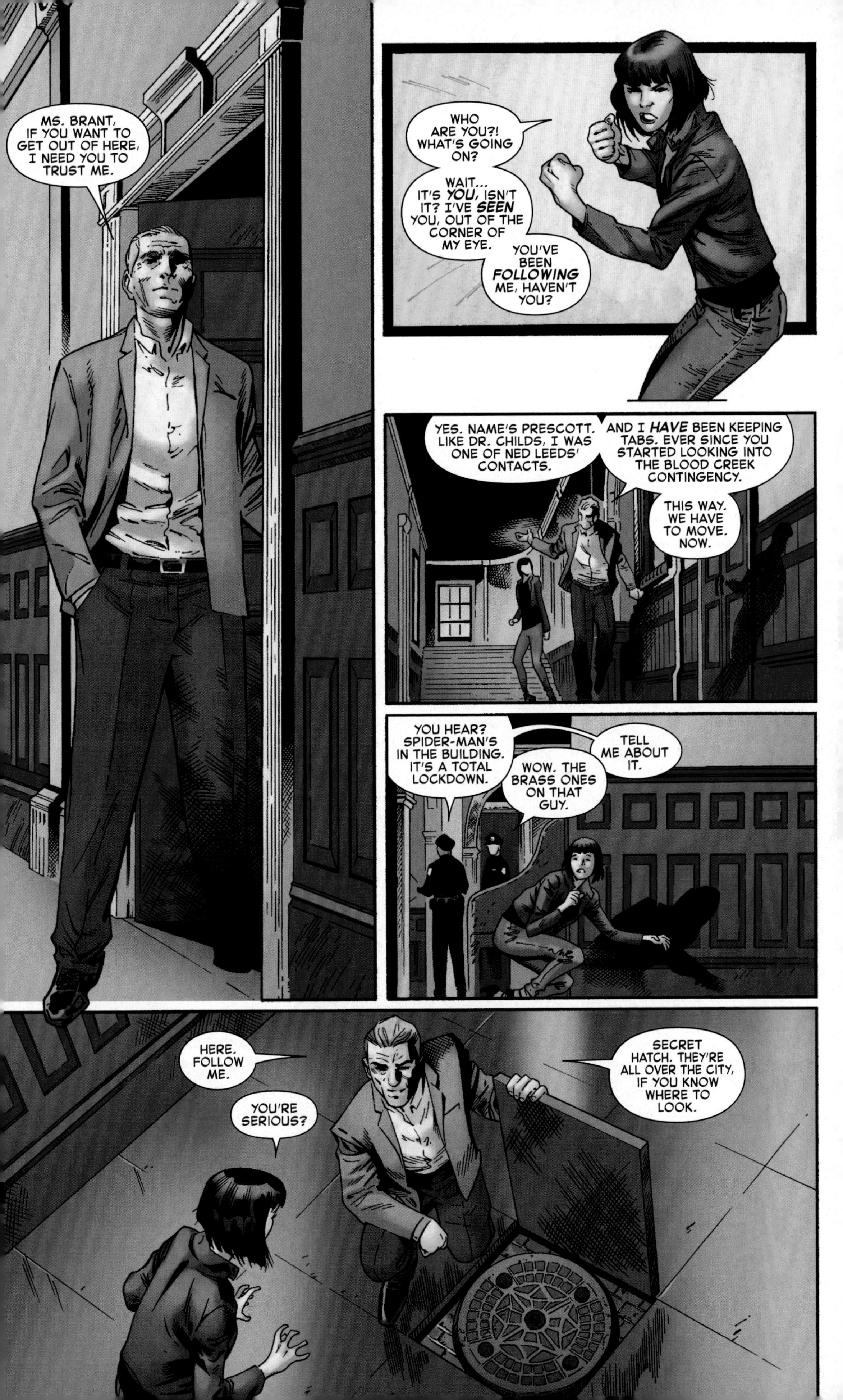
MS. BRANT, IF YOU WANT TO GET OUT OF HERE, I NEED YOU TO TRUST ME.
WHO ARE YOU?! WHAT'S GOING ON?
WAIT... IT'S YOU, ISN'T IT? I'VE SEEN YOU, OUT OF THE CORNER OF MY EYE.
YOU'VE BEEN FOLLOWING ME, HAVEN'T YOU?
YES. NAME'S PRESCOTT. LIKE DR. CHILDS, I WAS ONE OF NED LEEDS' CONTACTS.
AND I HAVE BEEN KEEPING TABS. EVER SINCE YOU STARTED LOOKING INTO THE BLOOD CREEK CONTINGENCY.
THIS WAY. WE HAVE TO MOVE. NOW.
YOU HEAR? SPIDER-MAN'S IN THE BUILDING. IT'S A TOTAL LOCKDOWN.
TELL ME ABOUT IT.
WOW. THE BRASS ONES ON THAT GUY.
HERE. FOLLOW ME.
YOU'RE SERIOUS?
SECRET HATCH. THEY'RE ALL OVER THE CITY, IF YOU KNOW WHERE TO LOOK.

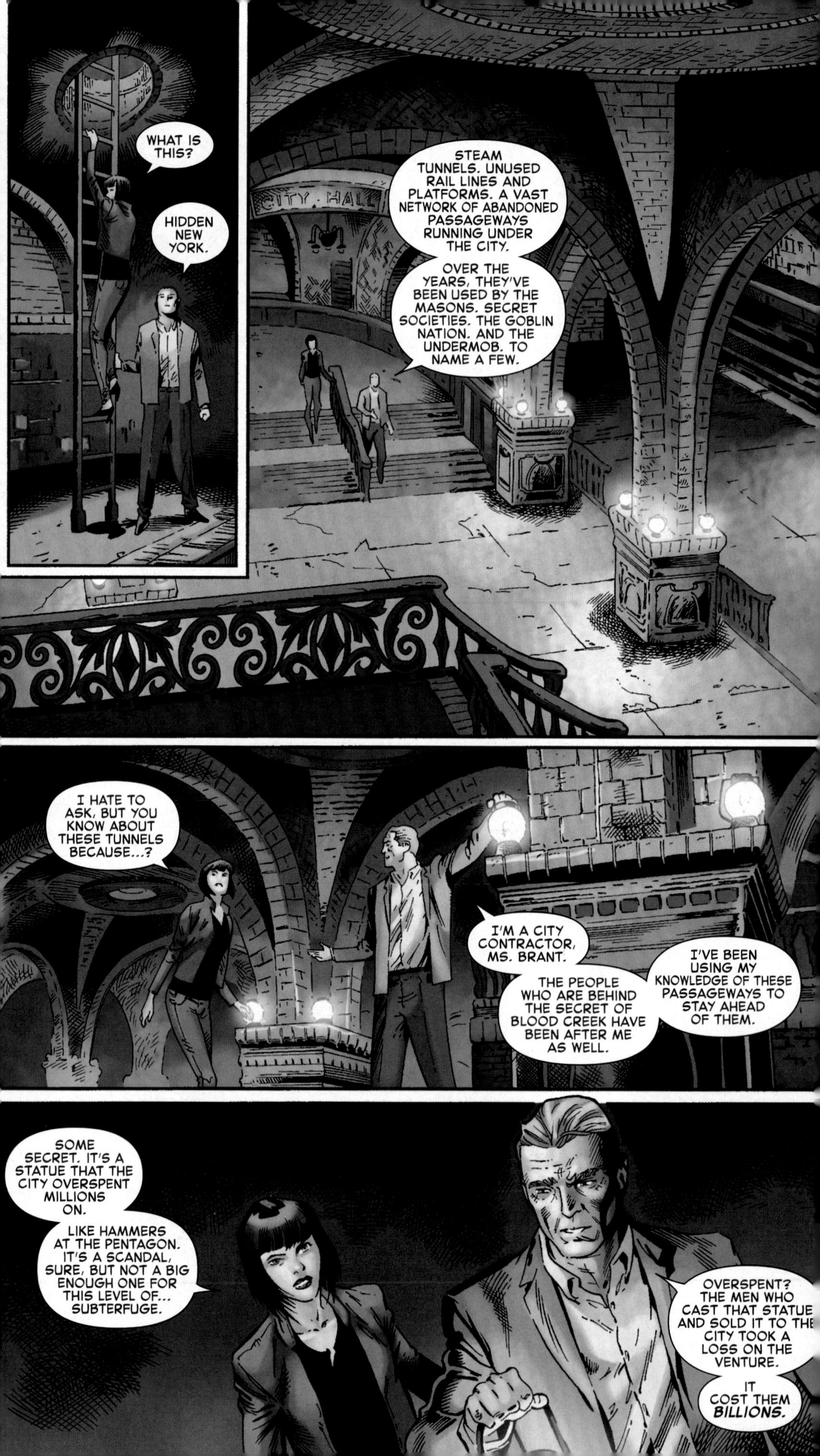
WHAT IS THIS?
HIDDEN NEW YORK.
CITY HALL
STEAM TUNNELS. UNUSED RAIL LINES AND PLATFORMS. A VAST NETWORK OF ABANDONED PASSAGEWAYS RUNNING UNDER THE CITY.
OVER THE YEARS, THEY'VE BEEN USED BY THE MASONS. SECRET SOCIETIES. THE GOBLIN NATION. AND THE UNDERMOB. TO NAME A FEW.
I HATE TO ASK, BUT YOU KNOW ABOUT THESE TUNNELS BECAUSE...?
I'M A CITY CONTRACTOR, MS. BRANT.
THE PEOPLE WHO ARE BEHIND THE SECRET OF BLOOD CREEK HAVE BEEN AFTER ME AS WELL.
I'VE BEEN USING MY KNOWLEDGE OF THESE PASSAGEWAYS TO STAY AHEAD OF THEM.
SOME SECRET. IT'S A STATUE THAT THE CITY OVERSPENT MILLIONS ON.
LIKE HAMMERS AT THE PENTAGON. IT'S A SCANDAL, SURE, BUT NOT A BIG ENOUGH ONE FOR THIS LEVEL OF... SUBTERFUGE.
OVERSPENT? THE MEN WHO CAST THAT STATUE AND SOLD IT TO THE CITY TOOK A LOSS ON THE VENTURE.
IT COST THEM BILLIONS.

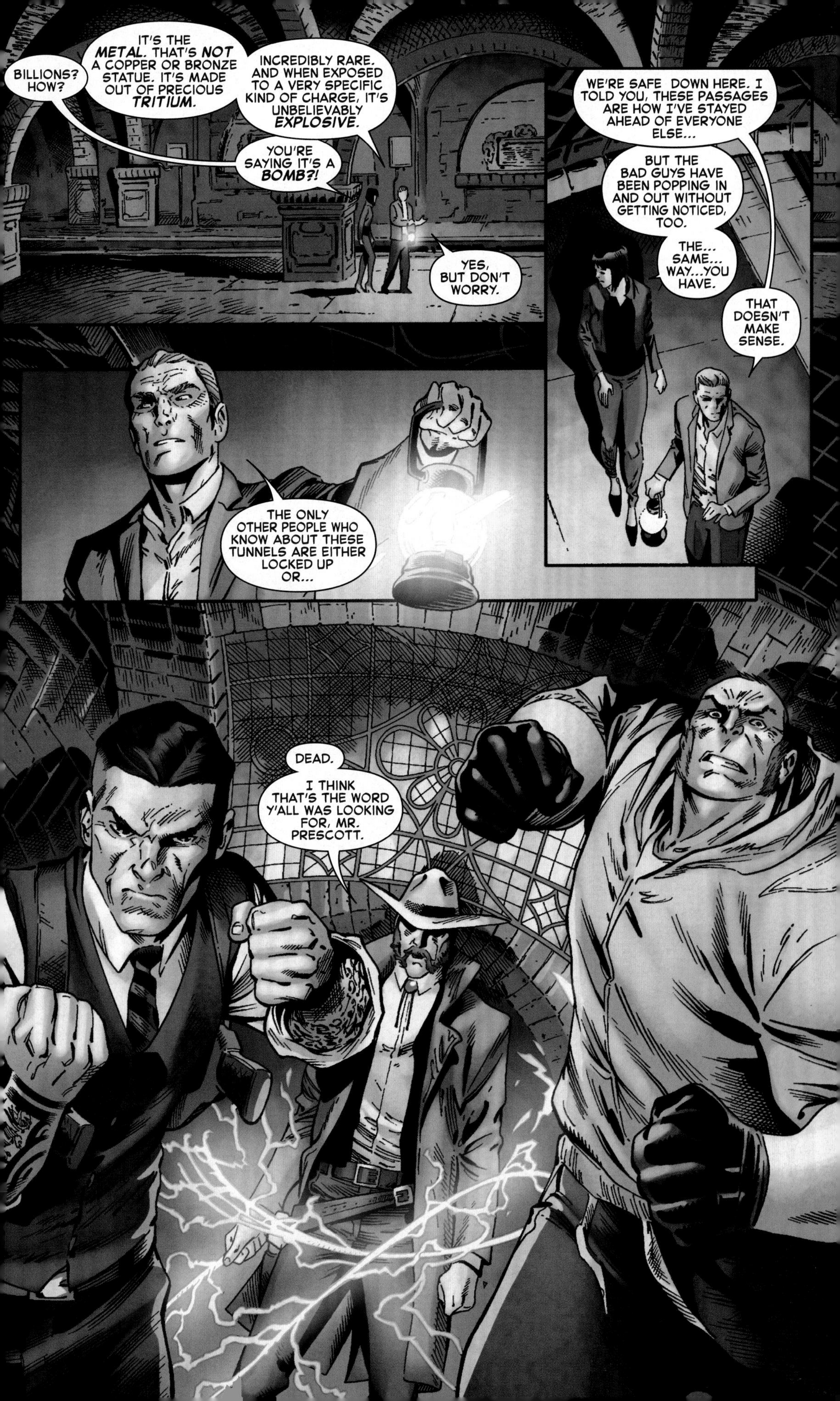

BILLIONS? HOW?
IT'S THE METAL. THAT'S NOT A COPPER OR BRONZE STATUE. IT'S MADE OUT OF PRECIOUS TRITIUM.
INCREDIBLY RARE. AND WHEN EXPOSED TO A VERY SPECIFIC KIND OF CHARGE, IT'S UNBELIEVABLY EXPLOSIVE.
YOU'RE SAYING IT'S A BOMB?!
YES, BUT DON'T WORRY.
WE'RE SAFE DOWN HERE. I TOLD YOU, THESE PASSAGES ARE HOW I'VE STAYED AHEAD OF EVERYONE ELSE...
BUT THE BAD GUYS HAVE BEEN POPPING IN AND OUT WITHOUT GETTING NOTICED, TOO.
THE... SAME... WAY...YOU HAVE.
THAT DOESN'T MAKE SENSE.
THE ONLY OTHER PEOPLE WHO KNOW ABOUT THESE TUNNELS ARE EITHER LOCKED UP OR...
DEAD.
I THINK THAT'S THE WORD Y'ALL WAS LOOKING FOR, MR. PRESCOTT.

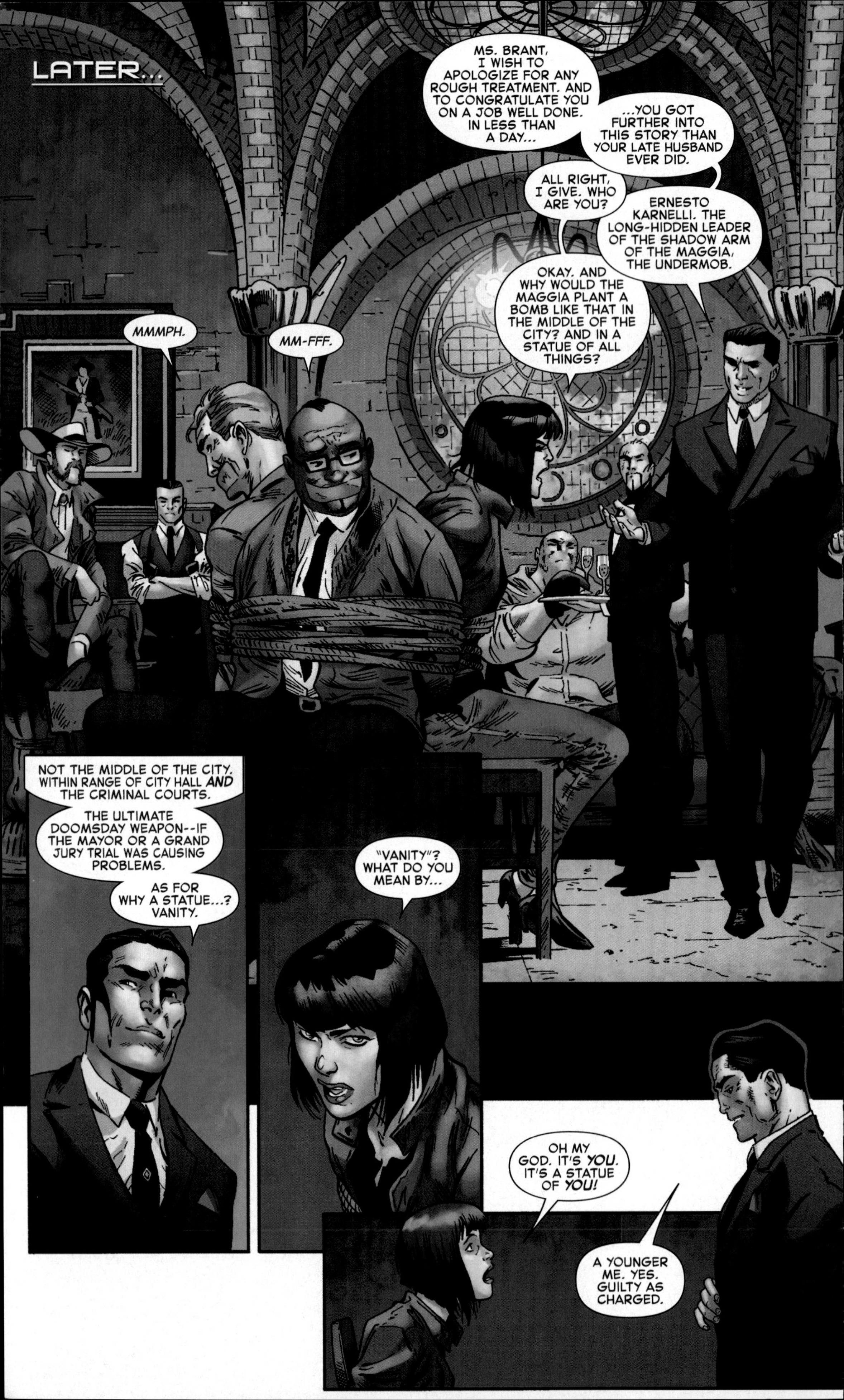
LATER...
MS. BRANT, I WISH TO APOLOGIZE FOR ANY ROUGH TREATMENT. AND TO CONGRATULATE YOU ON A JOB WELL DONE. IN LESS THAN A DAY...
...YOU GOT FURTHER INTO THIS STORY THAN YOUR LATE HUSBAND EVER DID.
ALL RIGHT, I GIVE. WHO ARE YOU?
ERNESTO KARNELLI. THE LONG-HIDDEN LEADER OF THE SHADOW ARM OF THE MAGGIA, THE UNDERMOB.
MMMPH.
MM-FFF.
OKAY. AND WHY WOULD THE MAGGIA PLANT A BOMB LIKE THAT IN THE MIDDLE OF THE CITY? AND IN A STATUE OF ALL THINGS?
NOT THE MIDDLE OF THE CITY. WITHIN RANGE OF CITY HALL AND THE CRIMINAL COURTS.
THE ULTIMATE DOOMSDAY WEAPON--IF THE MAYOR OR A GRAND JURY TRIAL WAS CAUSING PROBLEMS.
AS FOR WHY A STATUE...? VANITY.
"VANITY"? WHAT DO YOU MEAN BY...
OH MY GOD. IT'S YOU. IT'S A STATUE OF YOU!
A YOUNGER ME. YES. GUILTY AS CHARGED.

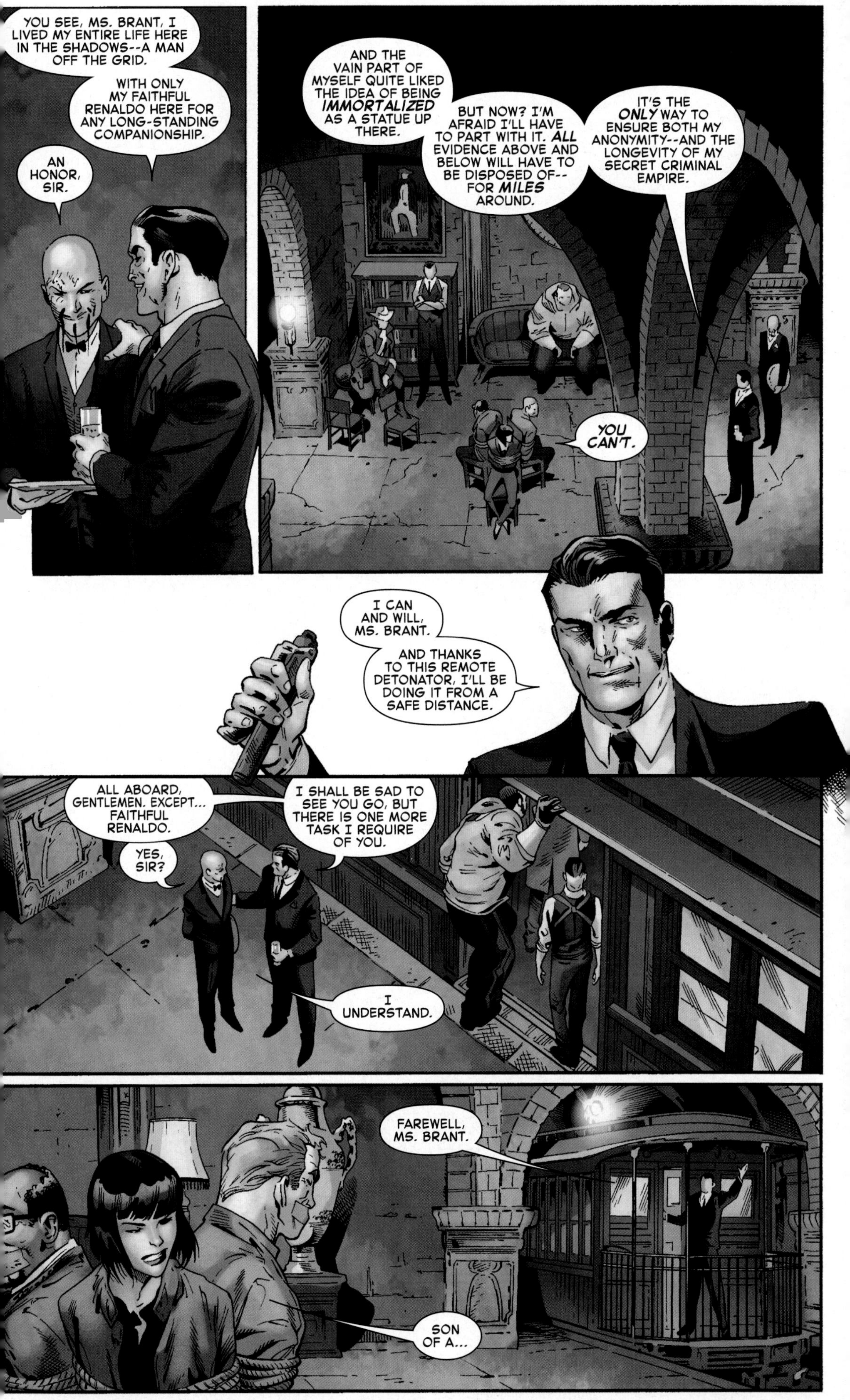
YOU SEE, MS. BRANT, I LIVED MY ENTIRE LIFE HERE IN THE SHADOWS--A MAN OFF THE GRID.
WITH ONLY MY FAITHFUL RENALDO HERE FOR ANY LONG-STANDING COMPANIONSHIP.
AN HONOR, SIR.
AND THE VAIN PART OF MYSELF QUITE LIKED THE IDEA OF BEING IMMORTALIZED AS A STATUE UP THERE.
BUT NOW? I'M AFRAID I'LL HAVE TO PART WITH IT. ALL EVIDENCE ABOVE AND BELOW WILL HAVE TO BE DISPOSED OF--FOR MILES AROUND.
IT'S THE ONLY WAY TO ENSURE BOTH MY ANONYMITY--AND THE LONGEVITY OF MY SECRET CRIMINAL EMPIRE.
YOU CAN'T.
I CAN AND WILL, MS. BRANT.
AND THANKS TO THIS REMOTE DETONATOR, I'LL BE DOING IT FROM A SAFE DISTANCE.
ALL ABOARD, GENTLEMEN. EXCEPT... FAITHFUL RENALDO.
YES, SIR?
I SHALL BE SAD TO SEE YOU GO, BUT THERE IS ONE MORE TASK I REQUIRE OF YOU.
I UNDERSTAND.
FAREWELL, MS. BRANT.
SON OF A...

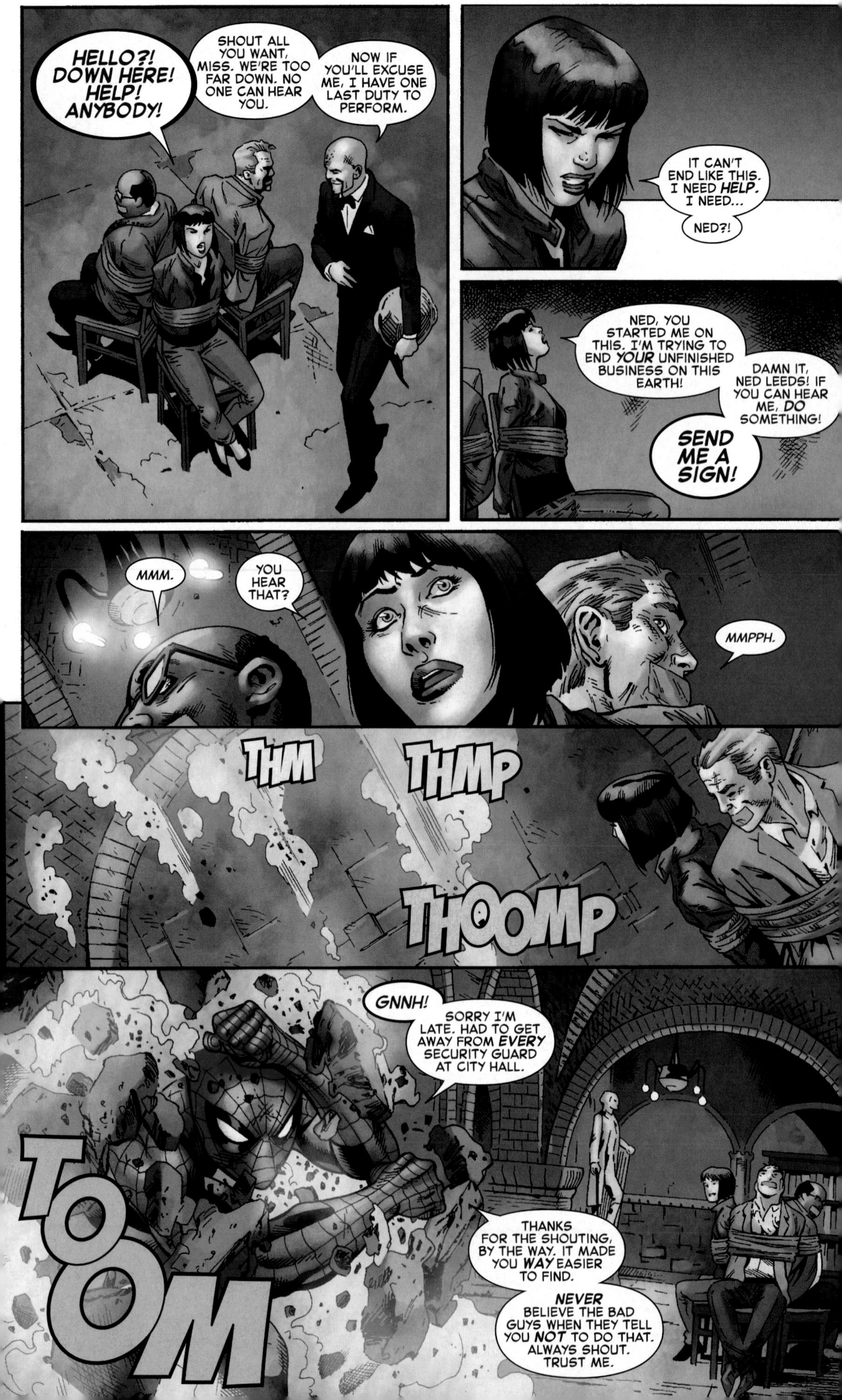
HELLO?! DOWN HERE! HELP! ANYBODY!
SHOUT ALL YOU WANT, MISS. WE'RE TOO FAR DOWN. NO ONE CAN HEAR YOU.
NOW IF YOU'LL EXCUSE ME, I HAVE ONE LAST DUTY TO PERFORM.
IT CAN'T END LIKE THIS. I NEED HELP. I NEED...
NED?!
NED, YOU STARTED ME ON THIS. I'M TRYING TO END YOUR UNFINISHED BUSINESS ON THIS EARTH!
DAMN IT, NED LEEDS! IF YOU CAN HEAR ME, DO SOMETHING!
SEND ME A SIGN!
MMM.
YOU HEAR THAT?
MMPPH.
THM
THMP
THOOMP
TOOM
GNNH!
SORRY I'M LATE. HAD TO GET AWAY FROM EVERY SECURITY GUARD AT CITY HALL.
THANKS FOR THE SHOUTING, BY THE WAY. IT MADE YOU WAY EASIER TO FIND.
NEVER BELIEVE THE BAD GUYS WHEN THEY TELL YOU NOT TO DO THAT. ALWAYS SHOUT. TRUST ME.

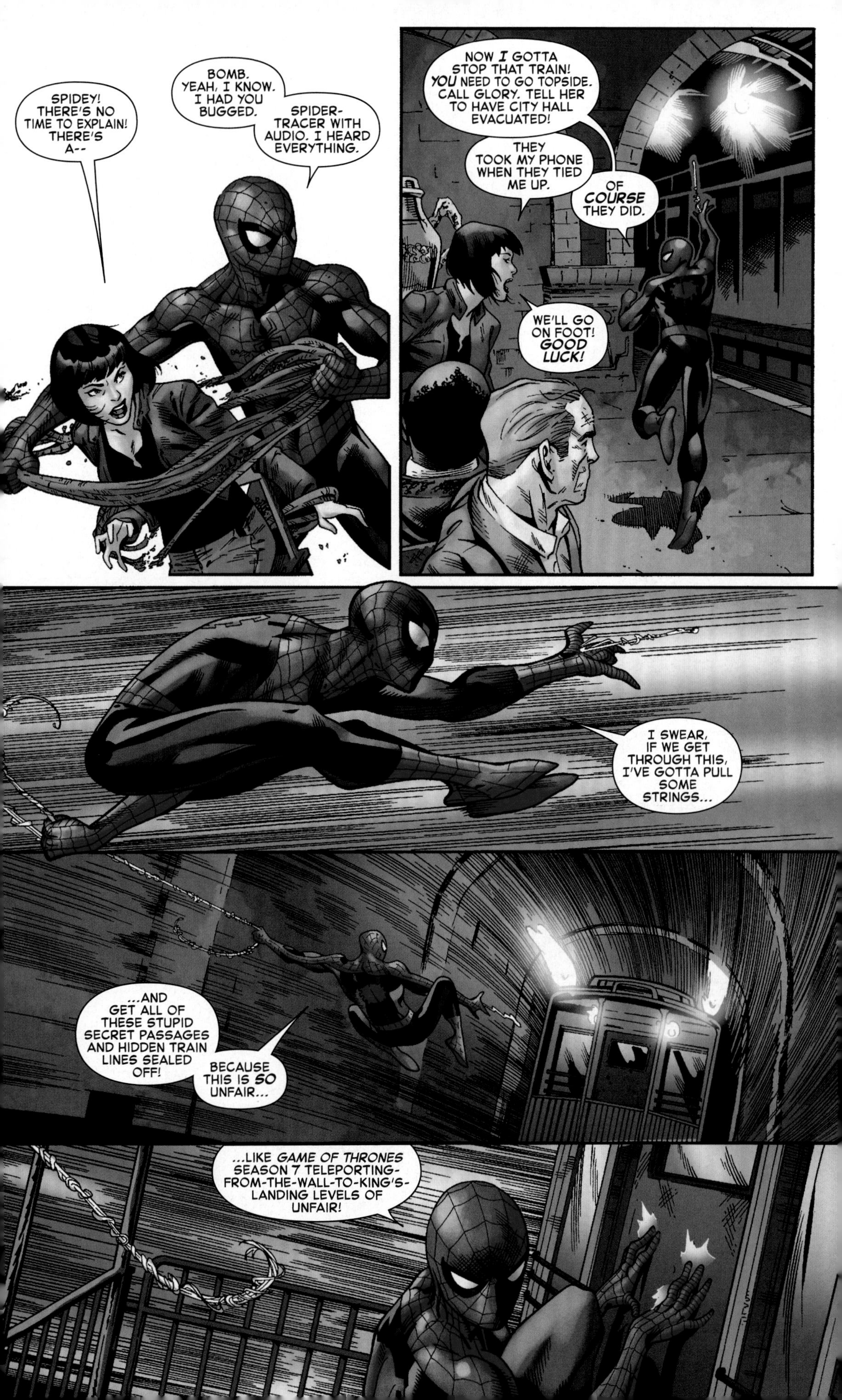
SPIDEY! THERE'S NO TIME TO EXPLAIN! THERE'S A--
BOMB. YEAH, I KNOW. I HAD YOU BUGGED.
SPIDER-TRACER WITH AUDIO. I HEARD EVERYTHING.
NOW I GOTTA STOP THAT TRAIN! YOU NEED TO GO TOPSIDE. CALL GLORY. TELL HER TO HAVE CITY HALL EVACUATED!
THEY TOOK MY PHONE WHEN THEY TIED ME UP.
OF COURSE THEY DID.
WE'LL GO ON FOOT! GOOD LUCK!
I SWEAR, IF WE GET THROUGH THIS, I'VE GOTTA PULL SOME STRINGS...
...AND GET ALL OF THESE STUPID SECRET PASSAGES AND HIDDEN TRAIN LINES SEALED OFF!
BECAUSE THIS IS SO UNFAIR...
...LIKE GAME OF THRONES SEASON 7 TELEPORTING-FROM-THE-WALL-TO-KING'S-LANDING LEVELS OF UNFAIR!

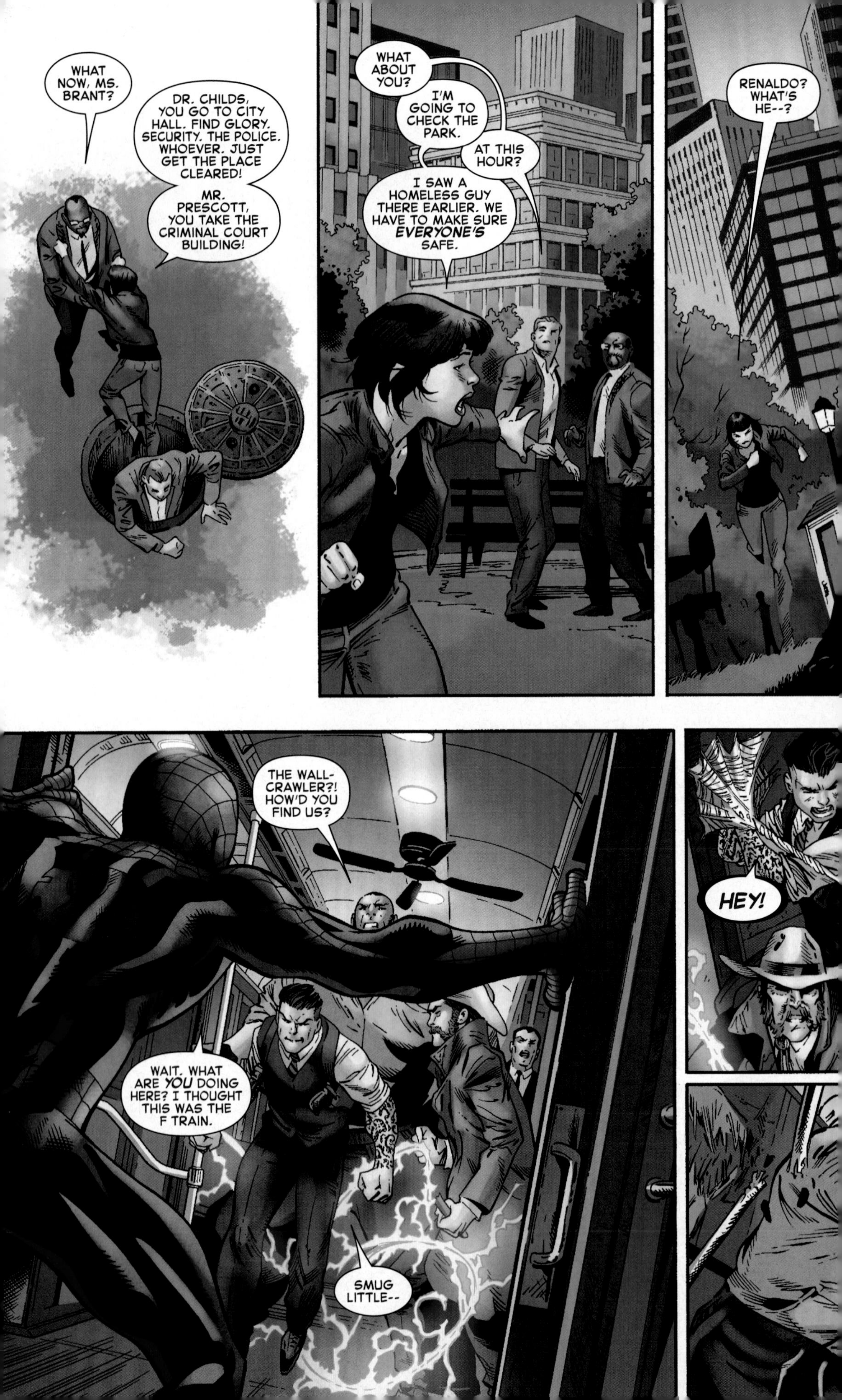
WHAT NOW, MS. BRANT?
DR. CHILDS, YOU GO TO CITY HALL. FIND GLORY. SECURITY. THE POLICE. WHOEVER. JUST GET THE PLACE CLEARED!
MR. PRESCOTT, YOU TAKE THE CRIMINAL COURT BUILDING!
WHAT ABOUT YOU?
I'M GOING TO CHECK THE PARK.
AT THIS HOUR?
I SAW A HOMELESS GUY THERE EARLIER. WE HAVE TO MAKE SURE EVERYONE'S SAFE.
RENALDO? WHAT'S HE--?
THE WALL-CRAWLER?! HOW'D YOU FIND US?
WAIT. WHAT ARE YOU DOING HERE? I THOUGHT THIS WAS THE F TRAIN.
SMUG LITTLE--
HEY!

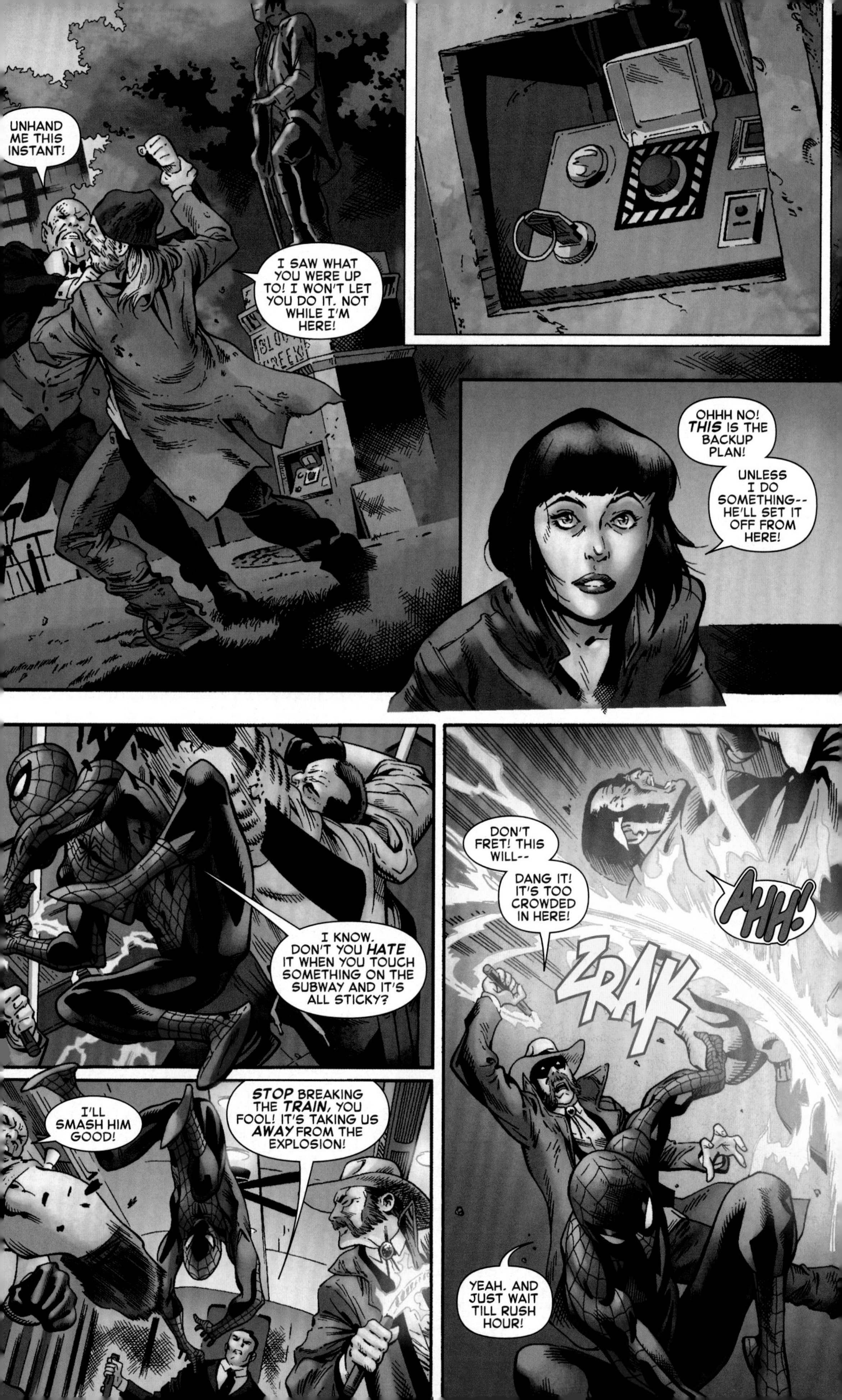

UNHAND ME THIS INSTANT!
I SAW WHAT YOU WERE UP TO! I WON'T LET YOU DO IT. NOT WHILE I'M HERE!
OHHH NO! THIS IS THE BACKUP PLAN!
UNLESS I DO SOMETHING-- HE'LL SET IT OFF FROM HERE!
I KNOW. DON'T YOU HATE IT WHEN YOU TOUCH SOMETHING ON THE SUBWAY AND IT'S ALL STICKY?
I'LL SMASH HIM GOOD!
STOP BREAKING THE TRAIN, YOU FOOL! IT'S TAKING US AWAY FROM THE EXPLOSION!
DON'T FRET! THIS WILL--
DANG IT! IT'S TOO CROWDED IN HERE!
AHH!
ZRAK
YEAH. AND JUST WAIT TILL RUSH HOUR!

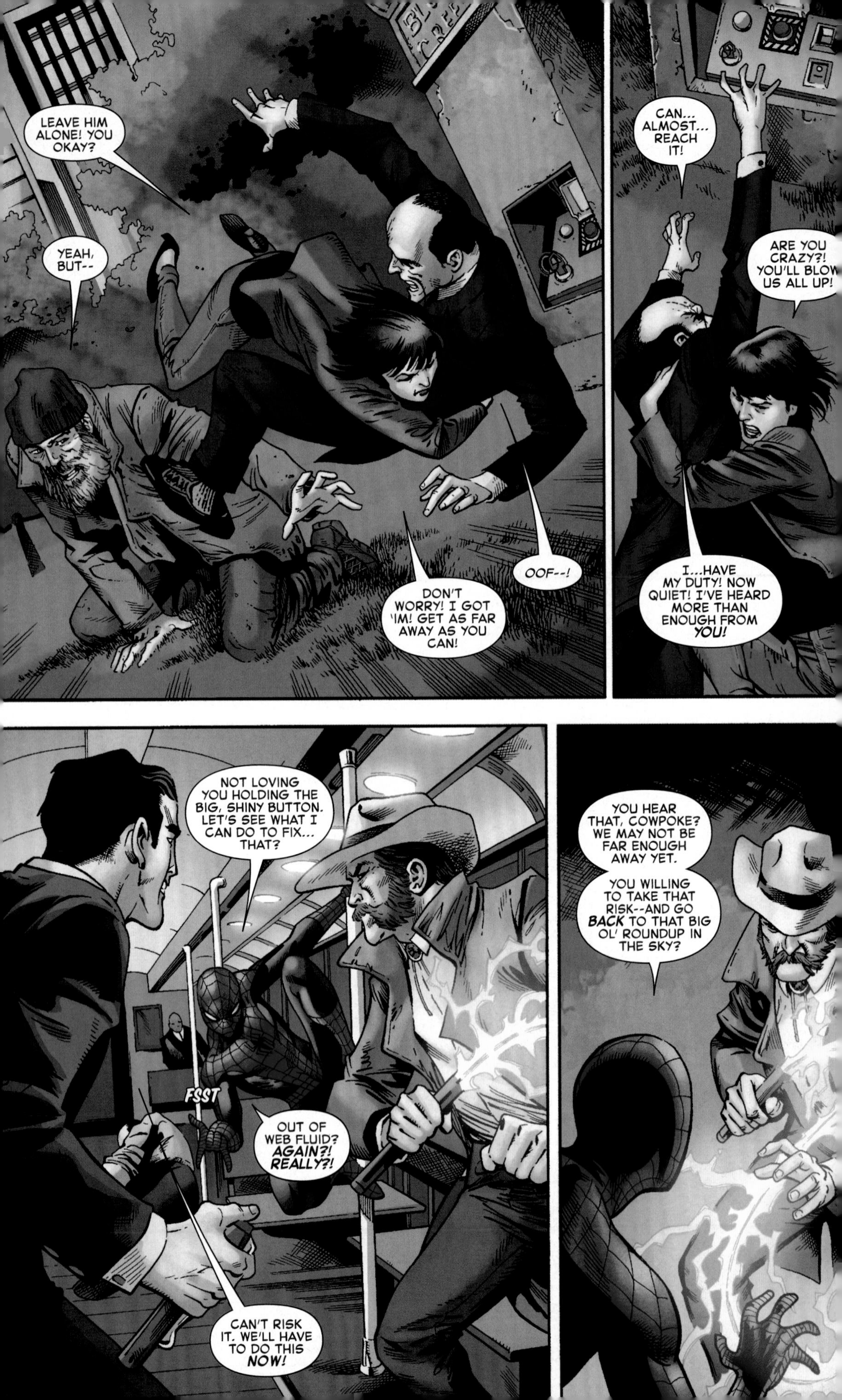
LEAVE HIM ALONE! YOU OKAY?
YEAH, BUT--
DON'T WORRY! I GOT 'IM! GET AS FAR AWAY AS YOU CAN!
OOF--!
CAN... ALMOST... REACH IT!
ARE YOU CRAZY?! YOU'LL BLOW US ALL UP!
I...HAVE MY DUTY! NOW QUIET! I'VE HEARD MORE THAN ENOUGH FROM *YOU!*
NOT LOVING YOU HOLDING THE BIG, SHINY BUTTON. LET'S SEE WHAT I CAN DO TO FIX... THAT?
FSST
OUT OF WEB FLUID? *AGAIN?! REALLY?!*
CAN'T RISK IT. WE'LL HAVE TO DO THIS *NOW!*
YOU HEAR THAT, COWPOKE? WE MAY NOT BE FAR ENOUGH AWAY YET.
YOU WILLING TO TAKE THAT RISK--AND GO *BACK* TO THAT BIG OL' ROUNDUP IN THE SKY?

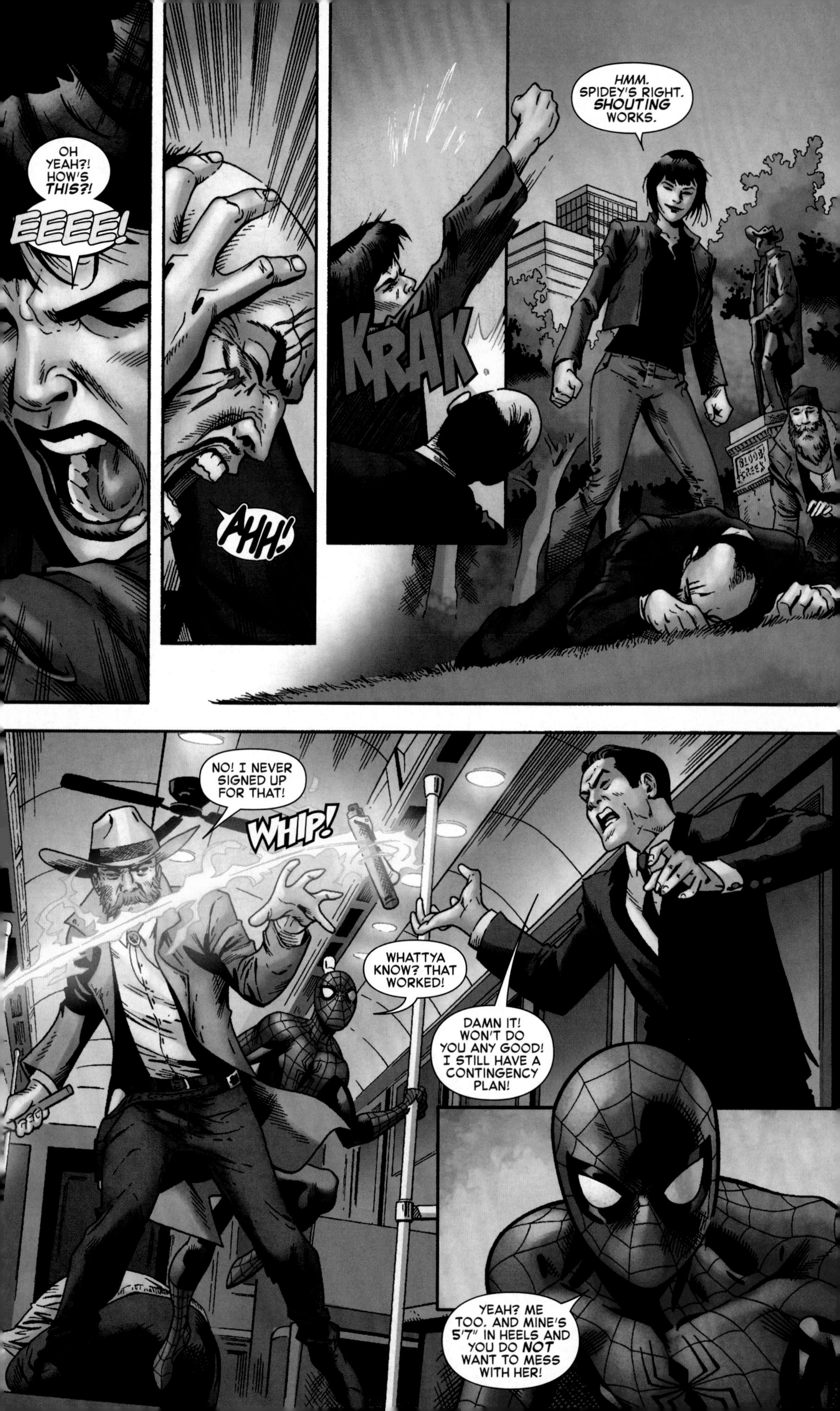
OH YEAH?! HOW'S THIS?!
EEEEE!
AHH!
KRAK
HMM. SPIDEY'S RIGHT. SHOUTING WORKS.
NO! I NEVER SIGNED UP FOR THAT!
WHIP!
WHATTYA KNOW? THAT WORKED!
DAMN IT! WON'T DO YOU ANY GOOD! I STILL HAVE A CONTINGENCY PLAN!
YEAH? ME TOO. AND MINE'S 5'7" IN HEELS AND YOU DO NOT WANT TO MESS WITH HER!

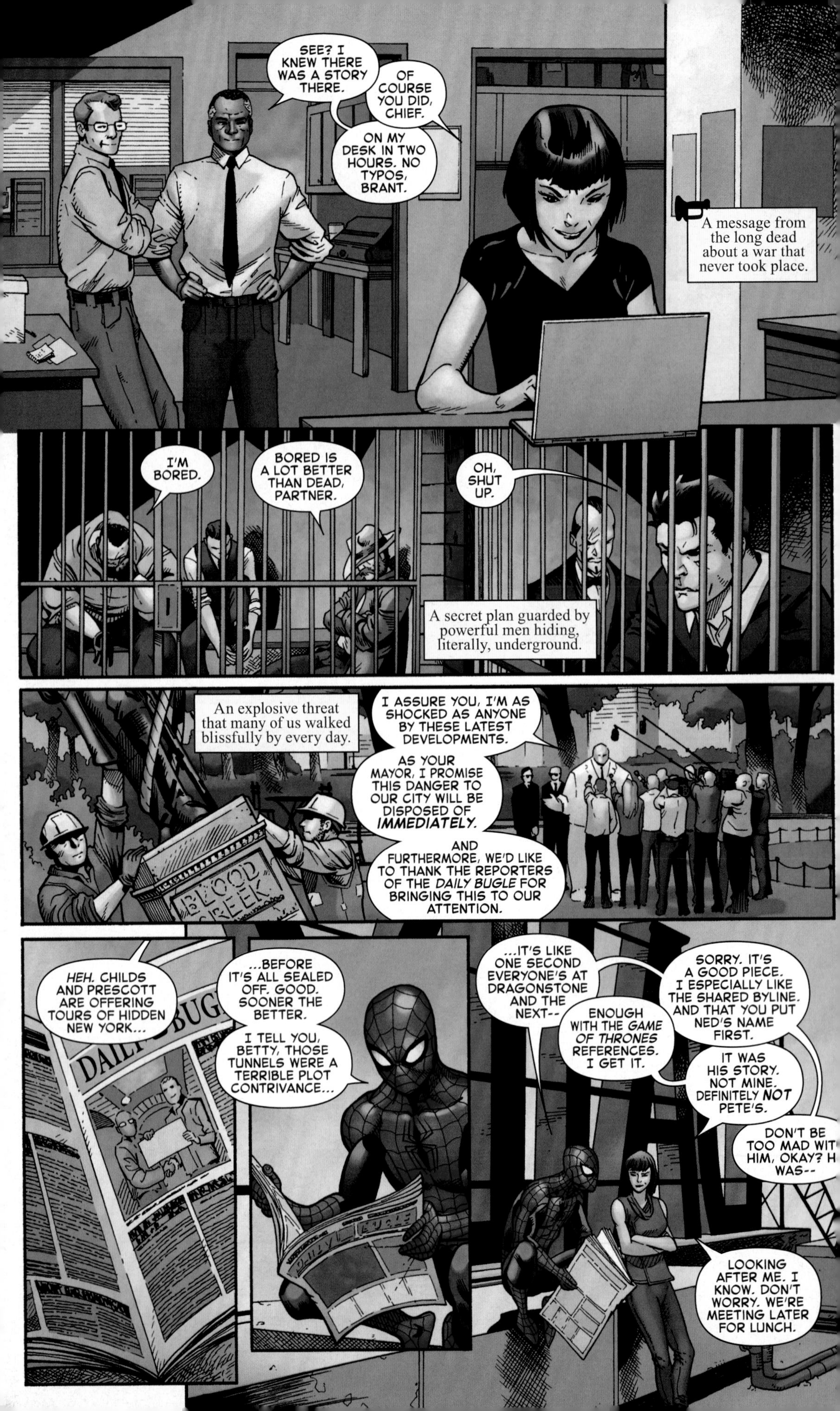
SEE? I KNEW THERE WAS A STORY THERE.
OF COURSE YOU DID, CHIEF.
ON MY DESK IN TWO HOURS. NO TYPOS, BRANT.
A message from the long dead about a war that never took place.
I'M BORED.
BORED IS A LOT BETTER THAN DEAD, PARTNER.
OH, SHUT UP.
A secret plan guarded by powerful men hiding, literally, underground.
An explosive threat that many of us walked blissfully by every day.
I ASSURE YOU, I'M AS SHOCKED AS ANYONE BY THESE LATEST DEVELOPMENTS.
AS YOUR MAYOR, I PROMISE THIS DANGER TO OUR CITY WILL BE DISPOSED OF *IMMEDIATELY.*
AND FURTHERMORE, WE'D LIKE TO THANK THE REPORTERS OF THE *DAILY BUGLE* FOR BRINGING THIS TO OUR ATTENTION.
BLOOD CREEK
HEH. CHILDS AND PRESCOTT ARE OFFERING TOURS OF HIDDEN NEW YORK...
...BEFORE IT'S ALL SEALED OFF. GOOD. SOONER THE BETTER.
I TELL YOU, BETTY, THOSE TUNNELS WERE A TERRIBLE PLOT CONTRIVANCE...
...IT'S LIKE ONE SECOND EVERYONE'S AT DRAGONSTONE AND THE NEXT--
ENOUGH WITH THE *GAME OF THRONES* REFERENCES. I GET IT.
SORRY. IT'S A GOOD PIECE. I ESPECIALLY LIKE THE SHARED BYLINE. AND THAT YOU PUT NED'S NAME FIRST.
IT WAS HIS STORY. NOT MINE. DEFINITELY *NOT* PETE'S.
DON'T BE TOO MAD WIT HIM, OKAY? H WAS--
LOOKING AFTER ME. I KNOW. DON'T WORRY. WE'RE MEETING LATER FOR LUNCH.

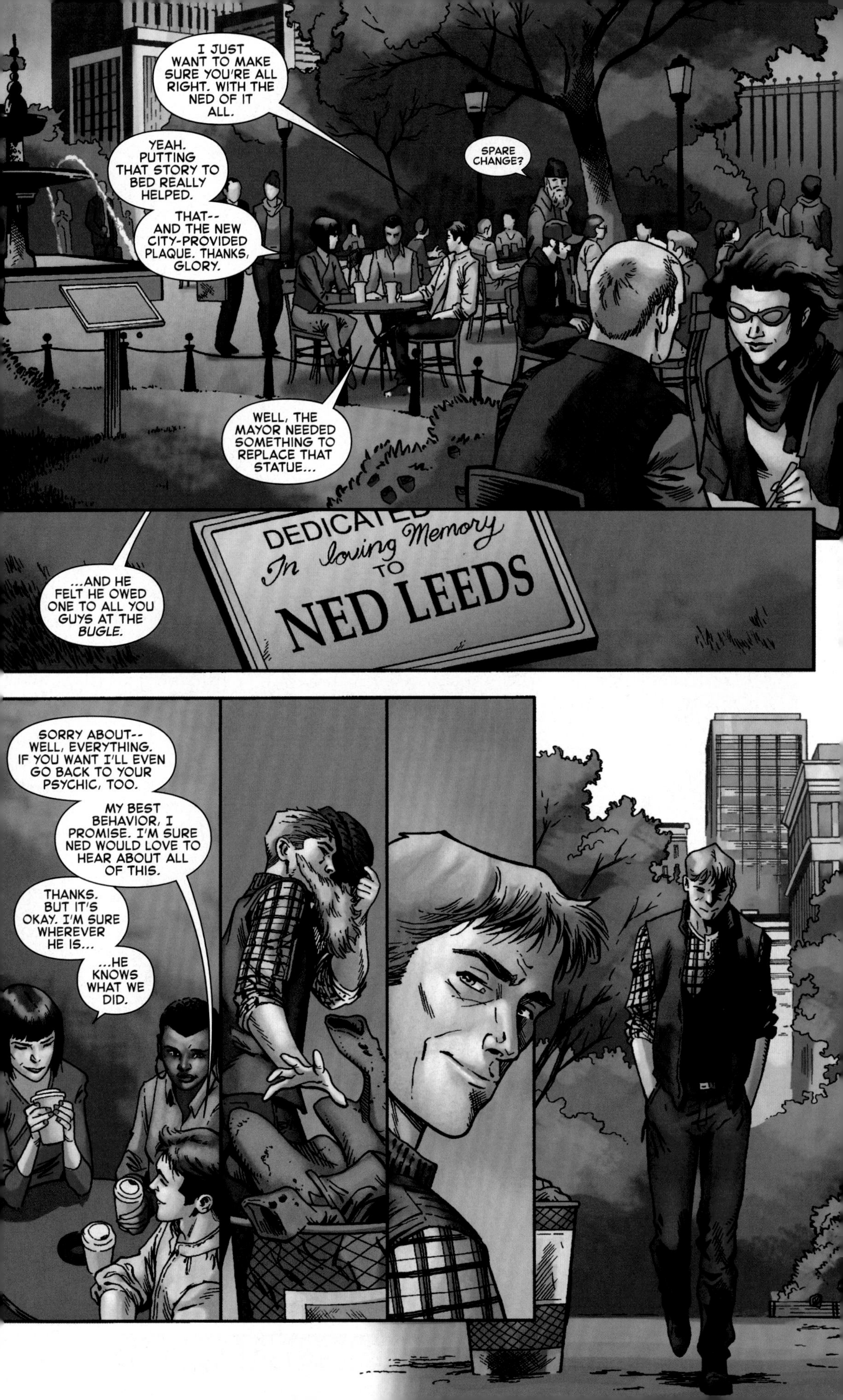

I JUST WANT TO MAKE SURE YOU'RE ALL RIGHT. WITH THE NED OF IT ALL.
YEAH. PUTTING THAT STORY TO BED REALLY HELPED.
THAT-- AND THE NEW CITY-PROVIDED PLAQUE. THANKS, GLORY.
SPARE CHANGE?
WELL, THE MAYOR NEEDED SOMETHING TO REPLACE THAT STATUE...
...AND HE FELT HE OWED ONE TO ALL YOU GUYS AT THE BUGLE.
DEDICATED
In loving Memory
TO
NED LEEDS
SORRY ABOUT-- WELL, EVERYTHING. IF YOU WANT I'LL EVEN GO BACK TO YOUR PSYCHIC, TOO.
MY BEST BEHAVIOR, I PROMISE. I'M SURE NED WOULD LOVE TO HEAR ABOUT ALL OF THIS.
THANKS. BUT IT'S OKAY. I'M SURE WHEREVER HE IS...
...HE KNOWS WHAT WE DID.

794

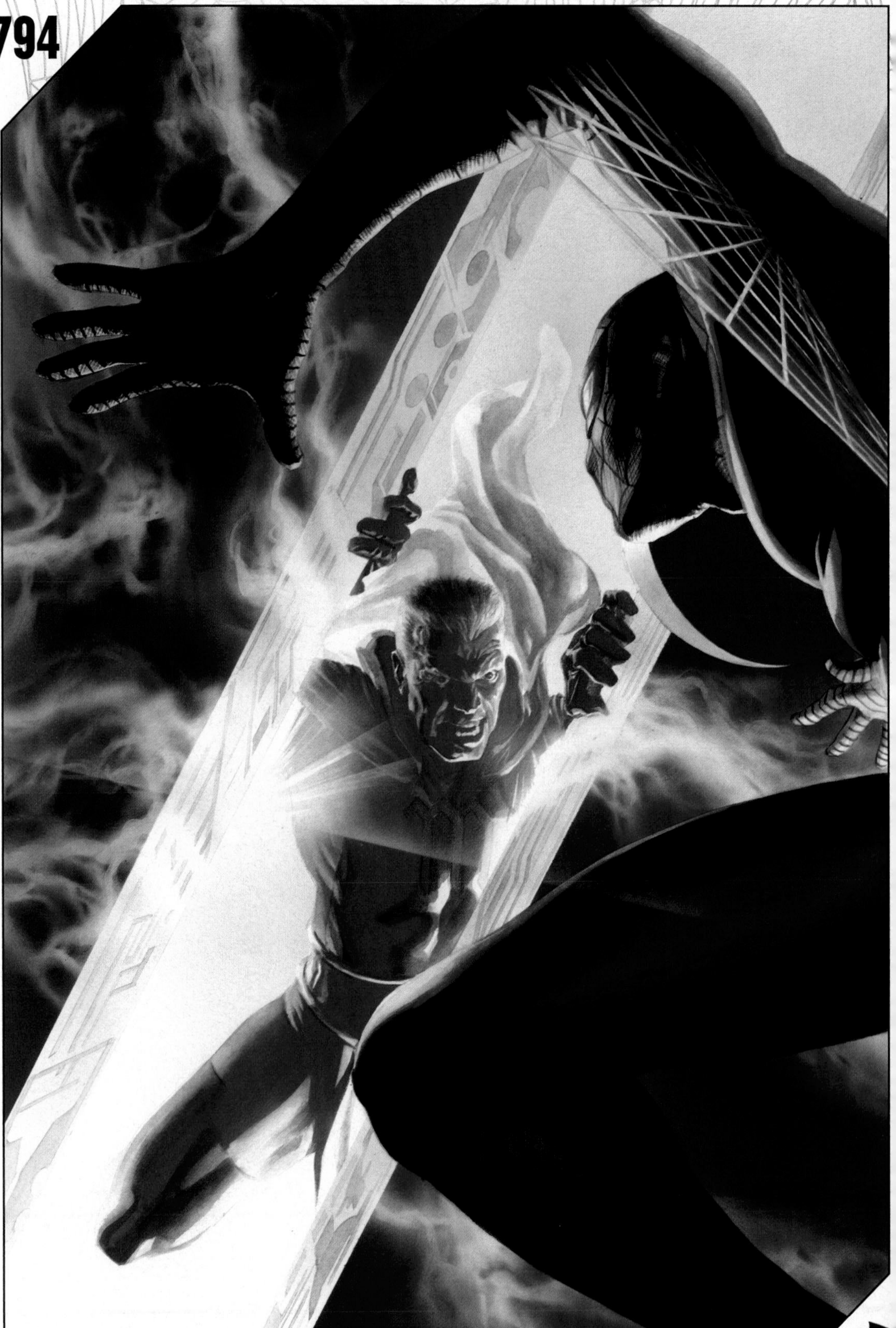

THREAT LEVEL: RED PART ONE "LAST CHANCE"

WHEN PETER PARKER WAS BITTEN BY A RADIOACTIVE SPIDER, HE GAINED THE PROPORTIONAL SPEED, STRENGTH AND AGILITY OF A SPIDER; ADHESIVE FINGERTIPS AND TOES; AND THE UNIQUE PRECOGNITIVE AWARENESS OF DANGER CALLED "SPIDER-SENSE"! AFTER LEARNING THAT WITH GREAT POWER THERE MUST ALSO COME GREAT RESPONSIBILITY, HE BECAME THE CRIME-FIGHTING SUPER HERO CALLED...

the AMAZING SPIDER-MAN

Since the downfall of Parker Industries, dejected and penniless former C.E.O. *PETER PARKER* has been crashing on the couch of *BOBBI MORSE A.K.A. MOCKINGBIRD*, with little to keep him happy save for his patrols as *THE AMAZING SPIDER-MAN*.

Almost exactly one year has passed since Spider-Man battled the Zodiac terrorist organization and its leader, *SCORPIO*. After obtaining the *ZODIAC KEY*, *Scorpio* used its power to unlock a gateway into the Zodiac Dimension, which granted him all knowledge of everything that would occur within the next year.

Spider-Man foiled the villain's plans to use this knowledge for evil and sealed Scorpio inside the mysterious dimension itself, buying the world precious time before the gateway would open once more 365 days later...TODAY!

PETER PARKER, A.K.A. THE AMAZING SPIDER-MAN

MOCKINGBIRD

MAX MODELL

SCORPIO

ANNA MARIA MARCONI

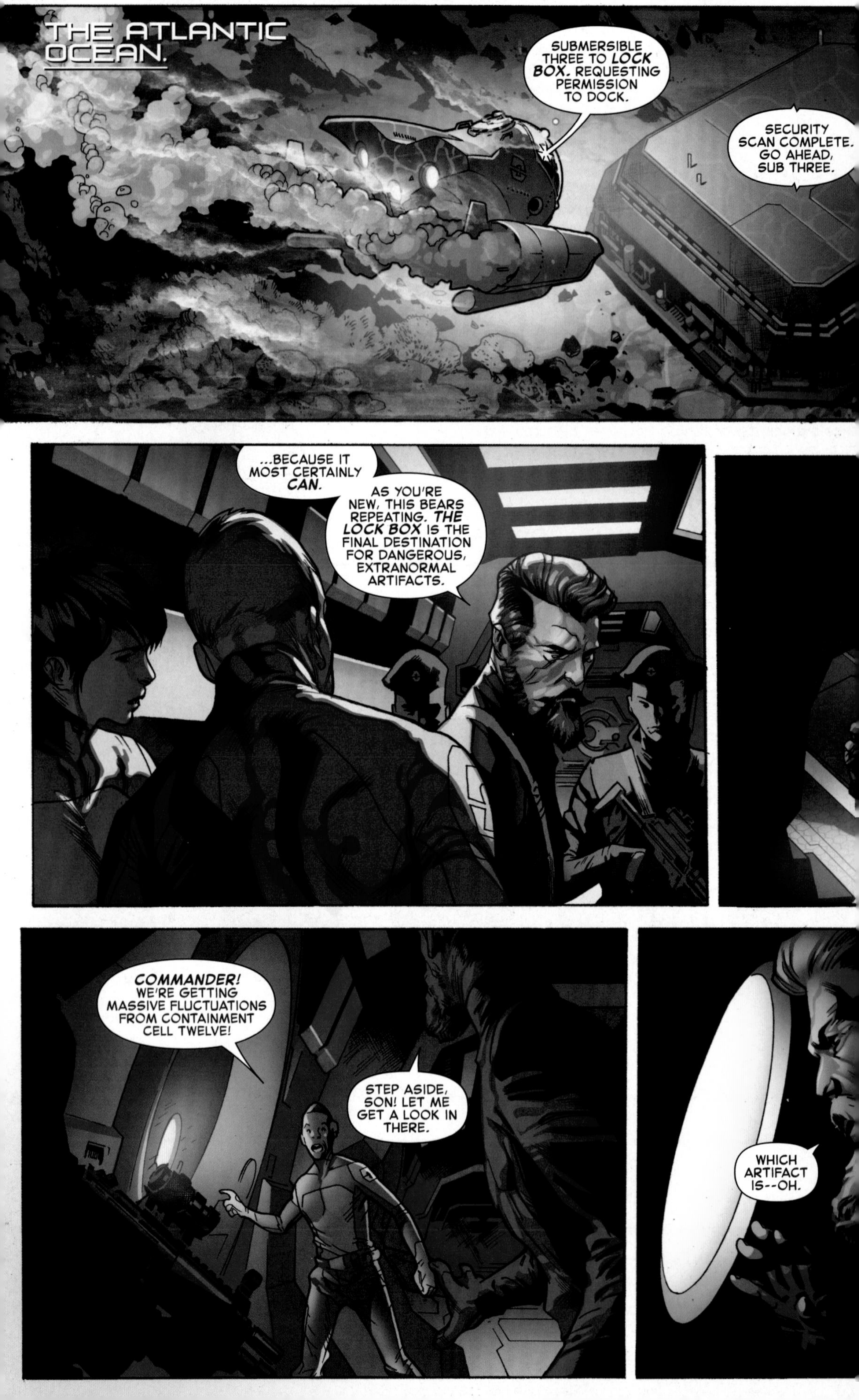
THE ATLANTIC OCEAN.
SUBMERSIBLE THREE TO LOCK BOX. REQUESTING PERMISSION TO DOCK.
SECURITY SCAN COMPLETE. GO AHEAD, SUB THREE.
...BECAUSE IT MOST CERTAINLY CAN.
AS YOU'RE NEW, THIS BEARS REPEATING. THE LOCK BOX IS THE FINAL DESTINATION FOR DANGEROUS, EXTRANORMAL ARTIFACTS.
COMMANDER! WE'RE GETTING MASSIVE FLUCTUATIONS FROM CONTAINMENT CELL TWELVE!
STEP ASIDE, SON! LET ME GET A LOOK IN THERE.
WHICH ARTIFACT IS--OH.

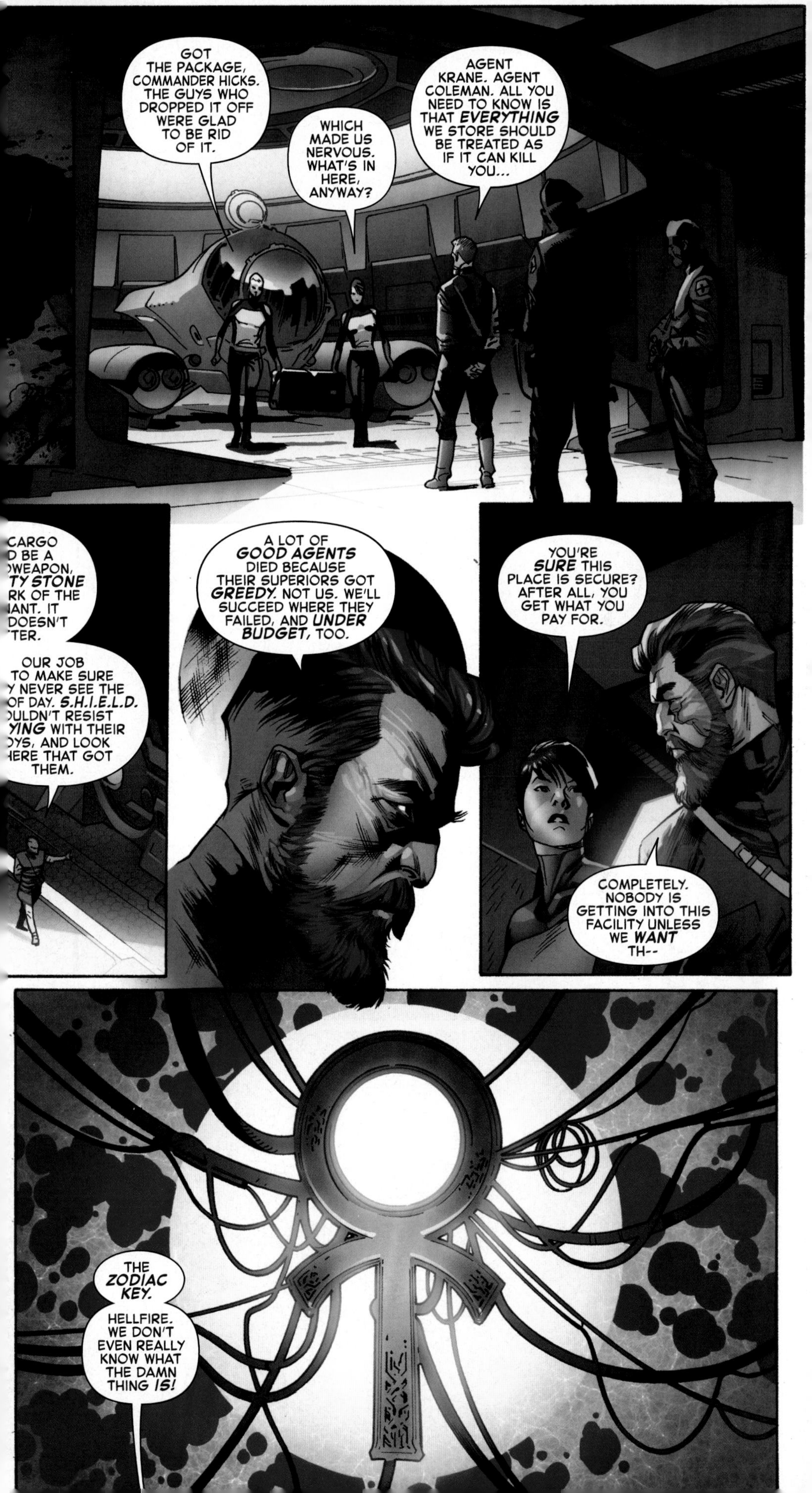
GOT THE PACKAGE, COMMANDER HICKS. THE GUYS WHO DROPPED IT OFF WERE GLAD TO BE RID OF IT.
WHICH MADE US NERVOUS. WHAT'S IN HERE, ANYWAY?
AGENT KRANE. AGENT COLEMAN. ALL YOU NEED TO KNOW IS THAT EVERYTHING WE STORE SHOULD BE TREATED AS IF IT CAN KILL YOU...
CARGO D BE A OWEAPON, TY STONE RK OF THE IANT. IT DOESN'T TER.
OUR JOB TO MAKE SURE Y NEVER SEE THE OF DAY. S.H.I.E.L.D. OULDN'T RESIST YING WITH THEIR OYS, AND LOOK HERE THAT GOT THEM.
A LOT OF GOOD AGENTS DIED BECAUSE THEIR SUPERIORS GOT GREEDY. NOT US. WE'LL SUCCEED WHERE THEY FAILED, AND UNDER BUDGET, TOO.
YOU'RE SURE THIS PLACE IS SECURE? AFTER ALL, YOU GET WHAT YOU PAY FOR.
COMPLETELY. NOBODY IS GETTING INTO THIS FACILITY UNLESS WE WANT TH--
THE ZODIAC KEY.
HELLFIRE. WE DON'T EVEN REALLY KNOW WHAT THE DAMN THING IS!

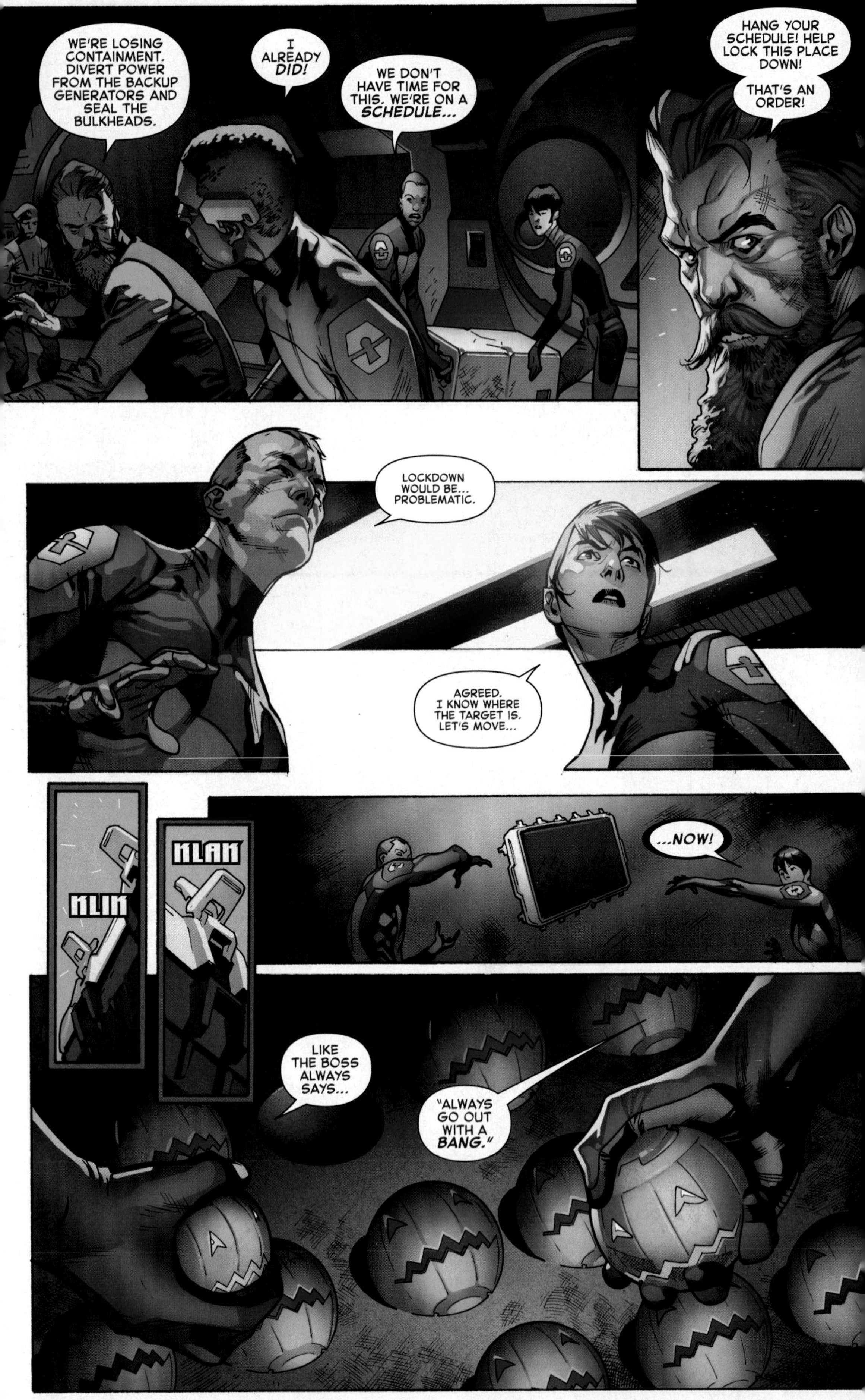

WE'RE LOSING CONTAINMENT. DIVERT POWER FROM THE BACKUP GENERATORS AND SEAL THE BULKHEADS.
I ALREADY DID!
WE DON'T HAVE TIME FOR THIS. WE'RE ON A SCHEDULE...
HANG YOUR SCHEDULE! HELP LOCK THIS PLACE DOWN!
THAT'S AN ORDER!
LOCKDOWN WOULD BE... PROBLEMATIC.
AGREED. I KNOW WHERE THE TARGET IS. LET'S MOVE...
KLIK
KLAK
...NOW!
LIKE THE BOSS ALWAYS SAYS...
"ALWAYS GO OUT WITH A BANG."

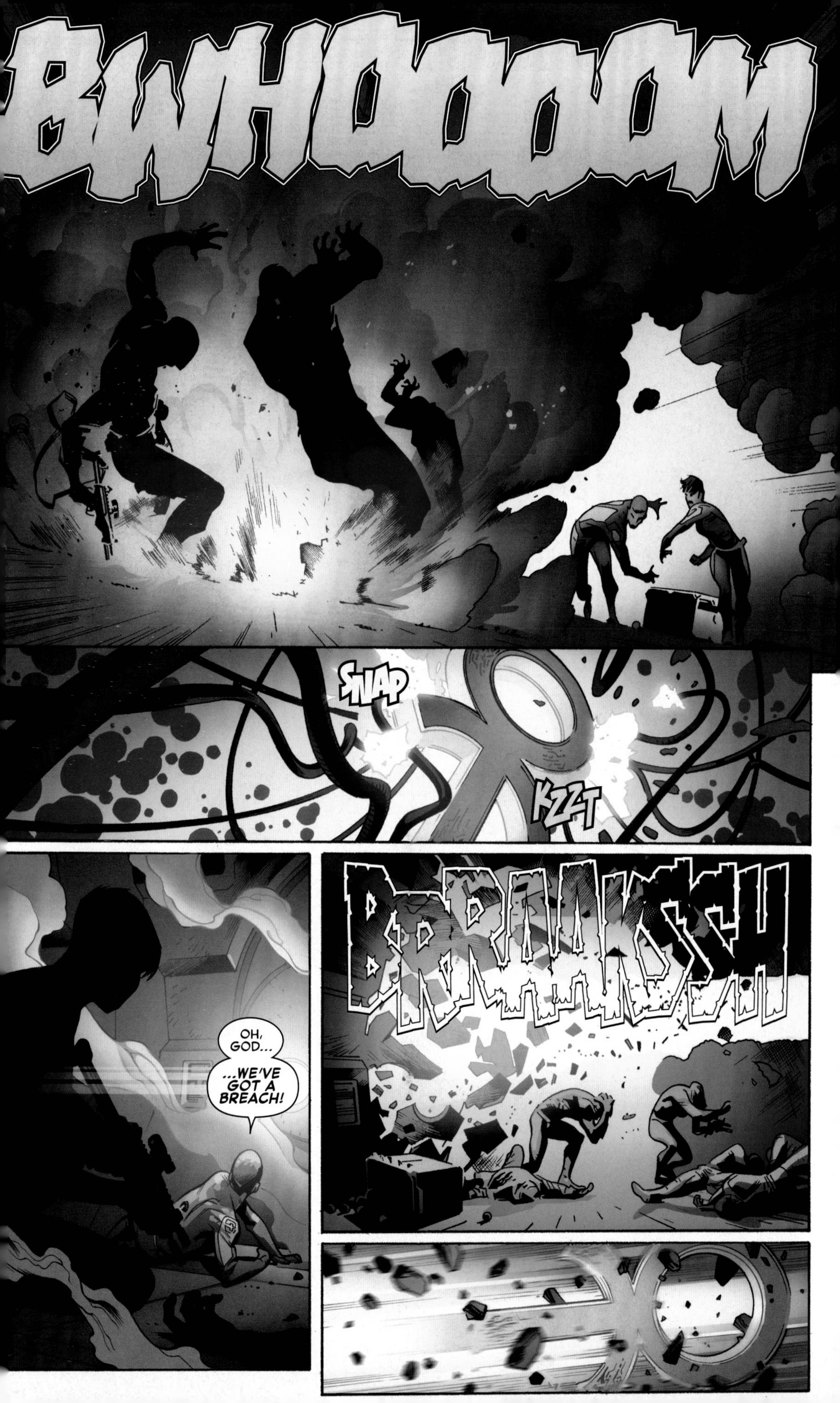
BWHOOOM
SNAP
KZZT
OH, GOD...
...WE'VE GOT A BREACH!
BRRAKKSSH

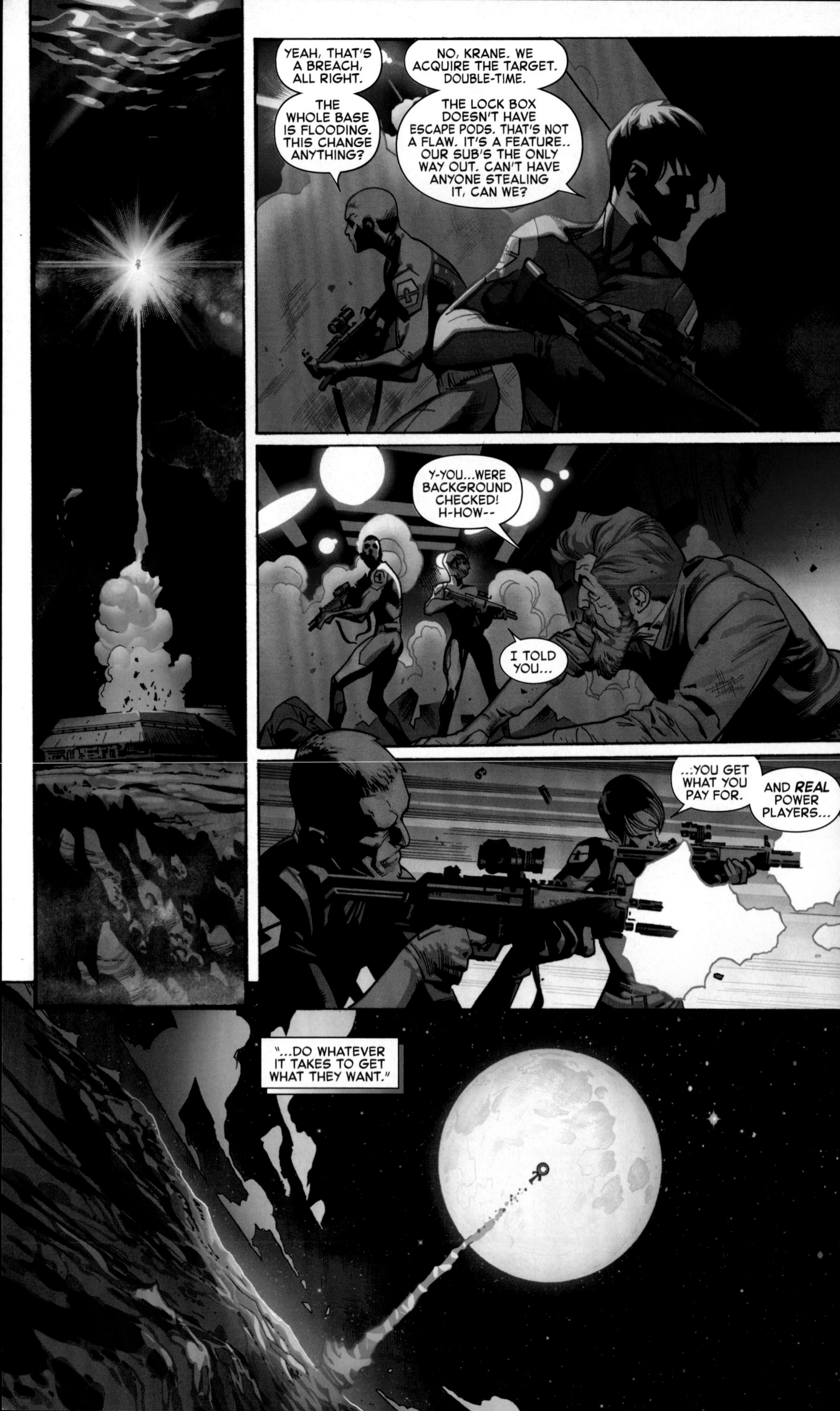
YEAH, THAT'S A BREACH, ALL RIGHT.
THE WHOLE BASE IS FLOODING. THIS CHANGE ANYTHING?
NO, KRANE. WE ACQUIRE THE TARGET. DOUBLE-TIME.
THE LOCK BOX DOESN'T HAVE ESCAPE PODS. THAT'S NOT A FLAW. IT'S A FEATURE.. OUR SUB'S THE ONLY WAY OUT. CAN'T HAVE ANYONE STEALING IT, CAN WE?
Y-YOU...WERE BACKGROUND CHECKED! H-HOW--
I TOLD YOU...
...YOU GET WHAT YOU PAY FOR.
AND REAL POWER PLAYERS...
"...DO WHATEVER IT TAKES TO GET WHAT THEY WANT."

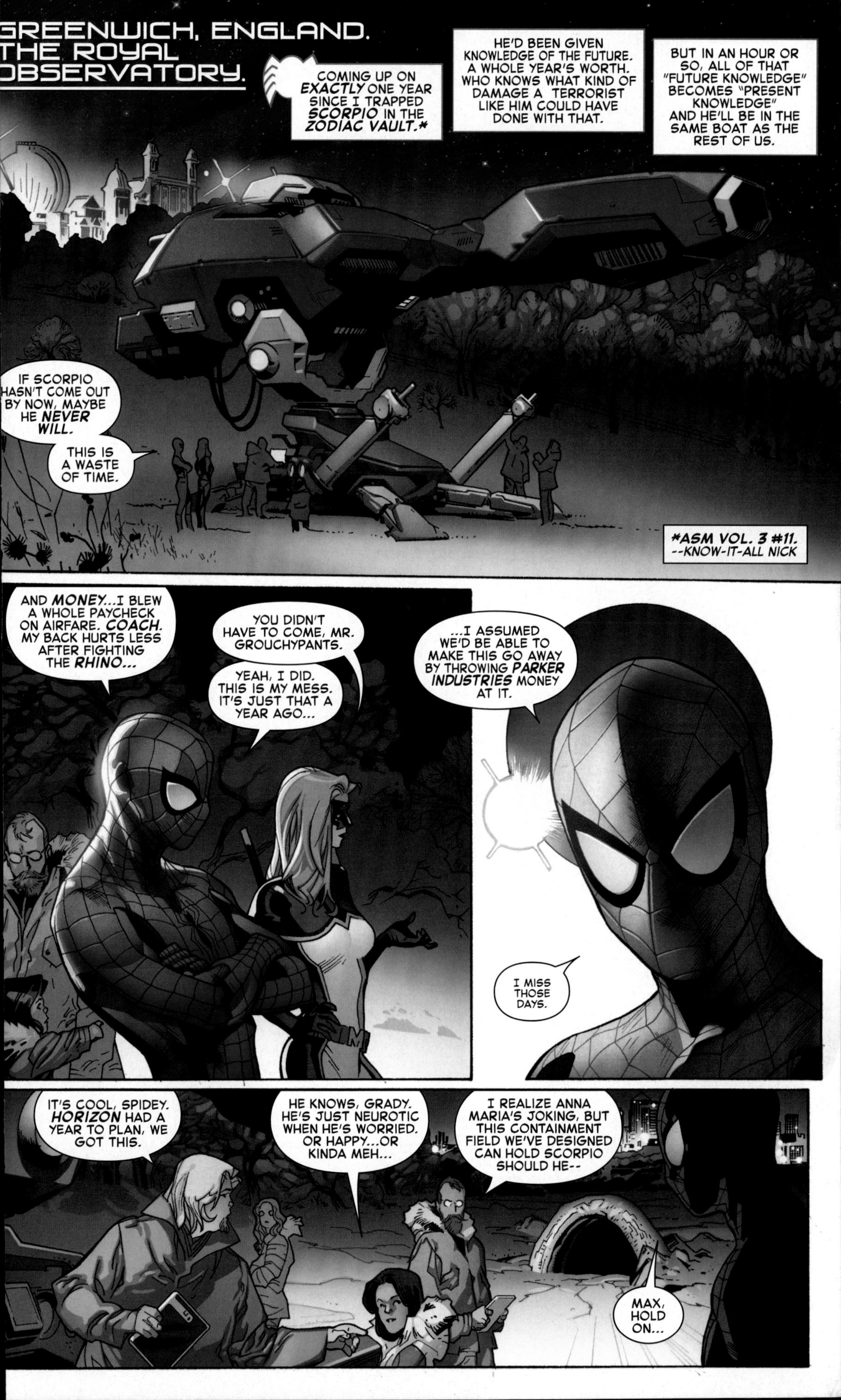

GREENWICH, ENGLAND. THE ROYAL OBSERVATORY.
COMING UP ON EXACTLY ONE YEAR SINCE I TRAPPED SCORPIO IN THE ZODIAC VAULT.*
HE'D BEEN GIVEN KNOWLEDGE OF THE FUTURE. A WHOLE YEAR'S WORTH. WHO KNOWS WHAT KIND OF DAMAGE A TERRORIST LIKE HIM COULD HAVE DONE WITH THAT.
BUT IN AN HOUR OR SO, ALL OF THAT "FUTURE KNOWLEDGE" BECOMES "PRESENT KNOWLEDGE" AND HE'LL BE IN THE SAME BOAT AS THE REST OF US.
IF SCORPIO HASN'T COME OUT BY NOW, MAYBE HE NEVER WILL.
THIS IS A WASTE OF TIME.
*ASM VOL. 3 #11. --KNOW-IT-ALL NICK
AND MONEY...I BLEW A WHOLE PAYCHECK ON AIRFARE. COACH. MY BACK HURTS LESS AFTER FIGHTING THE RHINO...
YOU DIDN'T HAVE TO COME, MR. GROUCHYPANTS.
YEAH, I DID. THIS IS MY MESS. IT'S JUST THAT A YEAR AGO...
...I ASSUMED WE'D BE ABLE TO MAKE THIS GO AWAY BY THROWING PARKER INDUSTRIES MONEY AT IT.
I MISS THOSE DAYS.
IT'S COOL, SPIDEY. HORIZON HAD A YEAR TO PLAN. WE GOT THIS.
HE KNOWS, GRADY. HE'S JUST NEUROTIC WHEN HE'S WORRIED. OR HAPPY...OR KINDA MEH...
I REALIZE ANNA MARIA'S JOKING, BUT THIS CONTAINMENT FIELD WE'VE DESIGNED CAN HOLD SCORPIO SHOULD HE--
MAX, HOLD ON...

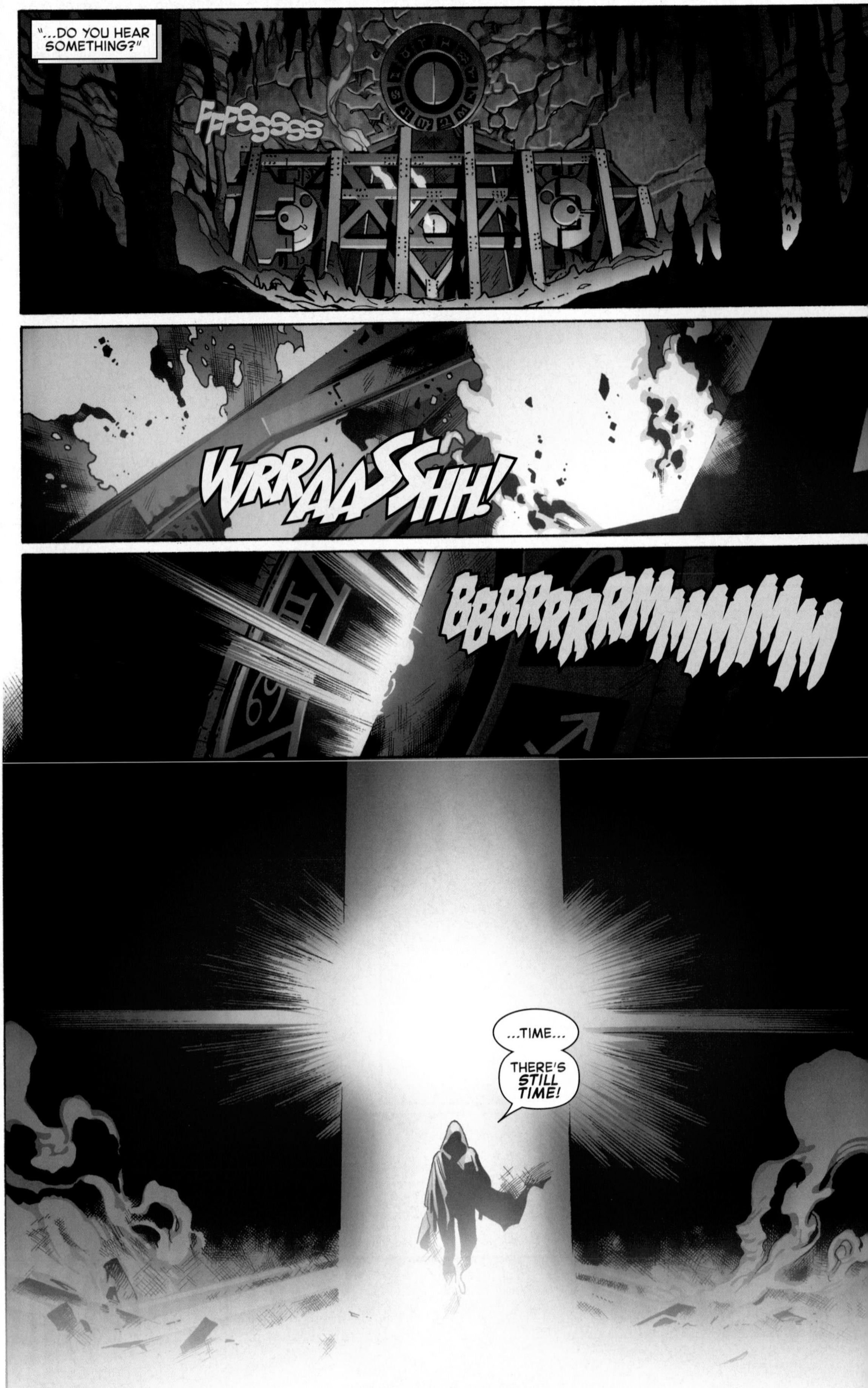
"...DO YOU HEAR SOMETHING?"
FFFSSSSSS
VVRRAASSHH!
BBBRRRRMMMMMM
...TIME...
THERE'S STILL TIME!

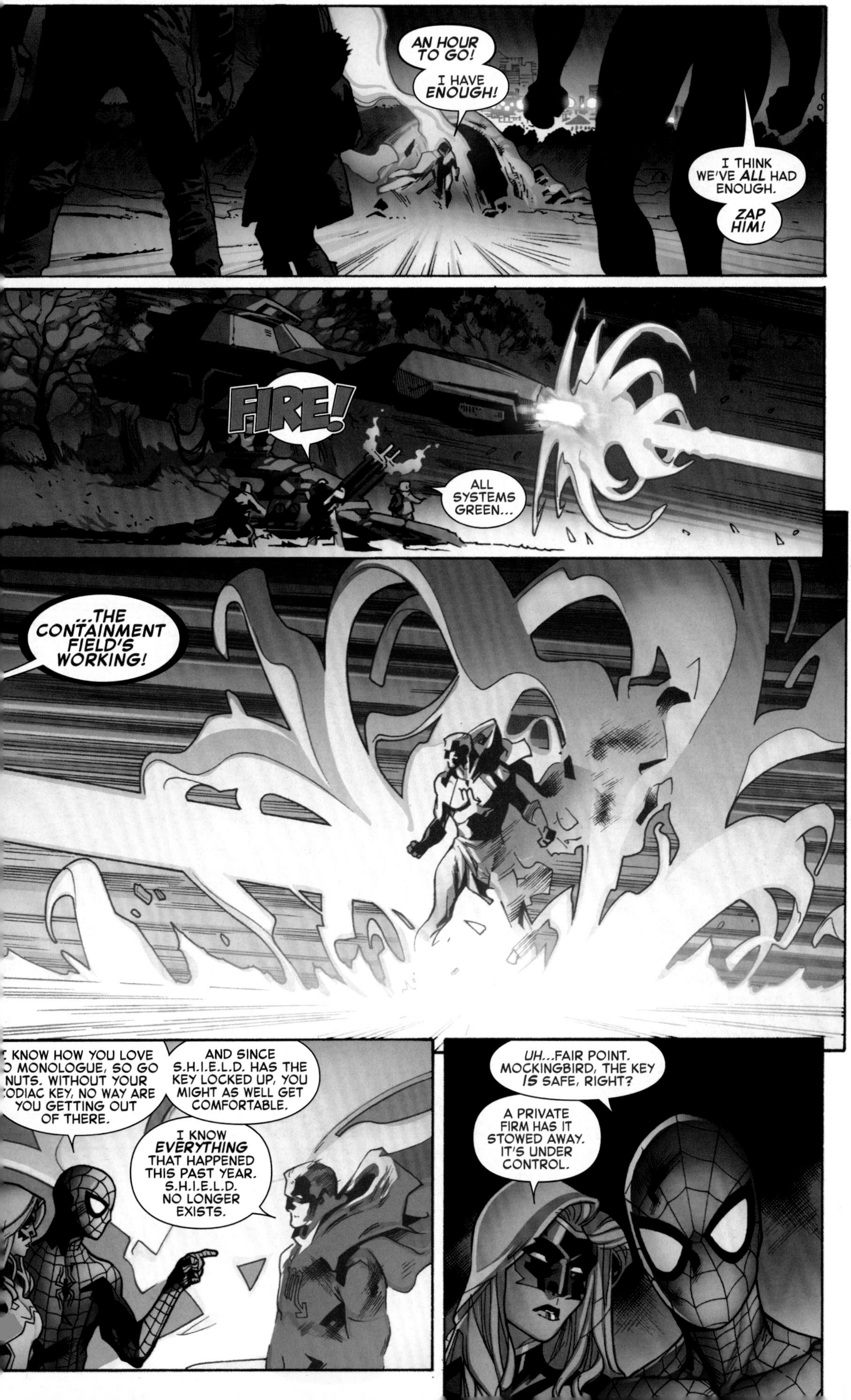
AN HOUR TO GO!
I HAVE ENOUGH!
I THINK WE'VE ALL HAD ENOUGH.
ZAP HIM!
FIRE!
ALL SYSTEMS GREEN...
...THE CONTAINMENT FIELD'S WORKING!
I KNOW HOW YOU LOVE TO MONOLOGUE, SO GO NUTS. WITHOUT YOUR ZODIAC KEY, NO WAY ARE YOU GETTING OUT OF THERE.
AND SINCE S.H.I.E.L.D. HAS THE KEY LOCKED UP, YOU MIGHT AS WELL GET COMFORTABLE.
I KNOW EVERYTHING THAT HAPPENED THIS PAST YEAR. S.H.I.E.L.D. NO LONGER EXISTS.
UH...FAIR POINT. MOCKINGBIRD, THE KEY IS SAFE, RIGHT?
A PRIVATE FIRM HAS IT STOWED AWAY. IT'S UNDER CONTROL.

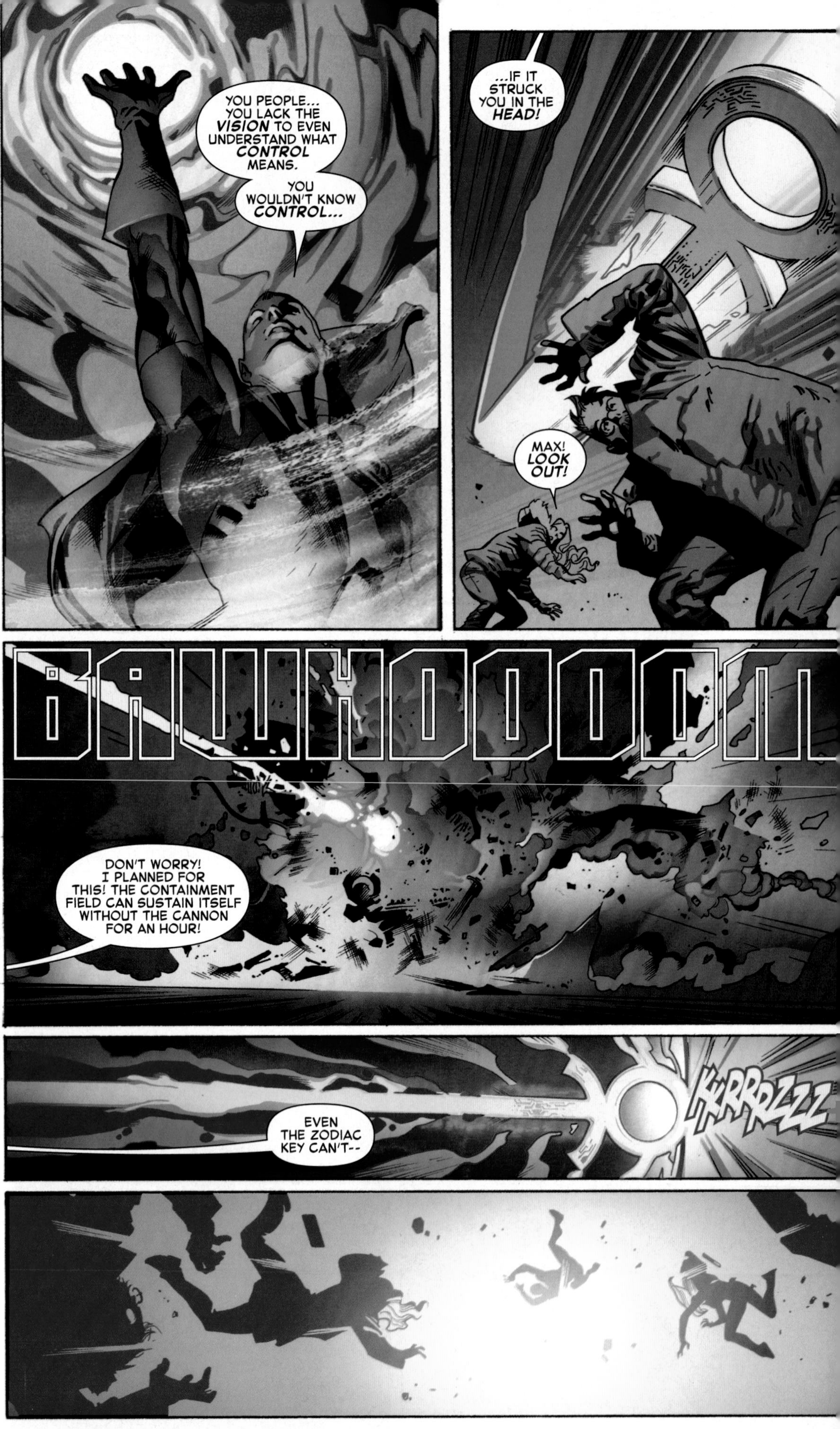
YOU PEOPLE... YOU LACK THE VISION TO EVEN UNDERSTAND WHAT CONTROL MEANS.
YOU WOULDN'T KNOW CONTROL...
...IF IT STRUCK YOU IN THE HEAD!
MAX! LOOK OUT!
BAWHOOOOM
DON'T WORRY! I PLANNED FOR THIS! THE CONTAINMENT FIELD CAN SUSTAIN ITSELF WITHOUT THE CANNON FOR AN HOUR!
EVEN THE ZODIAC KEY CAN'T--
KRRRZZZ

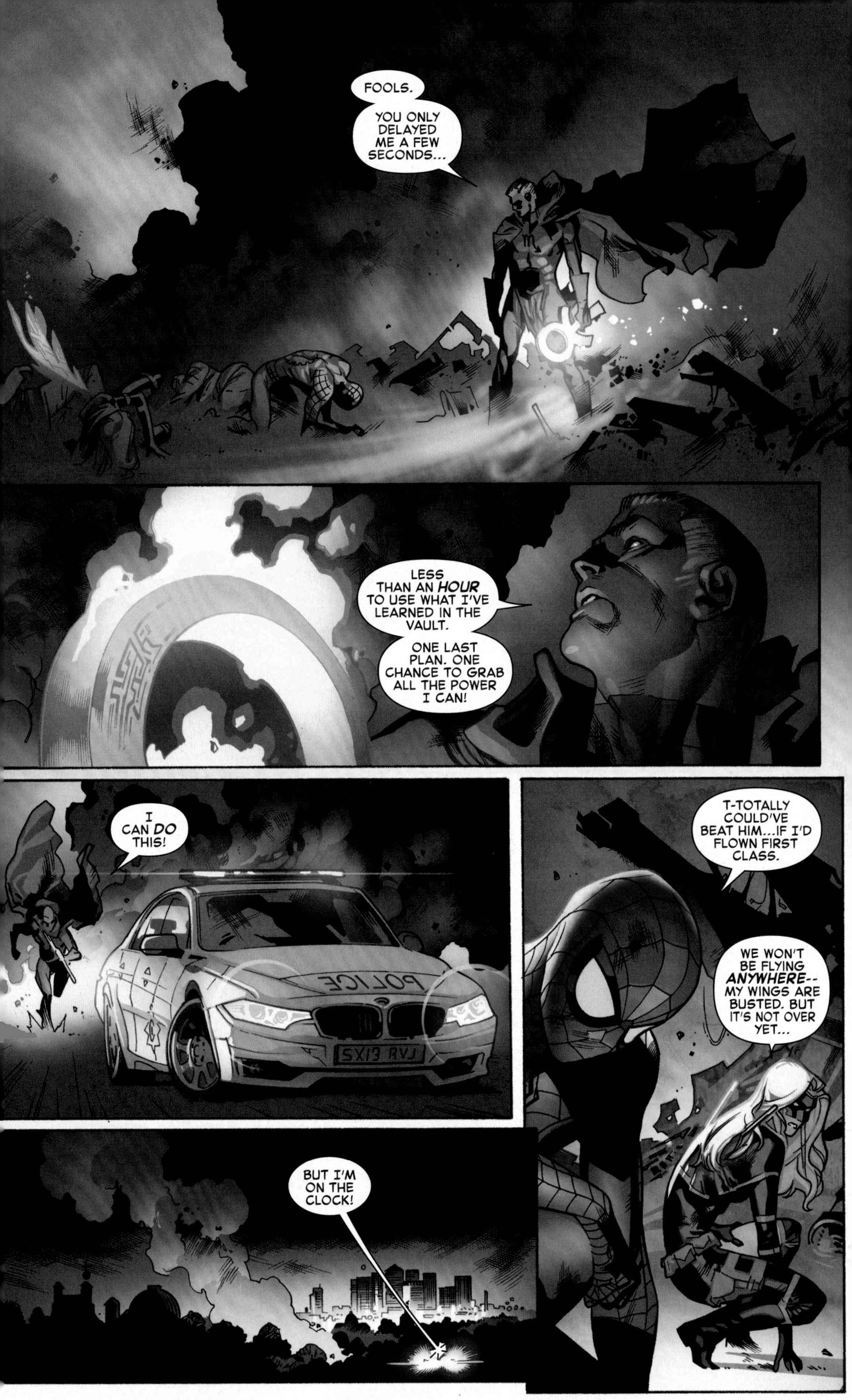
FOOLS.
YOU ONLY DELAYED ME A FEW SECONDS...
LESS THAN AN HOUR TO USE WHAT I'VE LEARNED IN THE VAULT.
ONE LAST PLAN. ONE CHANCE TO GRAB ALL THE POWER I CAN!
I CAN DO THIS!
POLICE
SX13 RVL
BUT I'M ON THE CLOCK!
T-TOTALLY COULD'VE BEAT HIM...IF I'D FLOWN FIRST CLASS.
WE WON'T BE FLYING ANYWHERE-- MY WINGS ARE BUSTED. BUT IT'S NOT OVER YET...

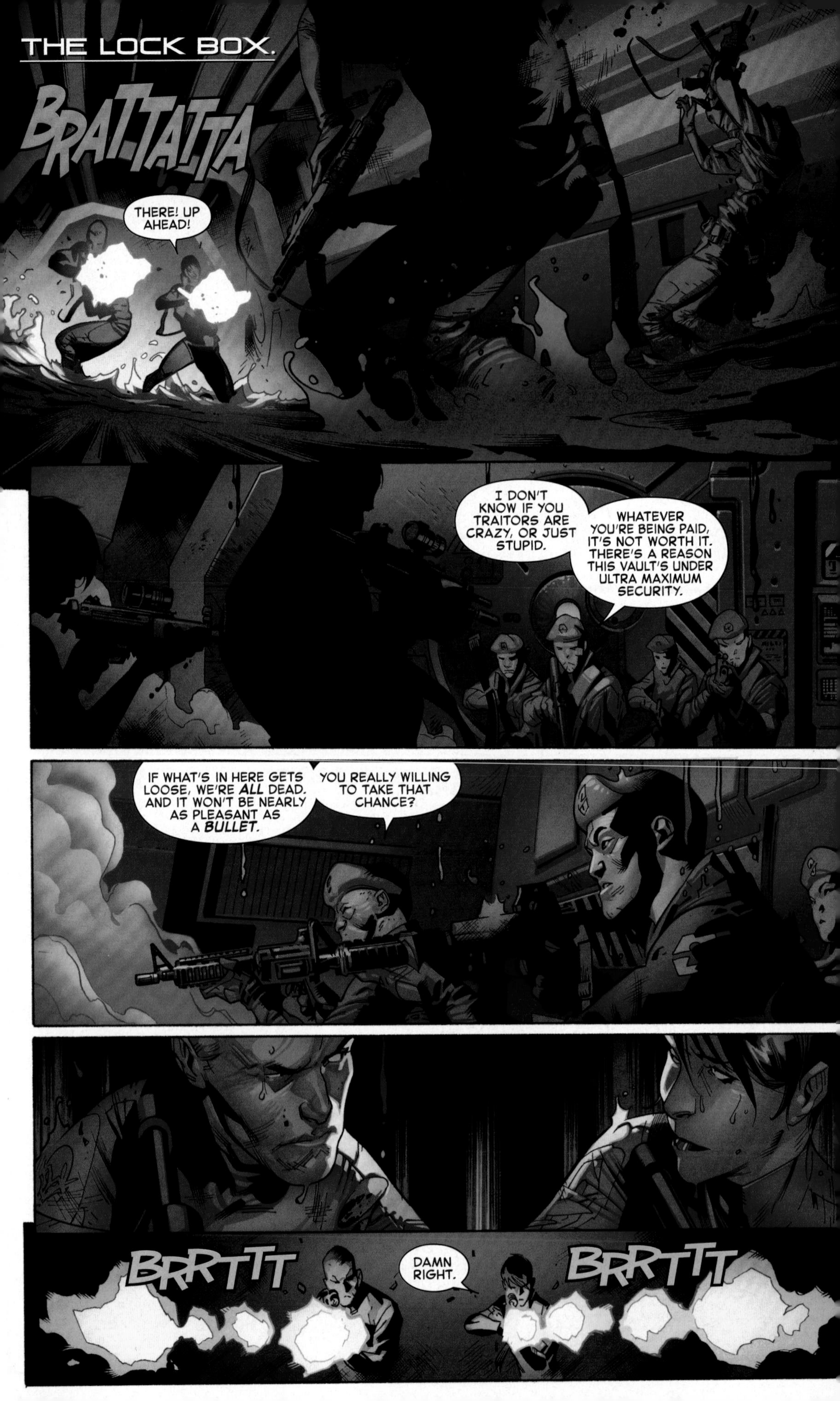
THE LOCK BOX.
BRATTATTA
THERE! UP AHEAD!
I DON'T KNOW IF YOU TRAITORS ARE CRAZY, OR JUST STUPID.
WHATEVER YOU'RE BEING PAID, IT'S NOT WORTH IT. THERE'S A REASON THIS VAULT'S UNDER ULTRA MAXIMUM SECURITY.
IF WHAT'S IN HERE GETS LOOSE, WE'RE ALL DEAD. AND IT WON'T BE NEARLY AS PLEASANT AS A BULLET.
YOU REALLY WILLING TO TAKE THAT CHANCE?
BRRTTT
DAMN RIGHT.
BRRTTT

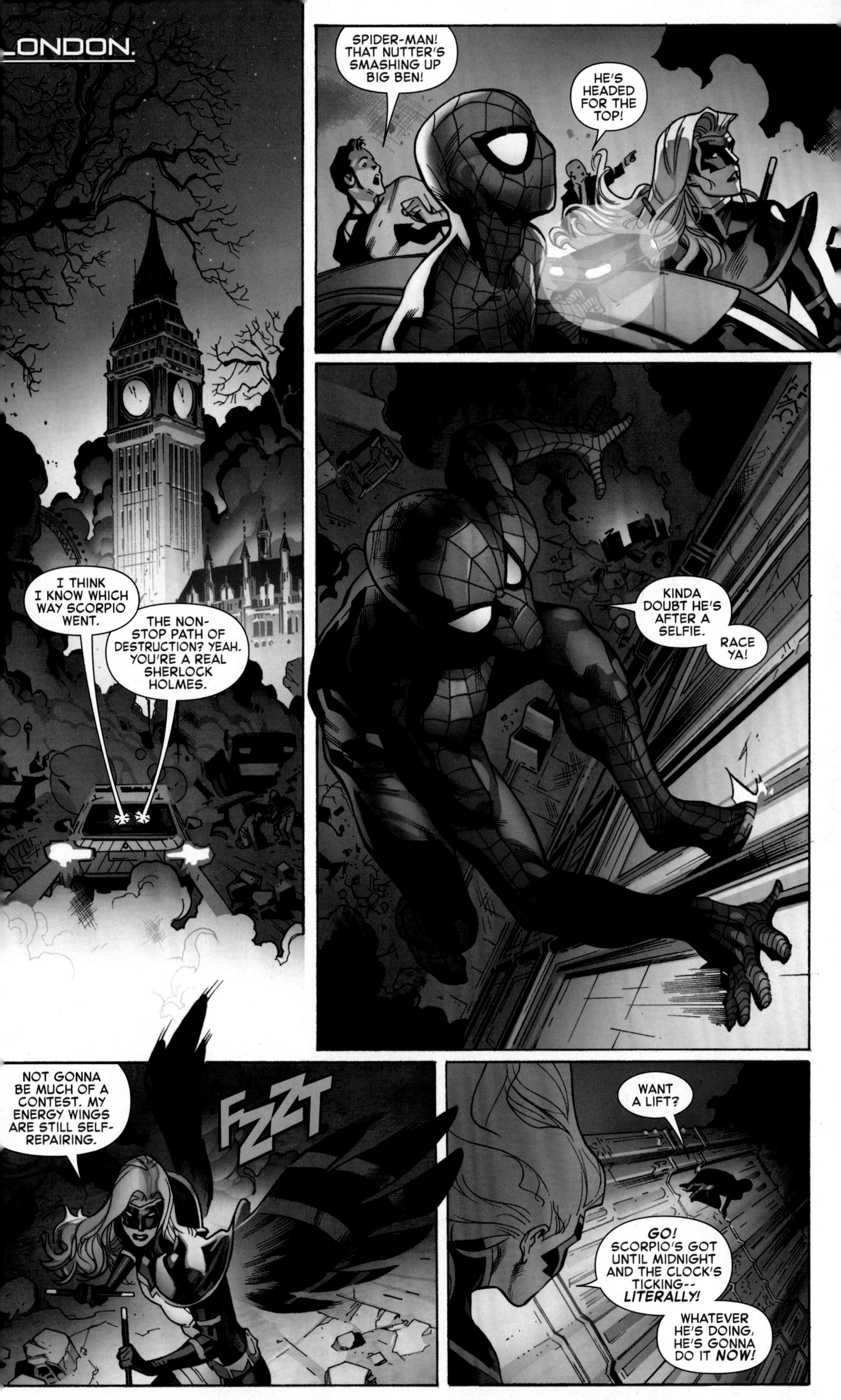
LONDON.
I THINK I KNOW WHICH WAY SCORPIO WENT.
THE NON-STOP PATH OF DESTRUCTION? YEAH. YOU'RE A REAL SHERLOCK HOLMES.
SPIDER-MAN! THAT NUTTER'S SMASHING UP BIG BEN!
HE'S HEADED FOR THE TOP!
KINDA DOUBT HE'S AFTER A SELFIE.
RACE YA!
NOT GONNA BE MUCH OF A CONTEST. MY ENERGY WINGS ARE STILL SELF-REPAIRING.
FZZT
WANT A LIFT?
GO! SCORPIO'S GOT UNTIL MIDNIGHT AND THE CLOCK'S TICKING-- LITERALLY!
WHATEVER HE'S DOING, HE'S GONNA DO IT NOW!

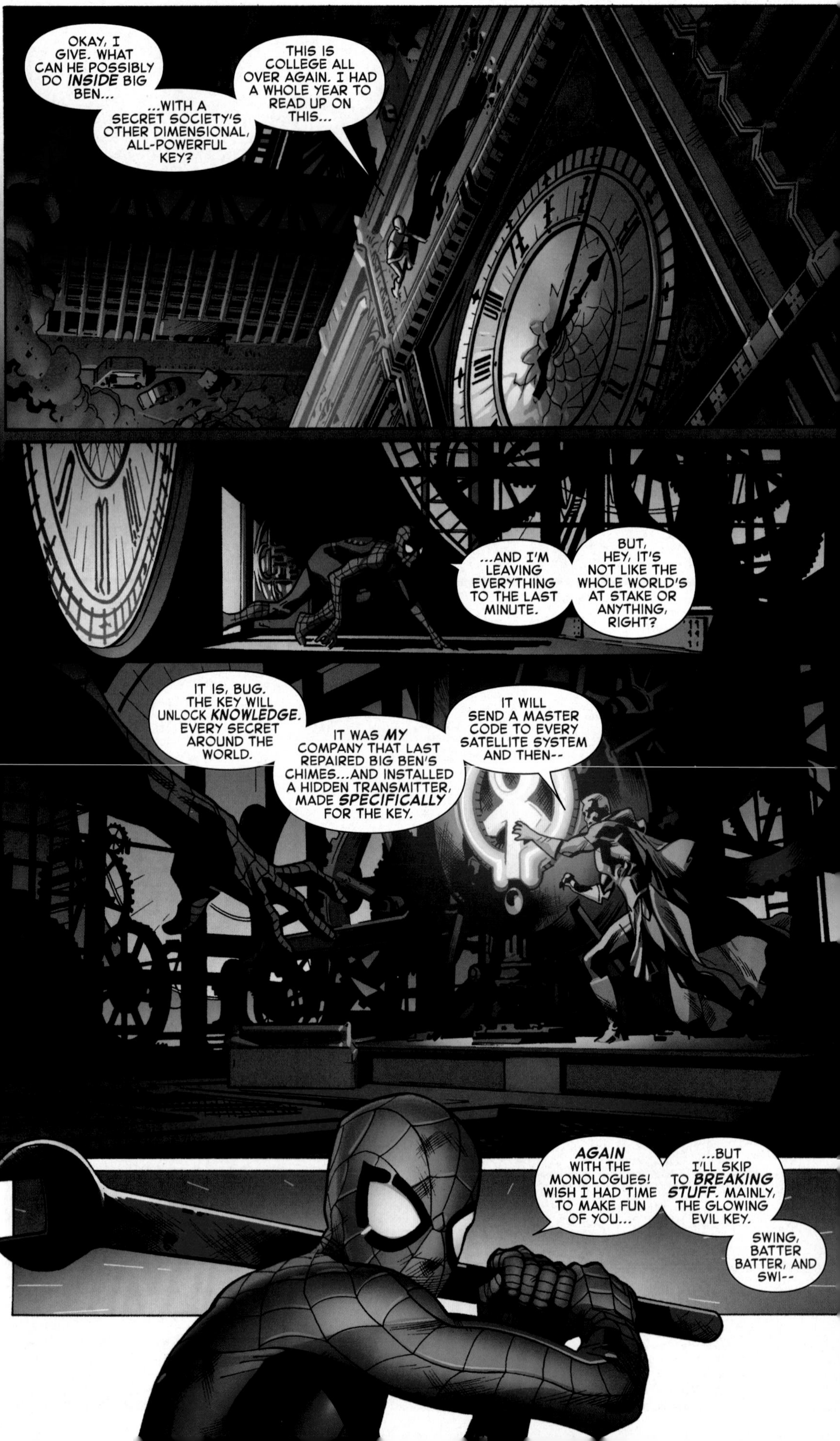
OKAY, I GIVE. WHAT CAN HE POSSIBLY DO INSIDE BIG BEN...
...WITH A SECRET SOCIETY'S OTHER DIMENSIONAL, ALL-POWERFUL KEY?
THIS IS COLLEGE ALL OVER AGAIN. I HAD A WHOLE YEAR TO READ UP ON THIS...
...AND I'M LEAVING EVERYTHING TO THE LAST MINUTE.
BUT, HEY, IT'S NOT LIKE THE WHOLE WORLD'S AT STAKE OR ANYTHING, RIGHT?
IT IS, BUG. THE KEY WILL UNLOCK KNOWLEDGE. EVERY SECRET AROUND THE WORLD.
IT WAS MY COMPANY THAT LAST REPAIRED BIG BEN'S CHIMES...AND INSTALLED A HIDDEN TRANSMITTER, MADE SPECIFICALLY FOR THE KEY.
IT WILL SEND A MASTER CODE TO EVERY SATELLITE SYSTEM AND THEN--
AGAIN WITH THE MONOLOGUES! WISH I HAD TIME TO MAKE FUN OF YOU...
...BUT I'LL SKIP TO BREAKING STUFF. MAINLY, THE GLOWING EVIL KEY.
SWING, BATTER BATTER, AND SWI--

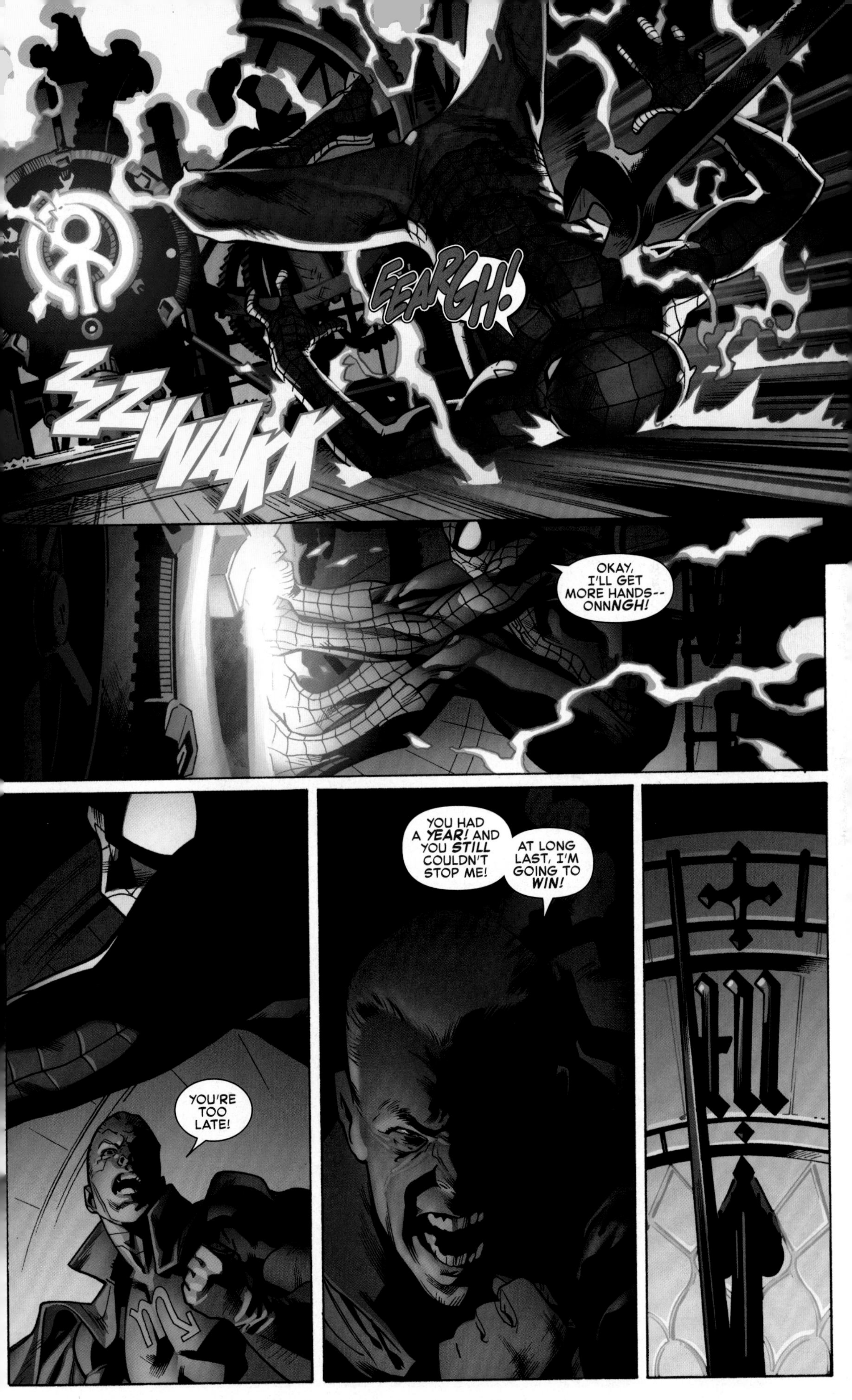
EEARGH!
ZZZVVAKK
OKAY, I'LL GET MORE HANDS-- ONNNGH!
YOU'RE TOO LATE!
YOU HAD A YEAR! AND YOU STILL COULDN'T STOP ME!
AT LONG LAST, I'M GOING TO WIN!

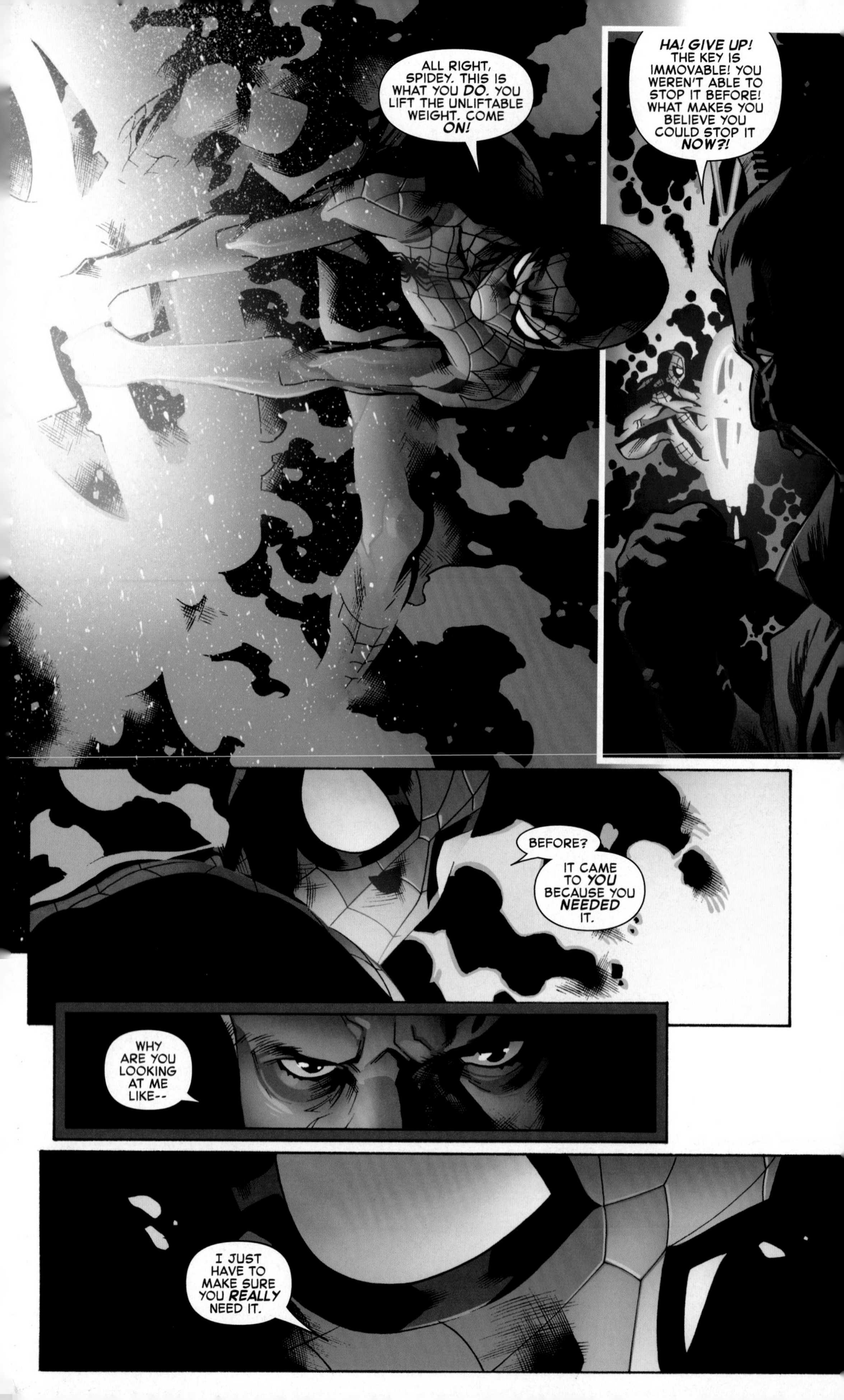
ALL RIGHT, SPIDEY. THIS IS WHAT YOU DO. YOU LIFT THE UNLIFTABLE WEIGHT. COME ON!
HA! GIVE UP! THE KEY IS IMMOVABLE! YOU WEREN'T ABLE TO STOP IT BEFORE! WHAT MAKES YOU BELIEVE YOU COULD STOP IT NOW?!
BEFORE?
IT CAME TO YOU BECAUSE YOU NEEDED IT.
WHY ARE YOU LOOKING AT ME LIKE--
I JUST HAVE TO MAKE SURE YOU REALLY NEED IT.

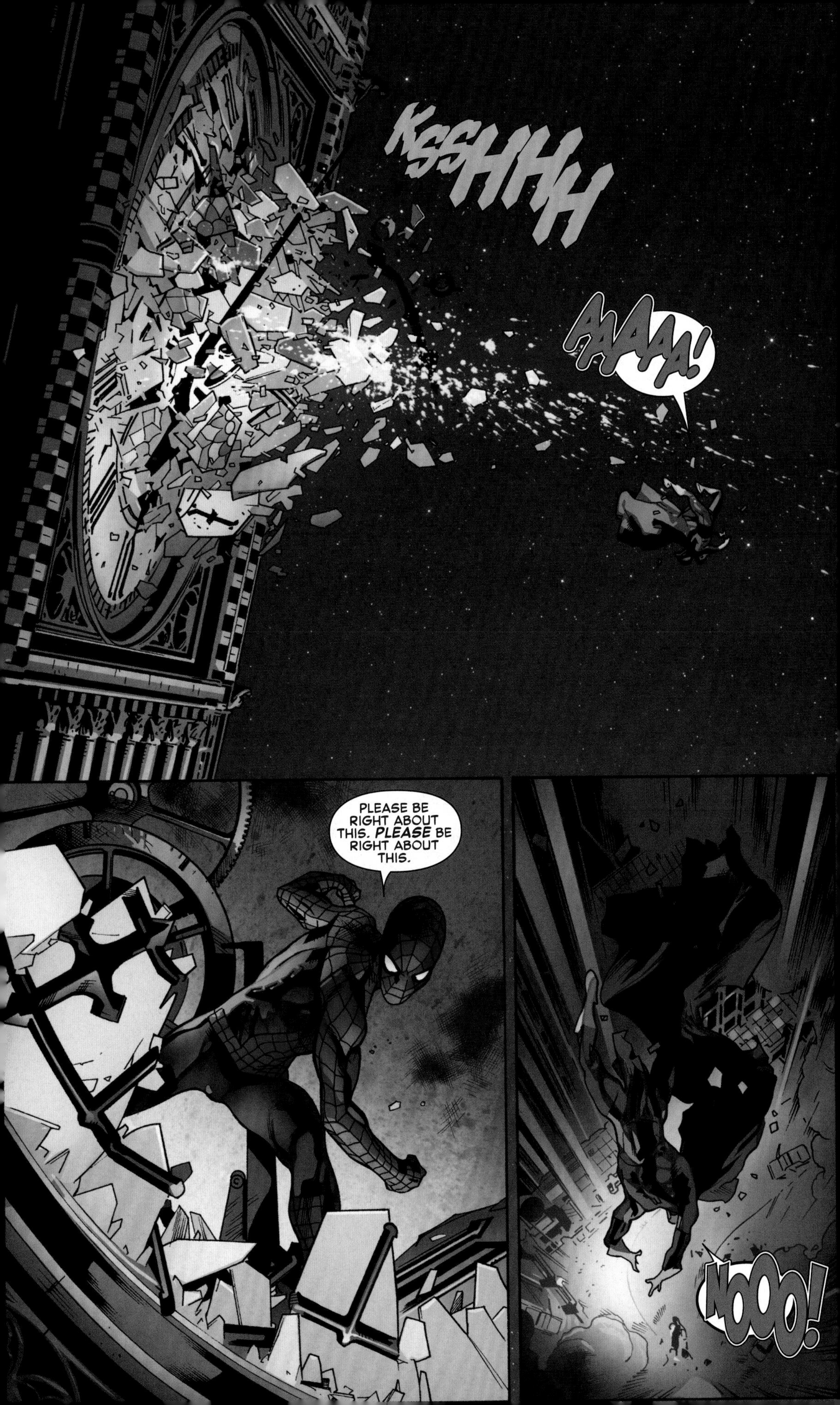
KSSHHH
AAAAA!
PLEASE BE RIGHT ABOUT THIS. PLEASE BE RIGHT ABOUT THIS.
NOOO!

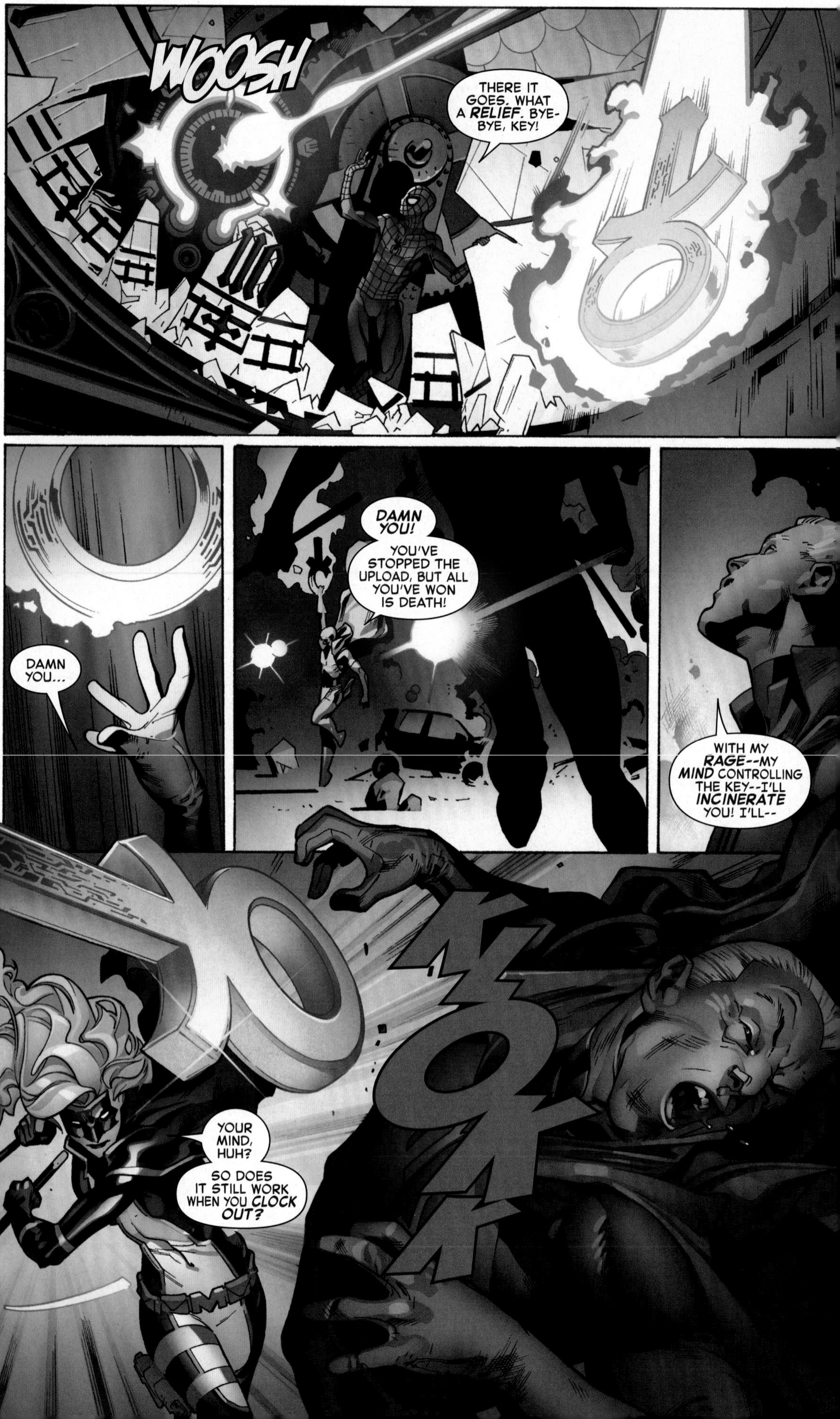
WOOSH
THERE IT GOES. WHAT A RELIEF. BYE-BYE, KEY!
DAMN YOU...
DAMN YOU!
YOU'VE STOPPED THE UPLOAD, BUT ALL YOU'VE WON IS DEATH!
WITH MY RAGE--MY MIND CONTROLLING THE KEY--I'LL INCINERATE YOU! I'LL--
YOUR MIND, HUH?
SO DOES IT STILL WORK WHEN YOU CLOCK OUT?

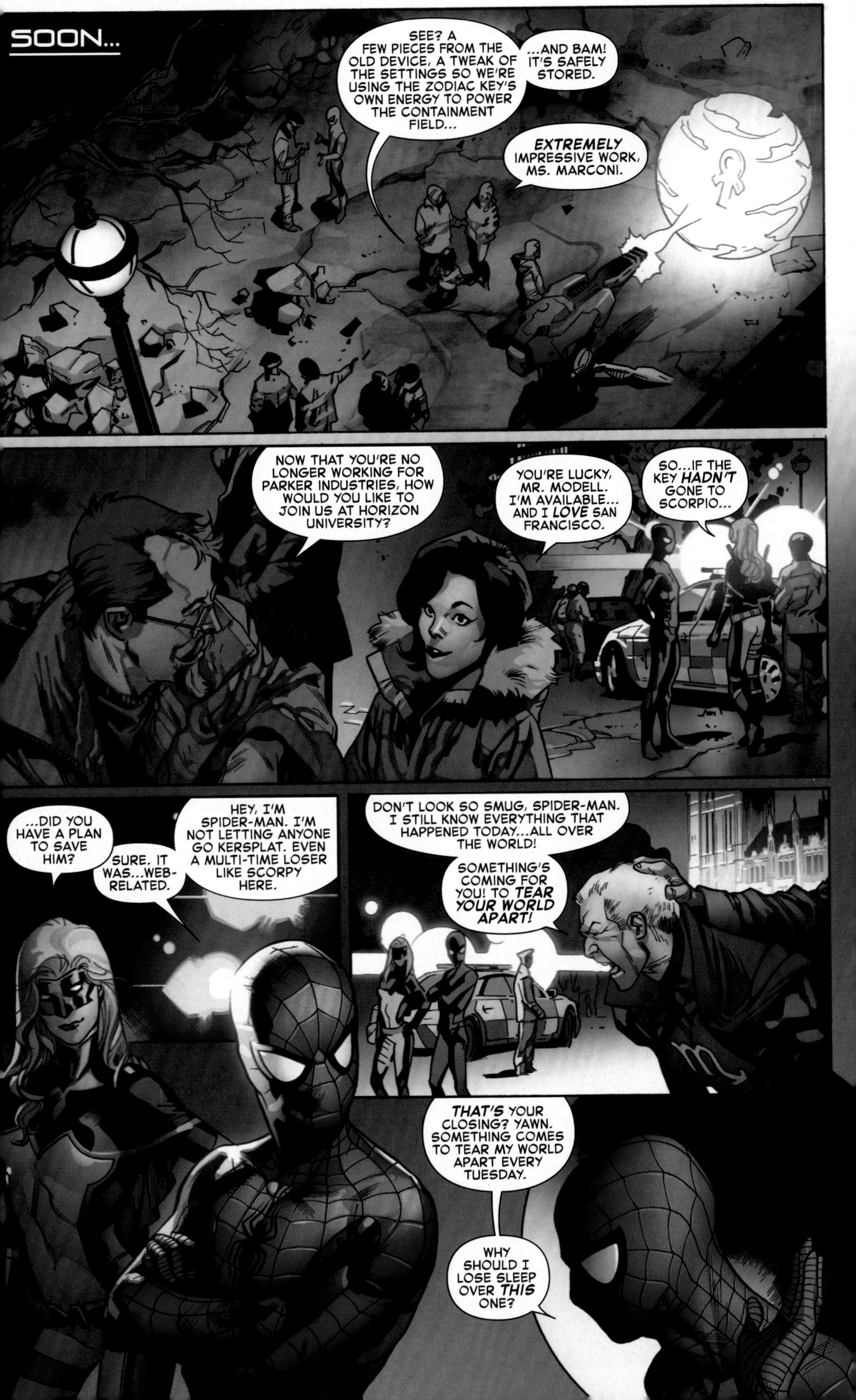
SOON...
SEE? A FEW PIECES FROM THE OLD DEVICE, A TWEAK OF THE SETTINGS SO WE'RE USING THE ZODIAC KEY'S OWN ENERGY TO POWER THE CONTAINMENT FIELD...
...AND BAM! IT'S SAFELY STORED.
EXTREMELY IMPRESSIVE WORK, MS. MARCONI.
NOW THAT YOU'RE NO LONGER WORKING FOR PARKER INDUSTRIES, HOW WOULD YOU LIKE TO JOIN US AT HORIZON UNIVERSITY?
YOU'RE LUCKY, MR. MODELL. I'M AVAILABLE... AND I LOVE SAN FRANCISCO.
SO...IF THE KEY HADN'T GONE TO SCORPIO...
...DID YOU HAVE A PLAN TO SAVE HIM?
SURE. IT WAS...WEB-RELATED.
HEY, I'M SPIDER-MAN. I'M NOT LETTING ANYONE GO KERSPLAT. EVEN A MULTI-TIME LOSER LIKE SCORPY HERE.
DON'T LOOK SO SMUG, SPIDER-MAN. I STILL KNOW EVERYTHING THAT HAPPENED TODAY...ALL OVER THE WORLD!
SOMETHING'S COMING FOR YOU! TO TEAR YOUR WORLD APART!
THAT'S YOUR CLOSING? YAWN. SOMETHING COMES TO TEAR MY WORLD APART EVERY TUESDAY.
WHY SHOULD I LOSE SLEEP OVER THIS ONE?

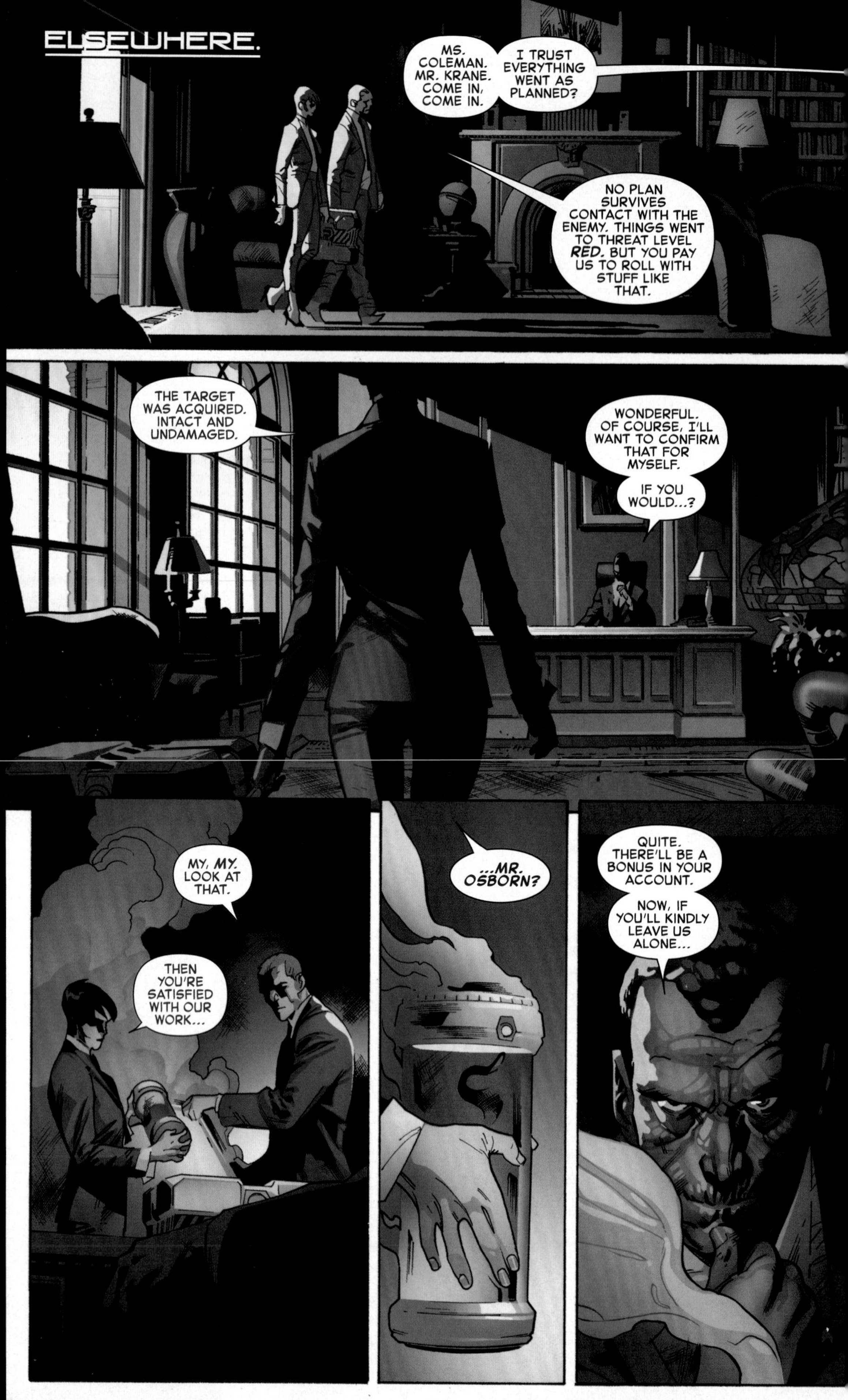
ELSEWHERE.
MS. COLEMAN. MR. KRANE. COME IN, COME IN.
I TRUST EVERYTHING WENT AS PLANNED?
NO PLAN SURVIVES CONTACT WITH THE ENEMY. THINGS WENT TO THREAT LEVEL RED. BUT YOU PAY US TO ROLL WITH STUFF LIKE THAT.
THE TARGET WAS ACQUIRED. INTACT AND UNDAMAGED.
WONDERFUL. OF COURSE, I'LL WANT TO CONFIRM THAT FOR MYSELF.
IF YOU WOULD...?
MY, MY. LOOK AT THAT.
THEN YOU'RE SATISFIED WITH OUR WORK...
...MR. OSBORN?
QUITE. THERE'LL BE A BONUS IN YOUR ACCOUNT.
NOW, IF YOU'LL KINDLY LEAVE US ALONE...

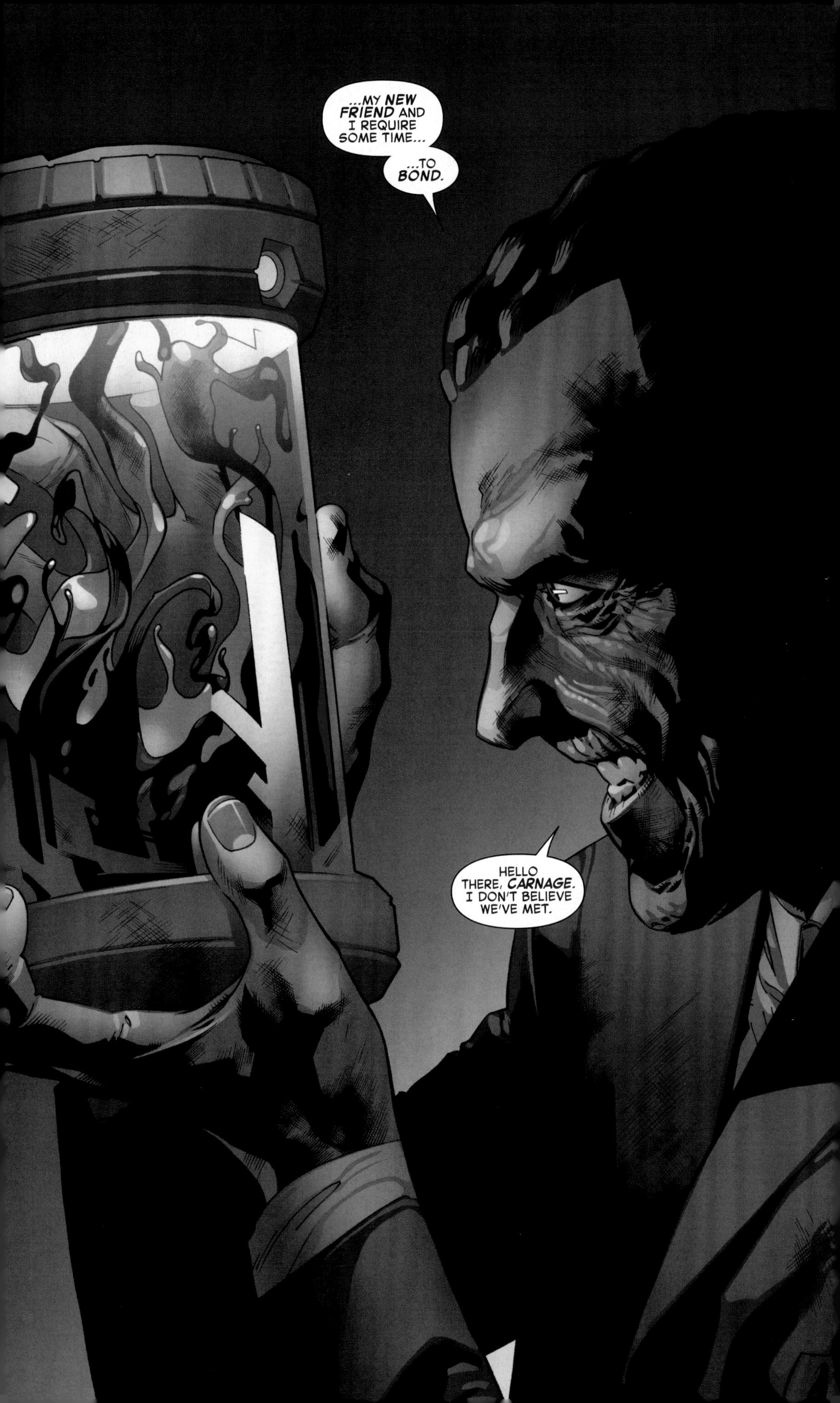
...MY NEW FRIEND AND I REQUIRE SOME TIME...
...TO BOND.
HELLO THERE, CARNAGE. I DON'T BELIEVE WE'VE MET.

795

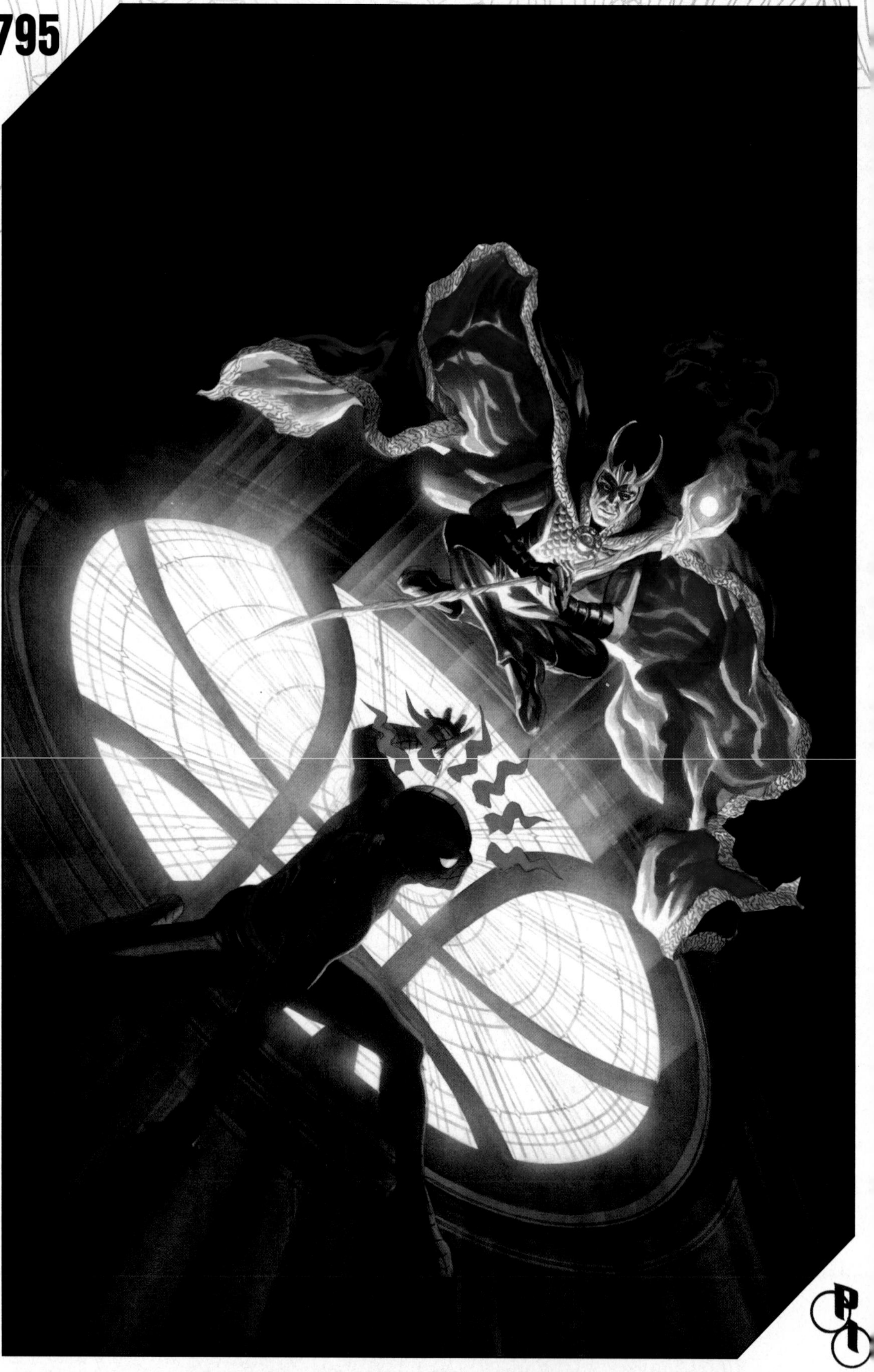

THREAT LEVEL: RED PART TWO "THE FAVOR"

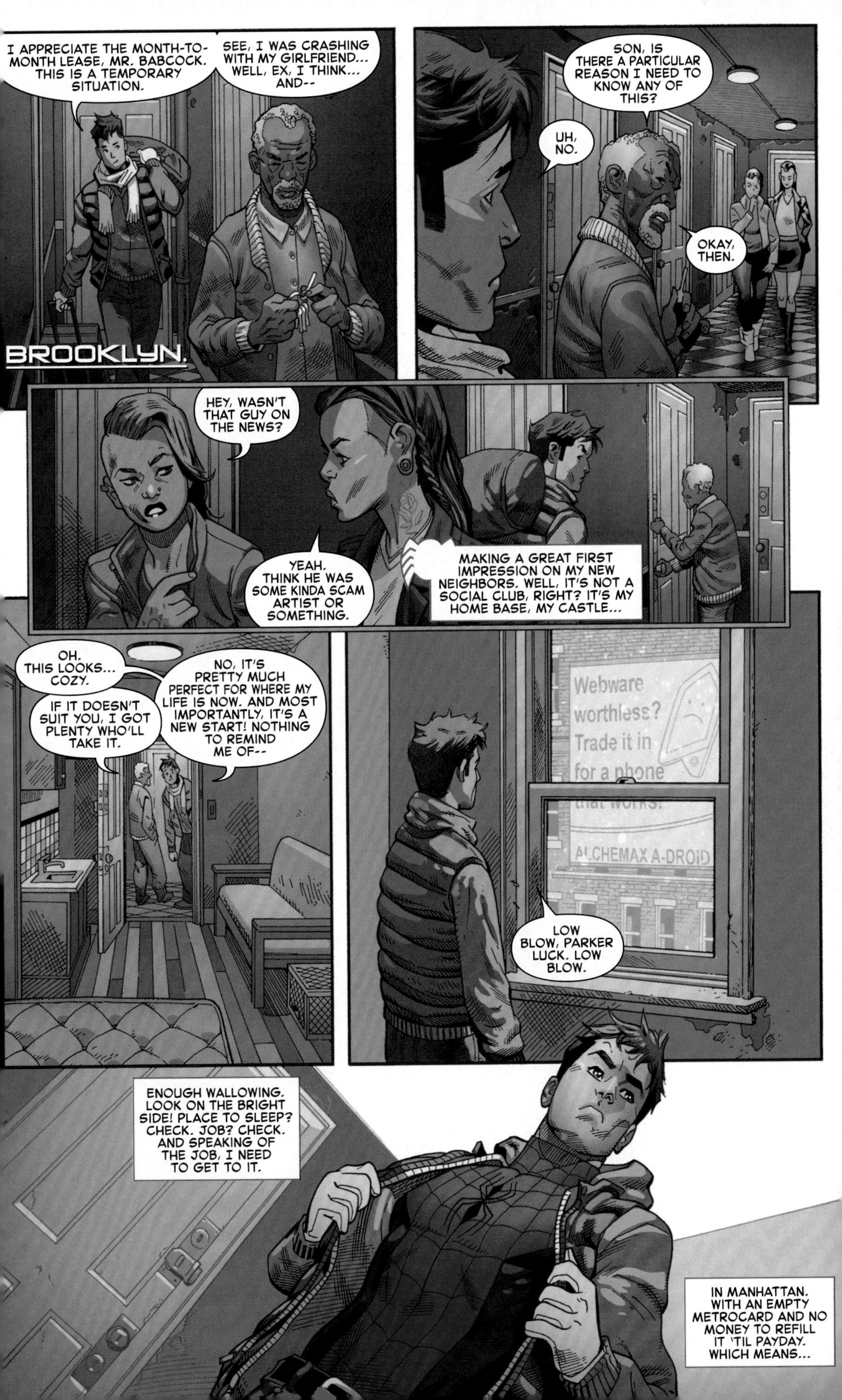
I APPRECIATE THE MONTH-TO-MONTH LEASE, MR. BABCOCK. THIS IS A TEMPORARY SITUATION.
SEE, I WAS CRASHING WITH MY GIRLFRIEND... WELL, EX, I THINK... AND--
BROOKLYN.
SON, IS THERE A PARTICULAR REASON I NEED TO KNOW ANY OF THIS?
UH, NO.
OKAY, THEN.
HEY, WASN'T THAT GUY ON THE NEWS?
YEAH. THINK HE WAS SOME KINDA SCAM ARTIST OR SOMETHING.
MAKING A GREAT FIRST IMPRESSION ON MY NEW NEIGHBORS. WELL, IT'S NOT A SOCIAL CLUB, RIGHT? IT'S MY HOME BASE, MY CASTLE...
OH. THIS LOOKS... COZY.
IF IT DOESN'T SUIT YOU, I GOT PLENTY WHO'LL TAKE IT.
NO, IT'S PRETTY MUCH PERFECT FOR WHERE MY LIFE IS NOW. AND MOST IMPORTANTLY, IT'S A NEW START! NOTHING TO REMIND ME OF--
Webware worthless? Trade it in for a phone
ALCHEMAX A-DROID
LOW BLOW, PARKER LUCK. LOW BLOW.
ENOUGH WALLOWING. LOOK ON THE BRIGHT SIDE! PLACE TO SLEEP? CHECK. JOB? CHECK. AND SPEAKING OF THE JOB, I NEED TO GET TO IT.
IN MANHATTAN. WITH AN EMPTY METROCARD AND NO MONEY TO REFILL IT 'TIL PAYDAY. WHICH MEANS...

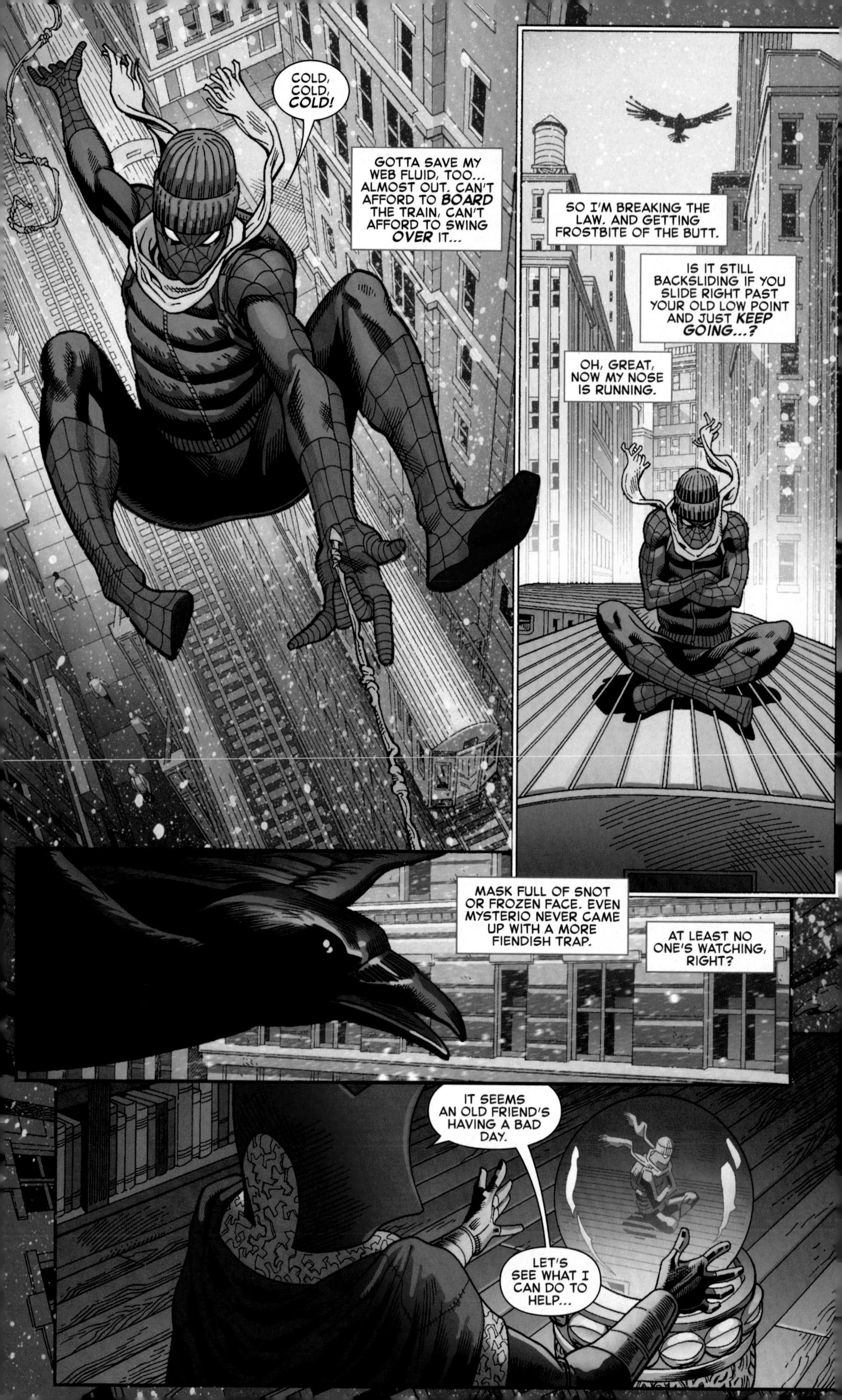
COLD, COLD, COLD!
GOTTA SAVE MY WEB FLUID, TOO... ALMOST OUT. CAN'T AFFORD TO BOARD THE TRAIN, CAN'T AFFORD TO SWING OVER IT...
SO I'M BREAKING THE LAW. AND GETTING FROSTBITE OF THE BUTT.
IS IT STILL BACKSLIDING IF YOU SLIDE RIGHT PAST YOUR OLD LOW POINT AND JUST KEEP GOING...?
OH, GREAT, NOW MY NOSE IS RUNNING.
MASK FULL OF SNOT OR FROZEN FACE. EVEN MYSTERIO NEVER CAME UP WITH A MORE FIENDISH TRAP.
AT LEAST NO ONE'S WATCHING, RIGHT?
IT SEEMS AN OLD FRIEND'S HAVING A BAD DAY.
LET'S SEE WHAT I CAN DO TO HELP...

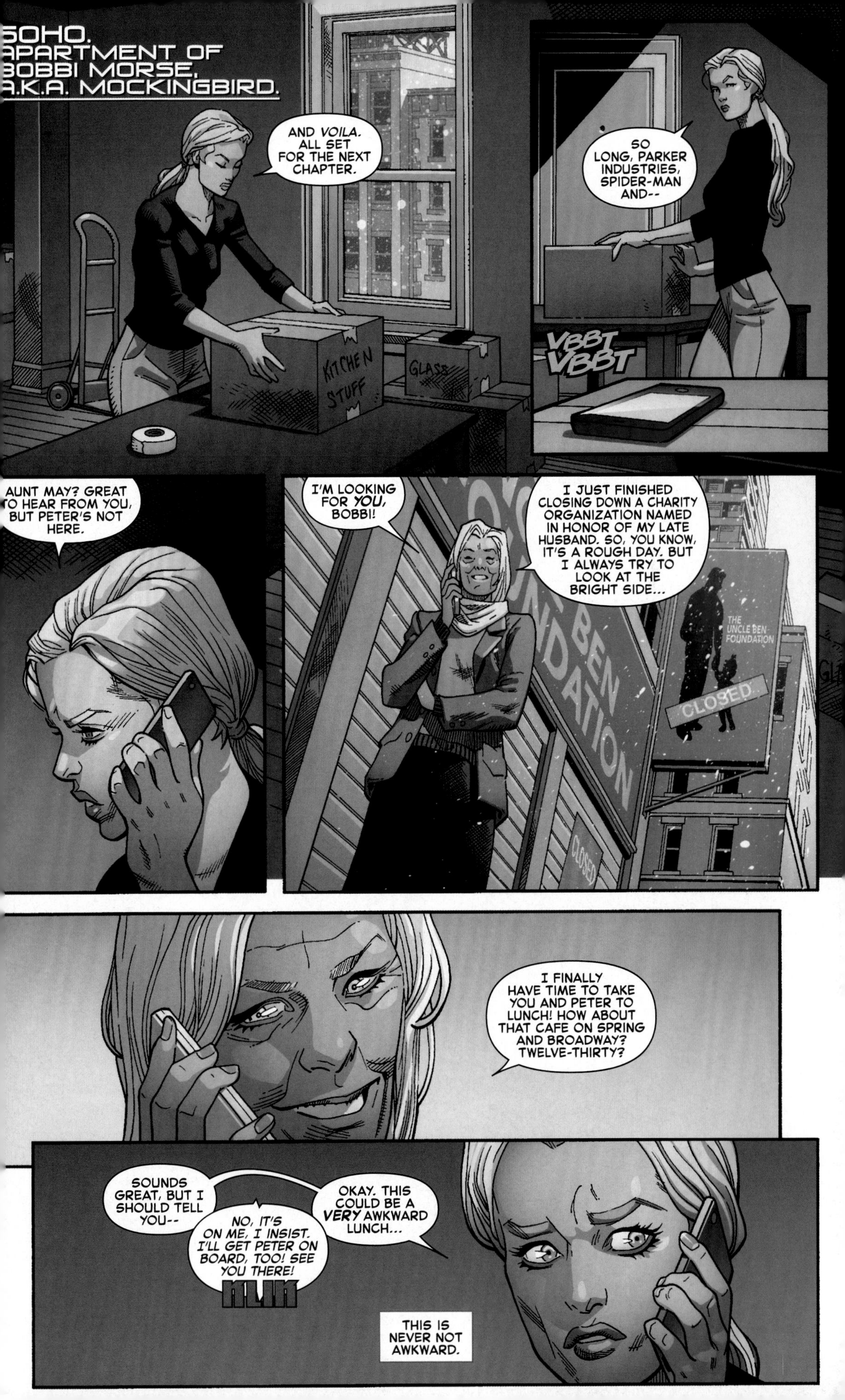
SOHO.
APARTMENT OF BOBBI MORSE, A.K.A. MOCKINGBIRD.
AND VOILA. ALL SET FOR THE NEXT CHAPTER.
KITCHEN STUFF
GLASS
SO LONG, PARKER INDUSTRIES, SPIDER-MAN AND--
VBBT VBBT
AUNT MAY? GREAT TO HEAR FROM YOU, BUT PETER'S NOT HERE.
I'M LOOKING FOR YOU, BOBBI!
I JUST FINISHED CLOSING DOWN A CHARITY ORGANIZATION NAMED IN HONOR OF MY LATE HUSBAND. SO, YOU KNOW, IT'S A ROUGH DAY. BUT I ALWAYS TRY TO LOOK AT THE BRIGHT SIDE...
THE UNCLE BEN FOUNDATION
CLOSED
CLOSED
I FINALLY HAVE TIME TO TAKE YOU AND PETER TO LUNCH! HOW ABOUT THAT CAFE ON SPRING AND BROADWAY? TWELVE-THIRTY?
SOUNDS GREAT, BUT I SHOULD TELL YOU--
NO, IT'S ON ME, I INSIST. I'LL GET PETER ON BOARD, TOO! SEE YOU THERE!
KLIK
OKAY. THIS COULD BE A VERY AWKWARD LUNCH...
THIS IS NEVER NOT AWKWARD.

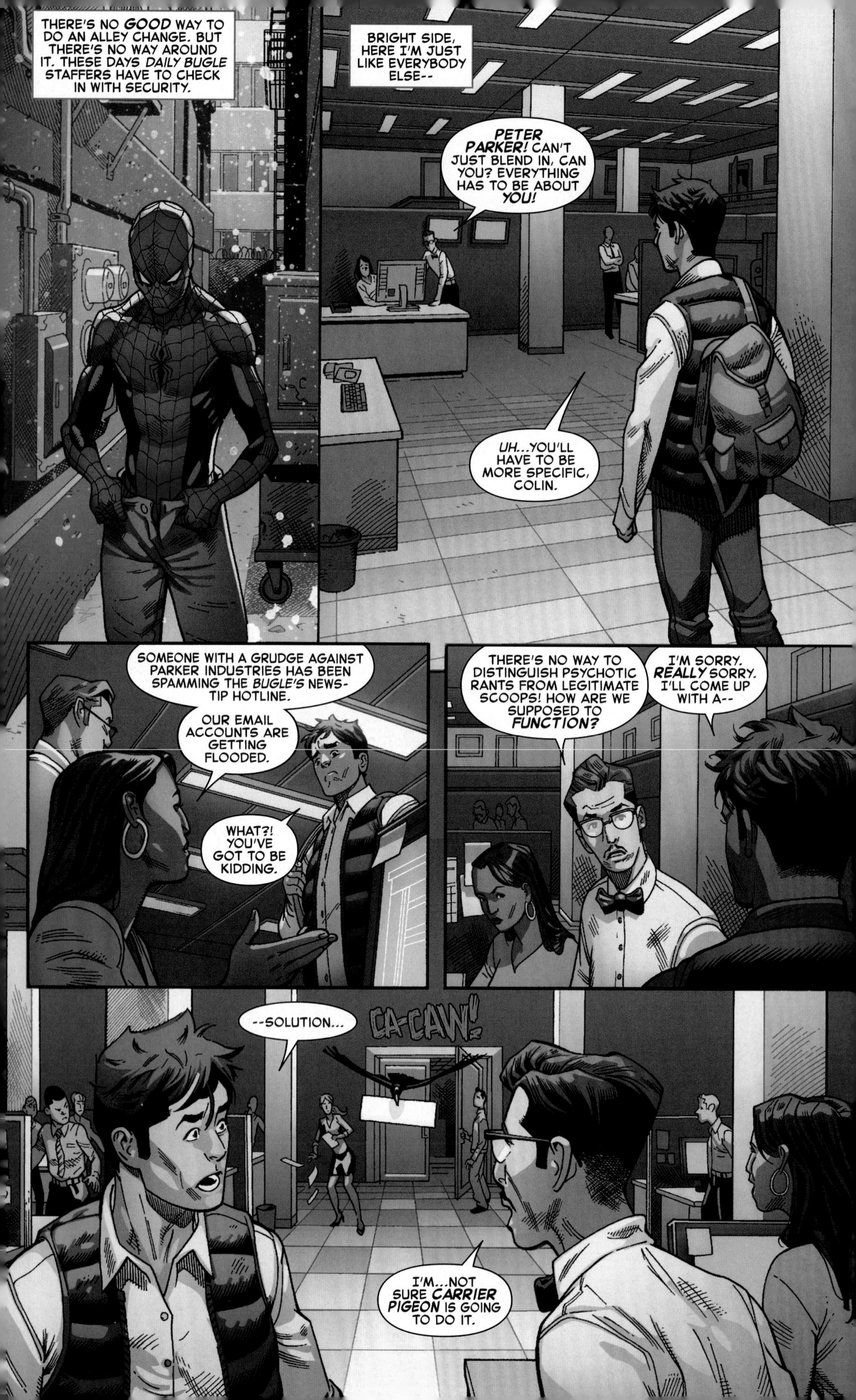
THERE'S NO GOOD WAY TO DO AN ALLEY CHANGE. BUT THERE'S NO WAY AROUND IT. THESE DAYS DAILY BUGLE STAFFERS HAVE TO CHECK IN WITH SECURITY.
BRIGHT SIDE, HERE I'M JUST LIKE EVERYBODY ELSE--
PETER PARKER! CAN'T JUST BLEND IN, CAN YOU? EVERYTHING HAS TO BE ABOUT YOU!
UH...YOU'LL HAVE TO BE MORE SPECIFIC, COLIN.
SOMEONE WITH A GRUDGE AGAINST PARKER INDUSTRIES HAS BEEN SPAMMING THE BUGLE'S NEWS-TIP HOTLINE.
OUR EMAIL ACCOUNTS ARE GETTING FLOODED.
WHAT?! YOU'VE GOT TO BE KIDDING.
THERE'S NO WAY TO DISTINGUISH PSYCHOTIC RANTS FROM LEGITIMATE SCOOPS! HOW ARE WE SUPPOSED TO FUNCTION?
I'M SORRY. REALLY SORRY. I'LL COME UP WITH A--
--SOLUTION...
CA-CAW!
I'M...NOT SURE CARRIER PIGEON IS GOING TO DO IT.

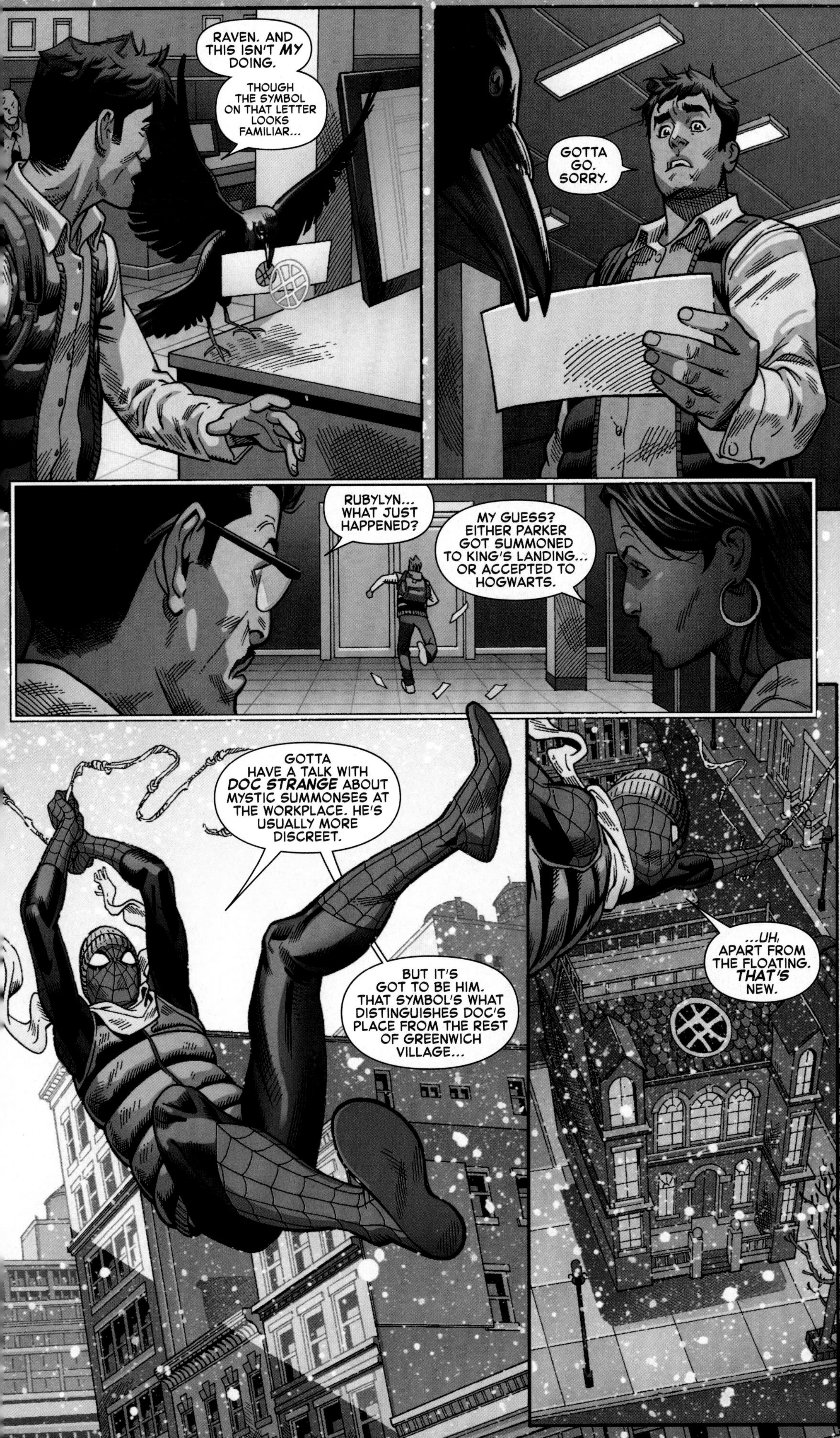
RAVEN. AND THIS ISN'T MY DOING.
THOUGH THE SYMBOL ON THAT LETTER LOOKS FAMILIAR...
GOTTA GO. SORRY.
RUBYLYN... WHAT JUST HAPPENED?
MY GUESS? EITHER PARKER GOT SUMMONED TO KING'S LANDING... OR ACCEPTED TO HOGWARTS.
GOTTA HAVE A TALK WITH DOC STRANGE ABOUT MYSTIC SUMMONSES AT THE WORKPLACE. HE'S USUALLY MORE DISCREET.
BUT IT'S GOT TO BE HIM. THAT SYMBOL'S WHAT DISTINGUISHES DOC'S PLACE FROM THE REST OF GREENWICH VILLAGE...
...UH, APART FROM THE FLOATING. THAT'S NEW.

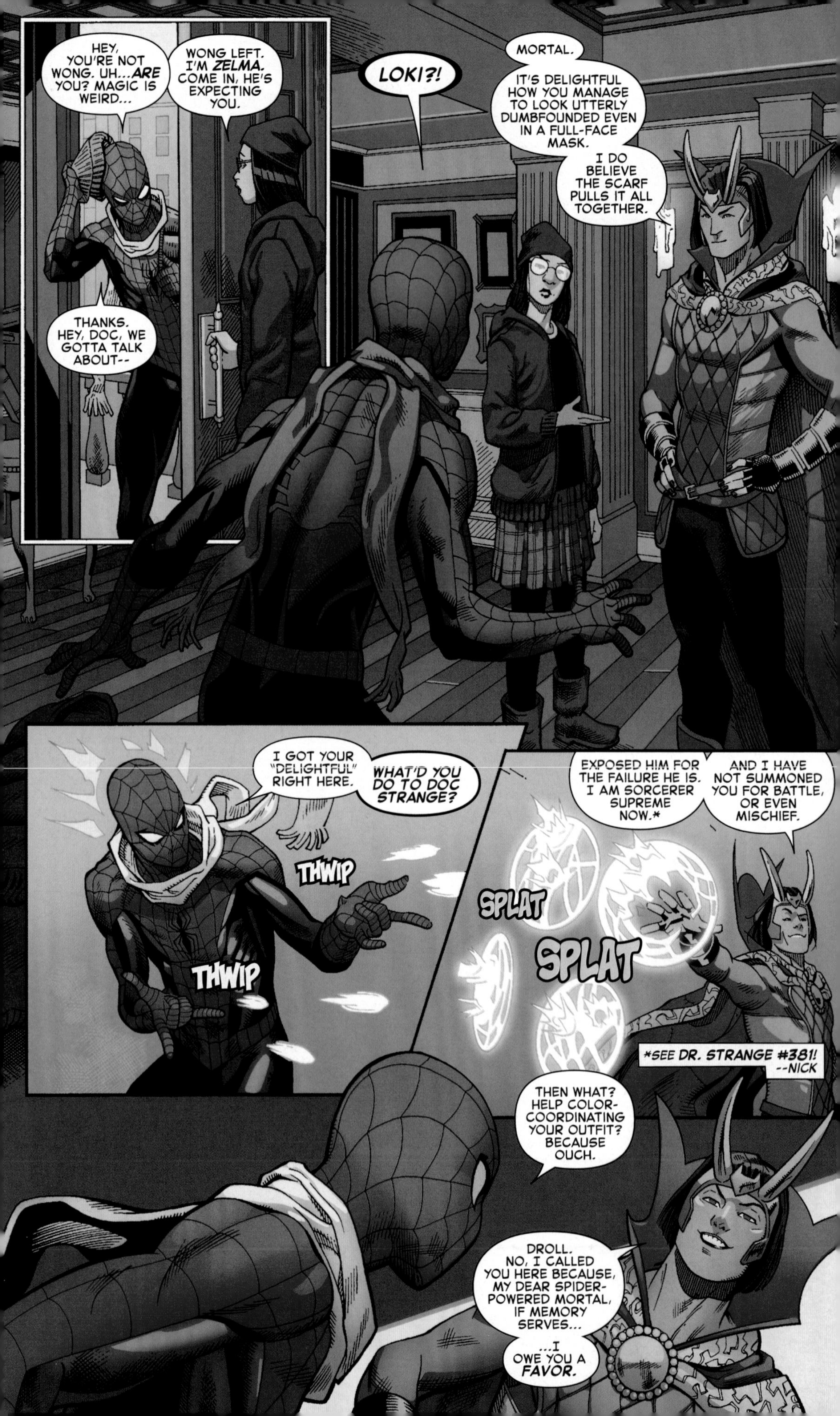
HEY, YOU'RE NOT WONG. UH...ARE YOU? MAGIC IS WEIRD...
WONG LEFT. I'M ZELMA. COME IN, HE'S EXPECTING YOU.
THANKS. HEY, DOC, WE GOTTA TALK ABOUT--
LOKI?!
MORTAL.
IT'S DELIGHTFUL HOW YOU MANAGE TO LOOK UTTERLY DUMBFOUNDED EVEN IN A FULL-FACE MASK.
I DO BELIEVE THE SCARF PULLS IT ALL TOGETHER.
I GOT YOUR "DELIGHTFUL" RIGHT HERE.
WHAT'D YOU DO TO DOC STRANGE?
THWIP
THWIP
EXPOSED HIM FOR THE FAILURE HE IS. I AM SORCERER SUPREME NOW.*
AND I HAVE NOT SUMMONED YOU FOR BATTLE, OR EVEN MISCHIEF.
SPLAT
SPLAT
*SEE DR. STRANGE #381! --NICK
THEN WHAT? HELP COLOR-COORDINATING YOUR OUTFIT? BECAUSE OUCH.
DROLL. NO, I CALLED YOU HERE BECAUSE, MY DEAR SPIDER-POWERED MORTAL, IF MEMORY SERVES...
...I OWE YOU A FAVOR.

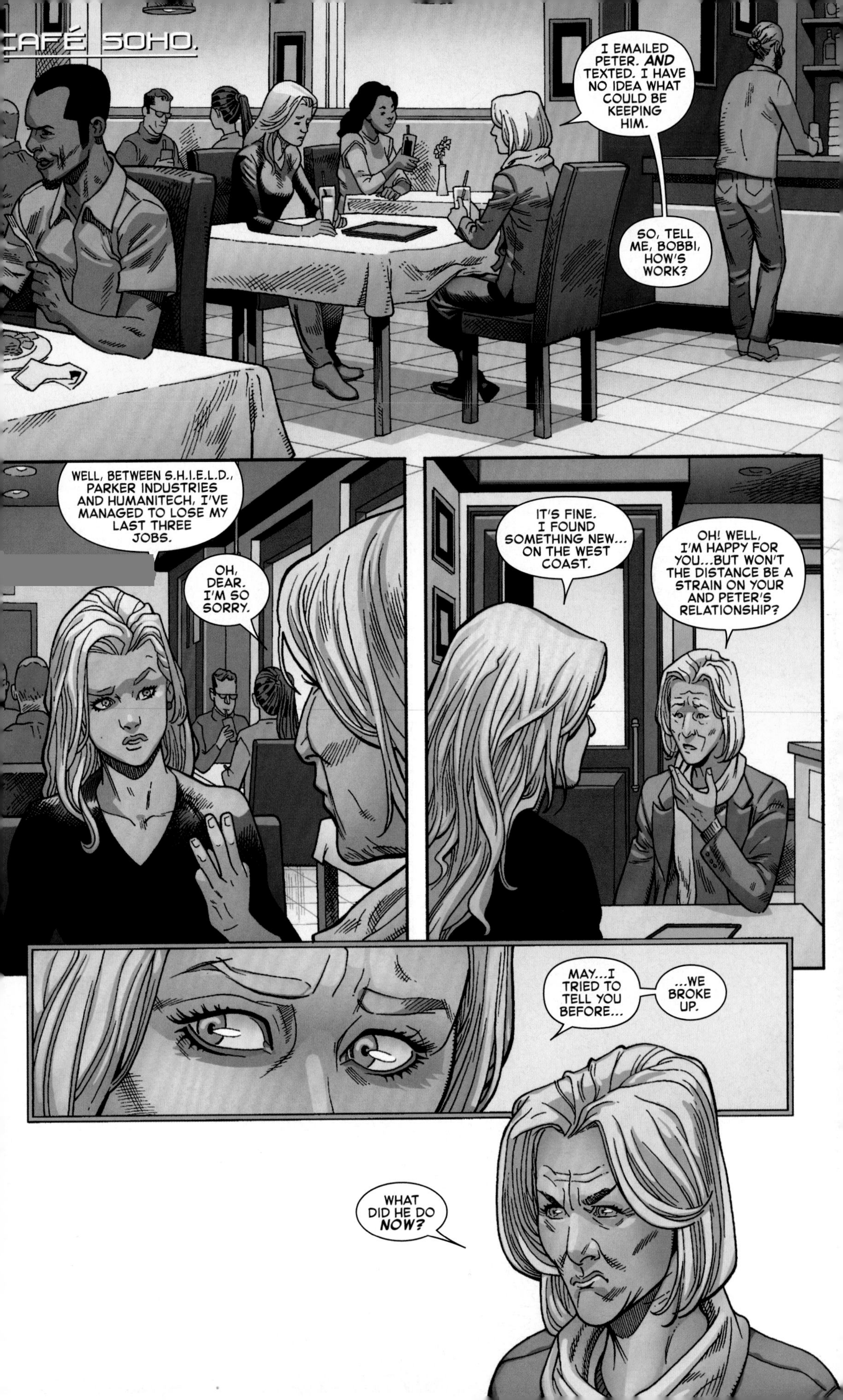
CAFÉ SOHO.
I EMAILED PETER. AND TEXTED. I HAVE NO IDEA WHAT COULD BE KEEPING HIM.
SO, TELL ME, BOBBI, HOW'S WORK?
WELL, BETWEEN S.H.I.E.L.D., PARKER INDUSTRIES AND HUMANITECH, I'VE MANAGED TO LOSE MY LAST THREE JOBS.
OH, DEAR. I'M SO SORRY.
IT'S FINE. I FOUND SOMETHING NEW... ON THE WEST COAST.
OH! WELL, I'M HAPPY FOR YOU...BUT WON'T THE DISTANCE BE A STRAIN ON YOUR AND PETER'S RELATIONSHIP?
MAY...I TRIED TO TELL YOU BEFORE...
...WE BROKE UP.
WHAT DID HE DO NOW?

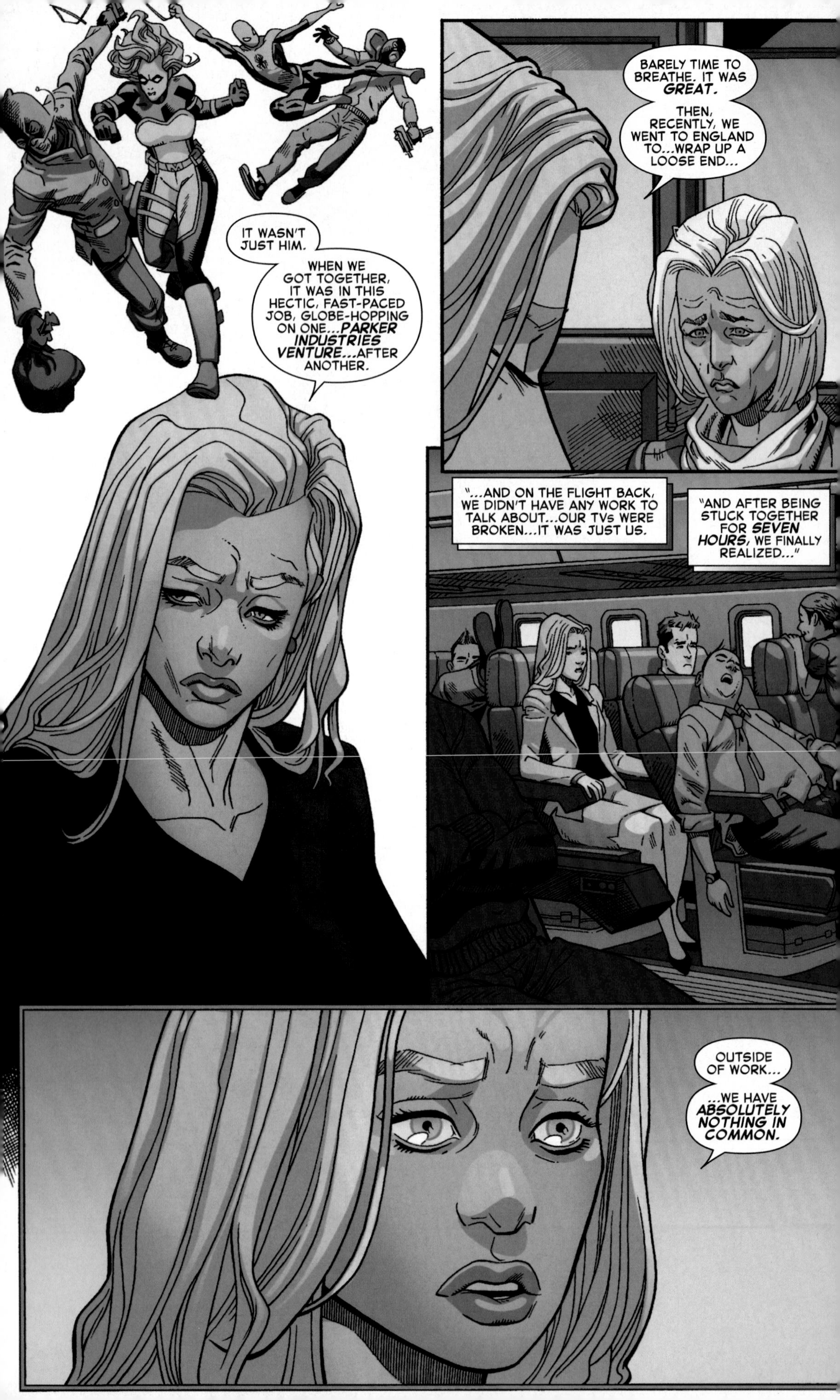

IT WASN'T JUST HIM.
WHEN WE GOT TOGETHER, IT WAS IN THIS HECTIC, FAST-PACED JOB, GLOBE-HOPPING ON ONE...PARKER INDUSTRIES VENTURE...AFTER ANOTHER.
BARELY TIME TO BREATHE. IT WAS GREAT.
THEN, RECENTLY, WE WENT TO ENGLAND TO...WRAP UP A LOOSE END...
"...AND ON THE FLIGHT BACK, WE DIDN'T HAVE ANY WORK TO TALK ABOUT...OUR TVs WERE BROKEN...IT WAS JUST US.
"AND AFTER BEING STUCK TOGETHER FOR SEVEN HOURS, WE FINALLY REALIZED..."
OUTSIDE OF WORK...
...WE HAVE ABSOLUTELY NOTHING IN COMMON.

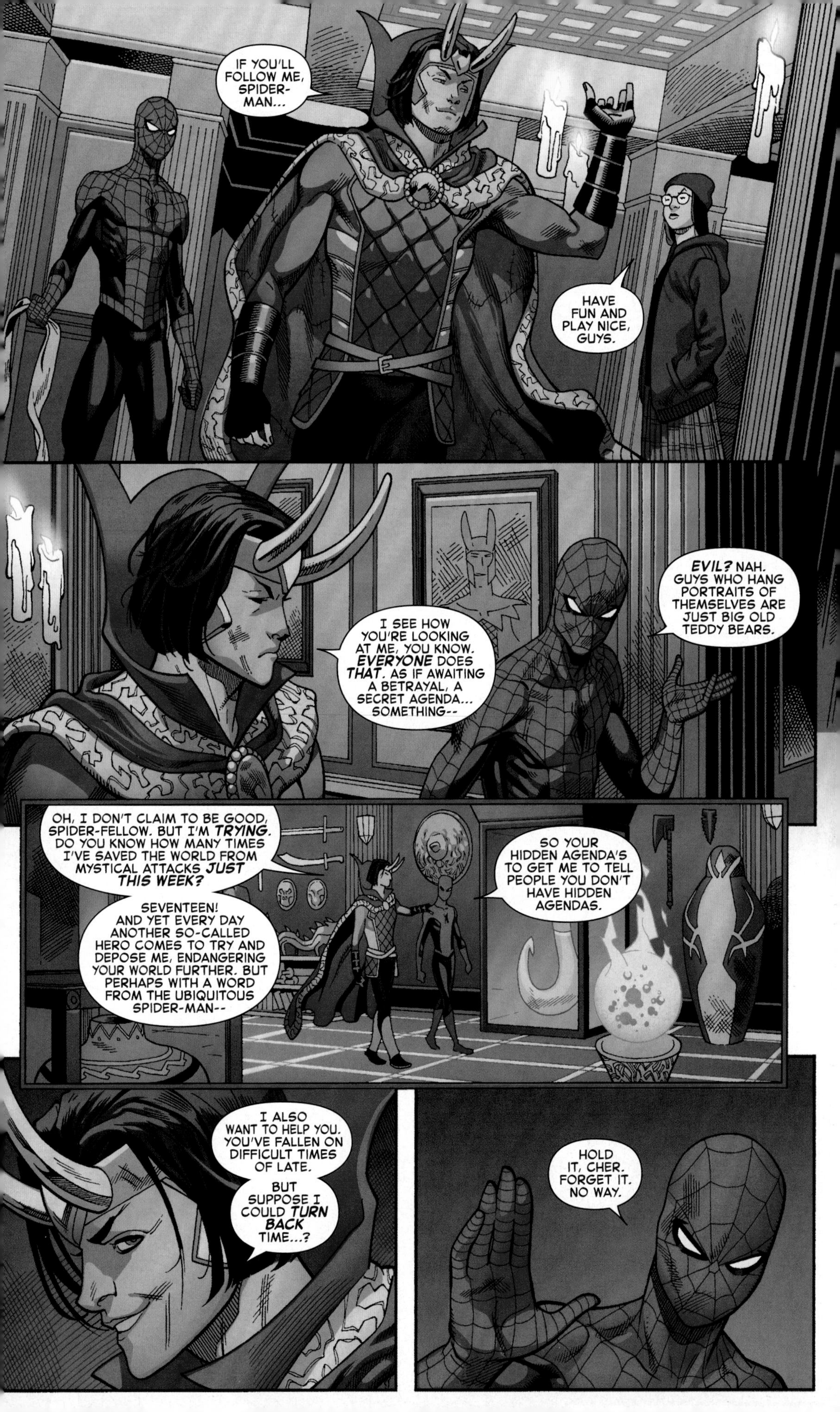

IF YOU'LL FOLLOW ME, SPIDER-MAN...
HAVE FUN AND PLAY NICE, GUYS.
I SEE HOW YOU'RE LOOKING AT ME, YOU KNOW. EVERYONE DOES THAT. AS IF AWAITING A BETRAYAL, A SECRET AGENDA... SOMETHING--
EVIL? NAH. GUYS WHO HANG PORTRAITS OF THEMSELVES ARE JUST BIG OLD TEDDY BEARS.
OH, I DON'T CLAIM TO BE GOOD, SPIDER-FELLOW. BUT I'M TRYING. DO YOU KNOW HOW MANY TIMES I'VE SAVED THE WORLD FROM MYSTICAL ATTACKS JUST THIS WEEK?
SEVENTEEN! AND YET EVERY DAY ANOTHER SO-CALLED HERO COMES TO TRY AND DEPOSE ME, ENDANGERING YOUR WORLD FURTHER. BUT PERHAPS WITH A WORD FROM THE UBIQUITOUS SPIDER-MAN--
SO YOUR HIDDEN AGENDA'S TO GET ME TO TELL PEOPLE YOU DON'T HAVE HIDDEN AGENDAS.
I ALSO WANT TO HELP YOU. YOU'VE FALLEN ON DIFFICULT TIMES OF LATE.
BUT SUPPOSE I COULD TURN BACK TIME...?
HOLD IT, CHER. FORGET IT. NO WAY.

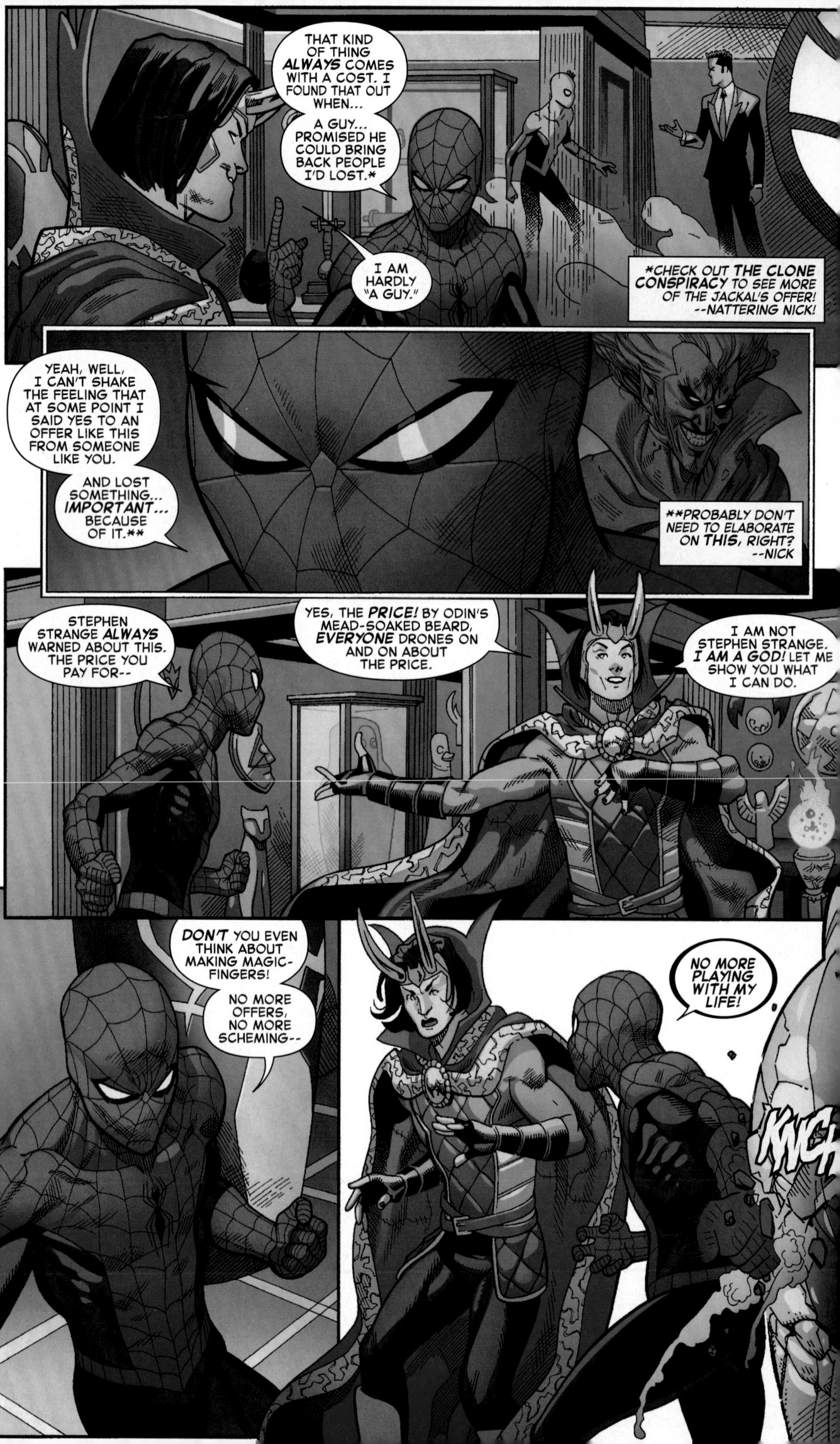
THAT KIND OF THING ALWAYS COMES WITH A COST. I FOUND THAT OUT WHEN...
A GUY... PROMISED HE COULD BRING BACK PEOPLE I'D LOST.*
I AM HARDLY "A GUY."
*CHECK OUT THE CLONE CONSPIRACY TO SEE MORE OF THE JACKAL'S OFFER! --NATTERING NICK!
YEAH, WELL, I CAN'T SHAKE THE FEELING THAT AT SOME POINT I SAID YES TO AN OFFER LIKE THIS FROM SOMEONE LIKE YOU.
AND LOST SOMETHING... IMPORTANT... BECAUSE OF IT.**
**PROBABLY DON'T NEED TO ELABORATE ON THIS, RIGHT? --NICK
STEPHEN STRANGE ALWAYS WARNED ABOUT THIS. THE PRICE YOU PAY FOR--
YES, THE PRICE! BY ODIN'S MEAD-SOAKED BEARD, EVERYONE DRONES ON AND ON ABOUT THE PRICE.
I AM NOT STEPHEN STRANGE. I AM A GOD! LET ME SHOW YOU WHAT I CAN DO.
DON'T YOU EVEN THINK ABOUT MAKING MAGIC-FINGERS!
NO MORE OFFERS, NO MORE SCHEMING--
NO MORE PLAYING WITH MY LIFE!

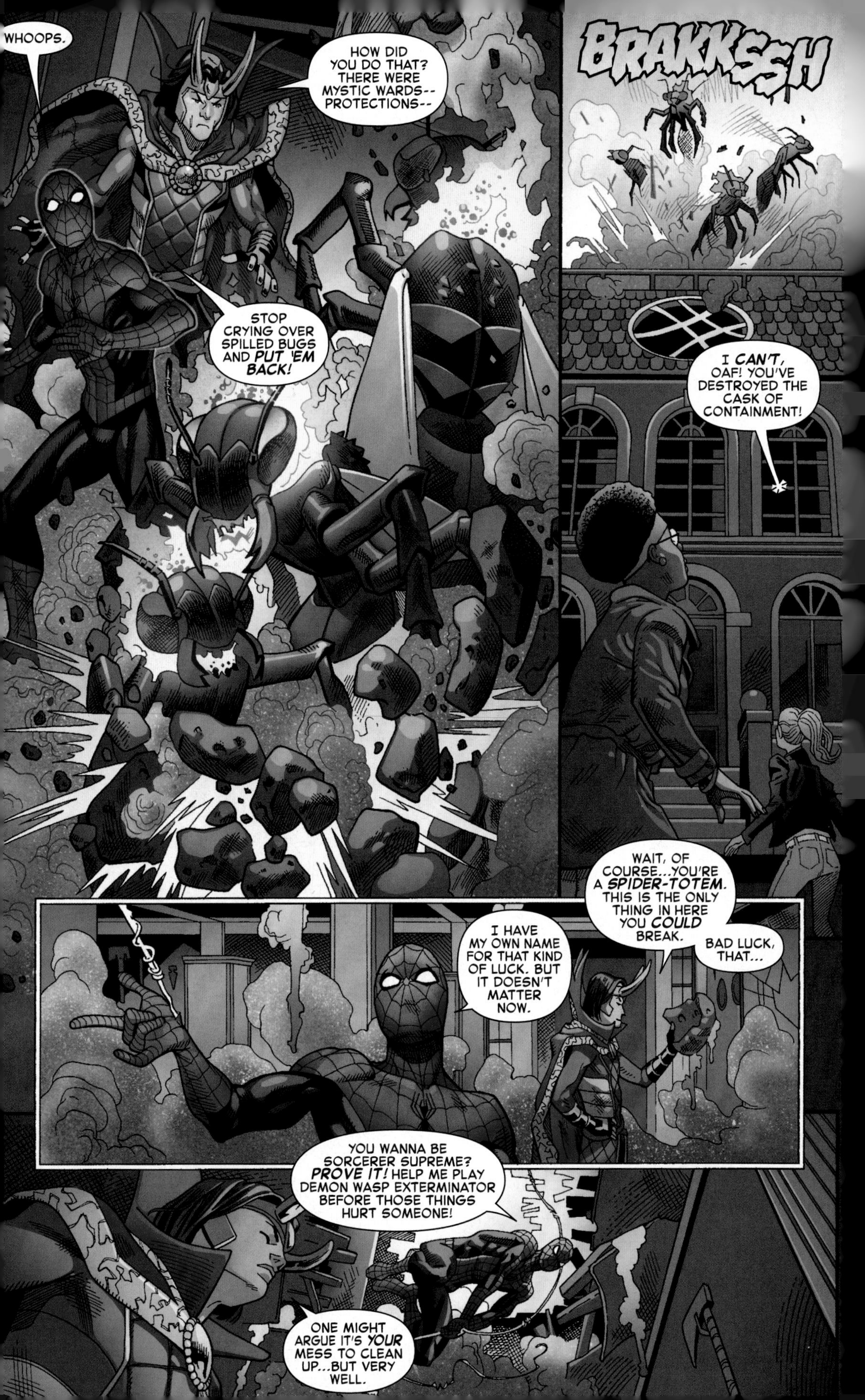
WHOOPS.
HOW DID YOU DO THAT? THERE WERE MYSTIC WARDS-- PROTECTIONS--
STOP CRYING OVER SPILLED BUGS AND PUT 'EM BACK!
BRAKKSSH
I CAN'T, OAF! YOU'VE DESTROYED THE CASK OF CONTAINMENT!
WAIT, OF COURSE...YOU'RE A SPIDER-TOTEM. THIS IS THE ONLY THING IN HERE YOU COULD BREAK.
BAD LUCK, THAT...
I HAVE MY OWN NAME FOR THAT KIND OF LUCK. BUT IT DOESN'T MATTER NOW.
YOU WANNA BE SORCERER SUPREME? PROVE IT! HELP ME PLAY DEMON WASP EXTERMINATOR BEFORE THOSE THINGS HURT SOMEONE!
ONE MIGHT ARGUE IT'S YOUR MESS TO CLEAN UP...BUT VERY WELL.

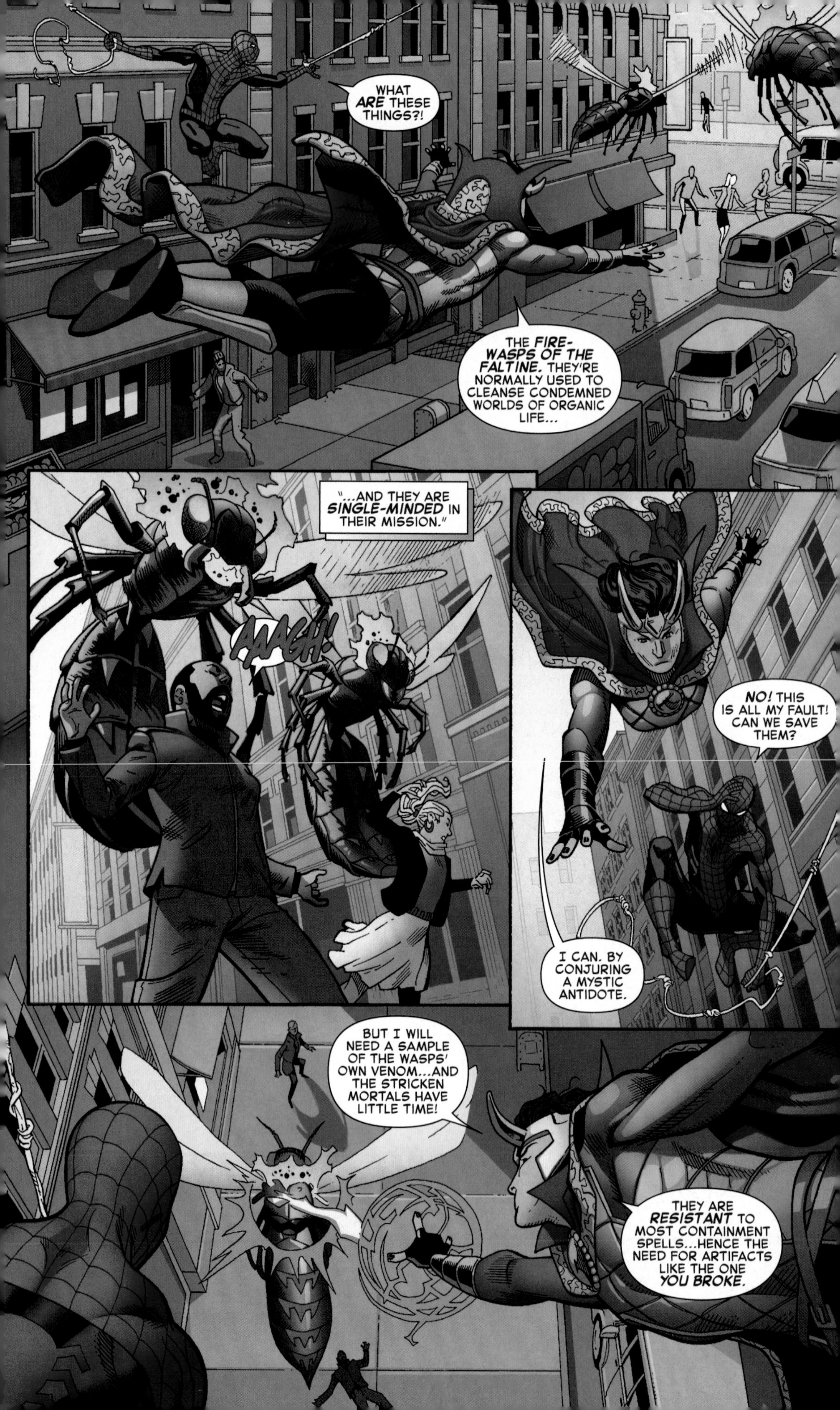
WHAT ARE THESE THINGS?!
THE FIRE-WASPS OF THE FALTINE. THEY'RE NORMALLY USED TO CLEANSE CONDEMNED WORLDS OF ORGANIC LIFE...
"...AND THEY ARE SINGLE-MINDED IN THEIR MISSION."
AAAGH!
NO! THIS IS ALL MY FAULT! CAN WE SAVE THEM?
I CAN. BY CONJURING A MYSTIC ANTIDOTE.
BUT I WILL NEED A SAMPLE OF THE WASPS' OWN VENOM...AND THE STRICKEN MORTALS HAVE LITTLE TIME!
THEY ARE RESISTANT TO MOST CONTAINMENT SPELLS...HENCE THE NEED FOR ARTIFACTS LIKE THE ONE YOU BROKE.

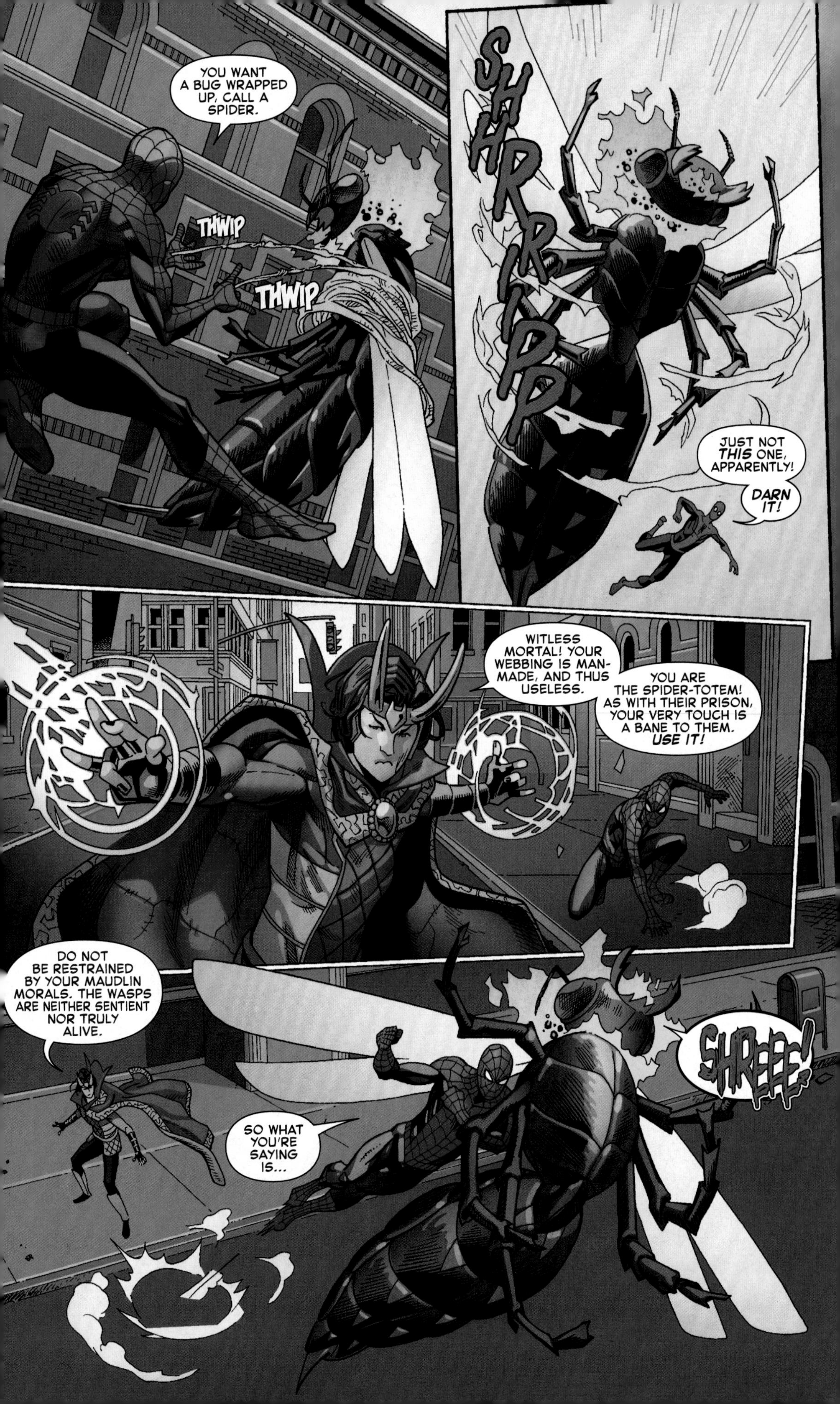
YOU WANT A BUG WRAPPED UP, CALL A SPIDER.
THWIP
THWIP
SHHRRIPP
JUST NOT THIS ONE, APPARENTLY!
DARN IT!
WITLESS MORTAL! YOUR WEBBING IS MAN-MADE, AND THUS USELESS.
YOU ARE THE SPIDER-TOTEM! AS WITH THEIR PRISON, YOUR VERY TOUCH IS A BANE TO THEM. USE IT!
DO NOT BE RESTRAINED BY YOUR MAUDLIN MORALS. THE WASPS ARE NEITHER SENTIENT NOR TRULY ALIVE.
SO WHAT YOU'RE SAYING IS...
SHREEE!

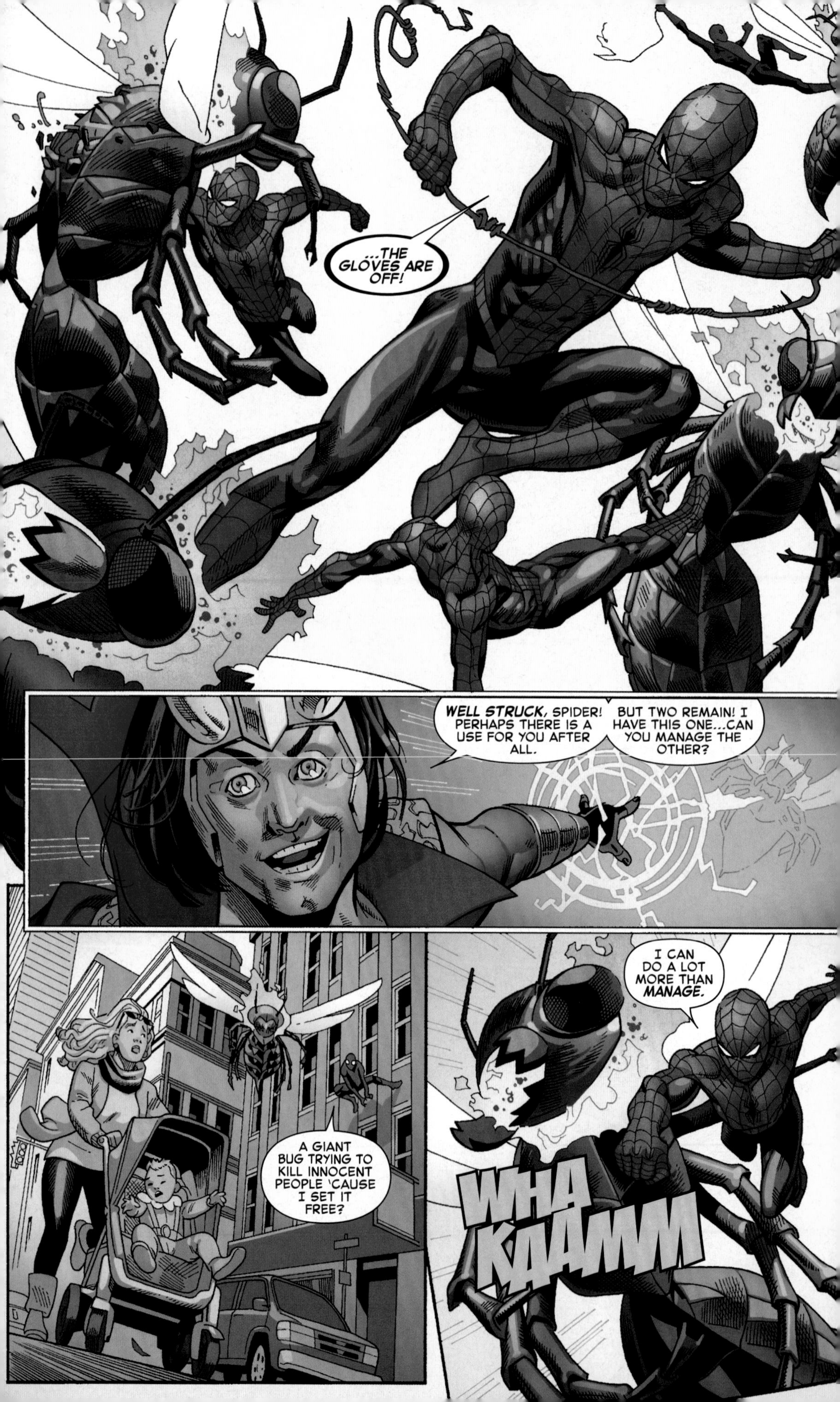
...THE GLOVES ARE OFF!
WELL STRUCK, SPIDER! PERHAPS THERE IS A USE FOR YOU AFTER ALL.
BUT TWO REMAIN! I HAVE THIS ONE...CAN YOU MANAGE THE OTHER?
A GIANT BUG TRYING TO KILL INNOCENT PEOPLE 'CAUSE I SET IT FREE?
I CAN DO A LOT MORE THAN MANAGE.
WHA KAAMM

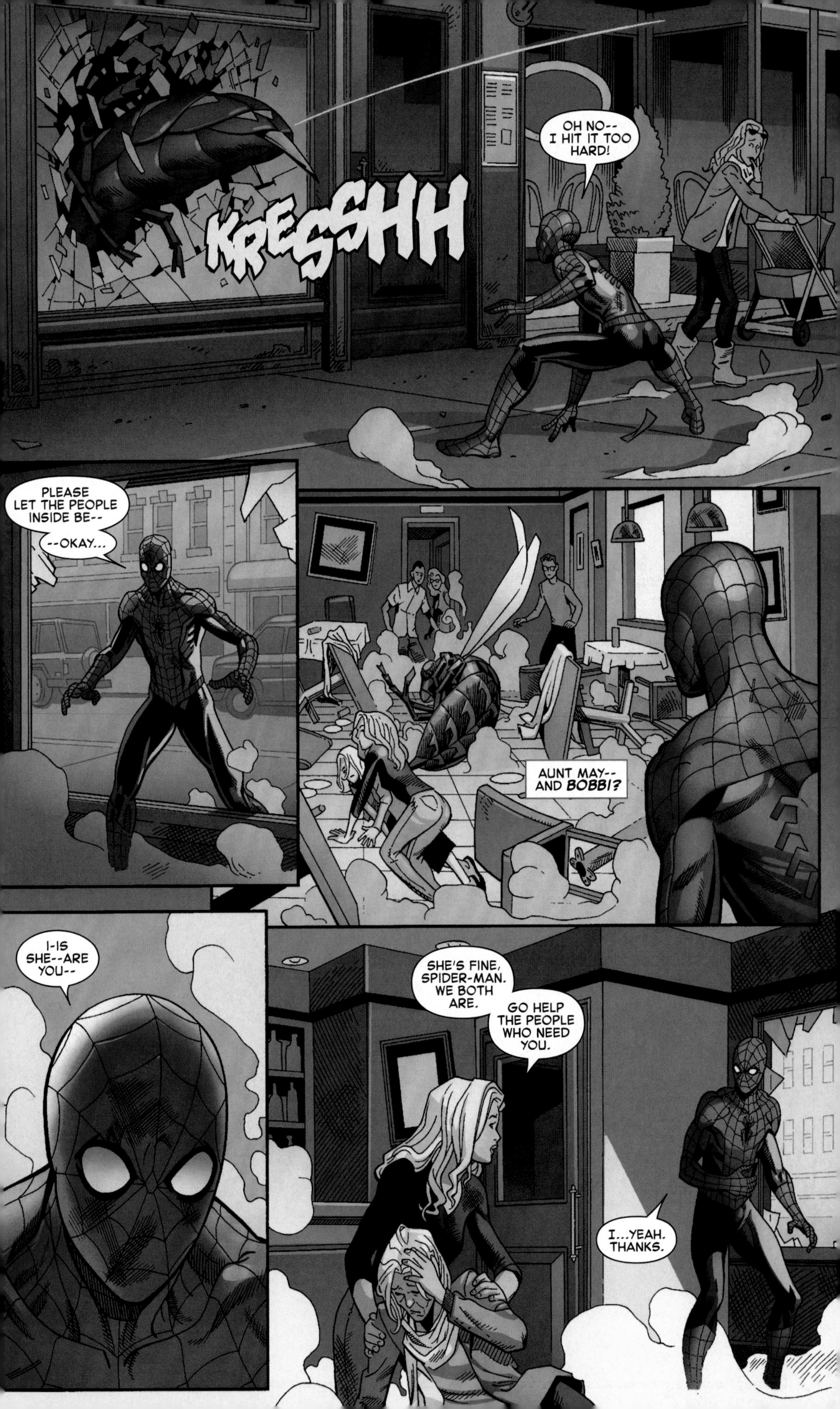
OH NO-- I HIT IT TOO HARD!
KRESSHH
PLEASE LET THE PEOPLE INSIDE BE--
--OKAY...
AUNT MAY-- AND BOBBI?
I-IS SHE--ARE YOU--
SHE'S FINE, SPIDER-MAN. WE BOTH ARE.
GO HELP THE PEOPLE WHO NEED YOU.
I...YEAH. THANKS.

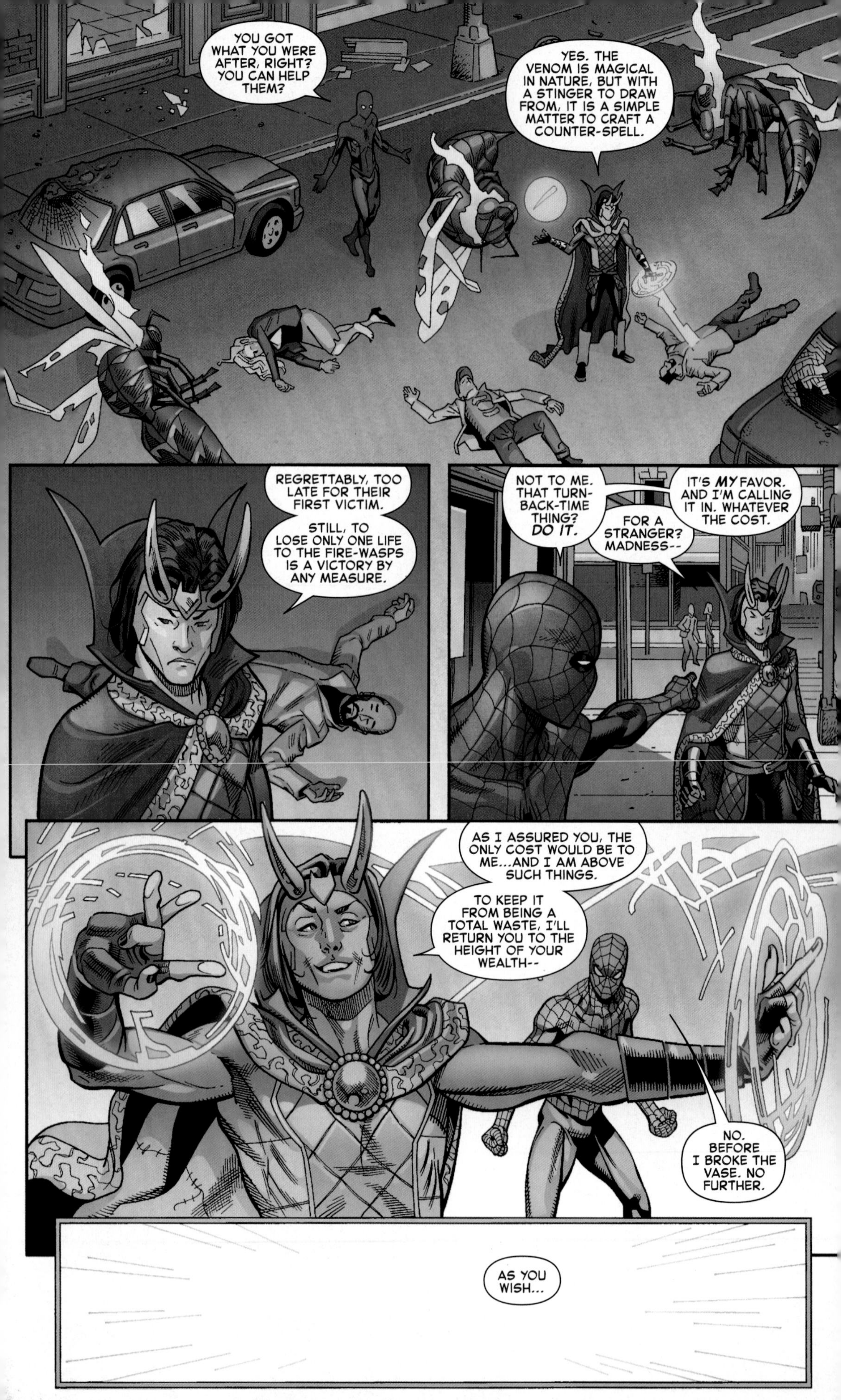
YOU GOT WHAT YOU WERE AFTER, RIGHT? YOU CAN HELP THEM?
YES. THE VENOM IS MAGICAL IN NATURE, BUT WITH A STINGER TO DRAW FROM, IT IS A SIMPLE MATTER TO CRAFT A COUNTER-SPELL.
REGRETTABLY, TOO LATE FOR THEIR FIRST VICTIM.
STILL, TO LOSE ONLY ONE LIFE TO THE FIRE-WASPS IS A VICTORY BY ANY MEASURE.
NOT TO ME. THAT TURN-BACK-TIME THING? *DO IT.*
FOR A STRANGER? MADNESS--
IT'S *MY* FAVOR. AND I'M CALLING IT IN. WHATEVER THE COST.
AS I ASSURED YOU, THE ONLY COST WOULD BE TO ME...AND I AM ABOVE SUCH THINGS.
TO KEEP IT FROM BEING A TOTAL WASTE, I'LL RETURN YOU TO THE HEIGHT OF YOUR WEALTH--
NO. BEFORE I BROKE THE VASE. NO FURTHER.
AS YOU WISH...

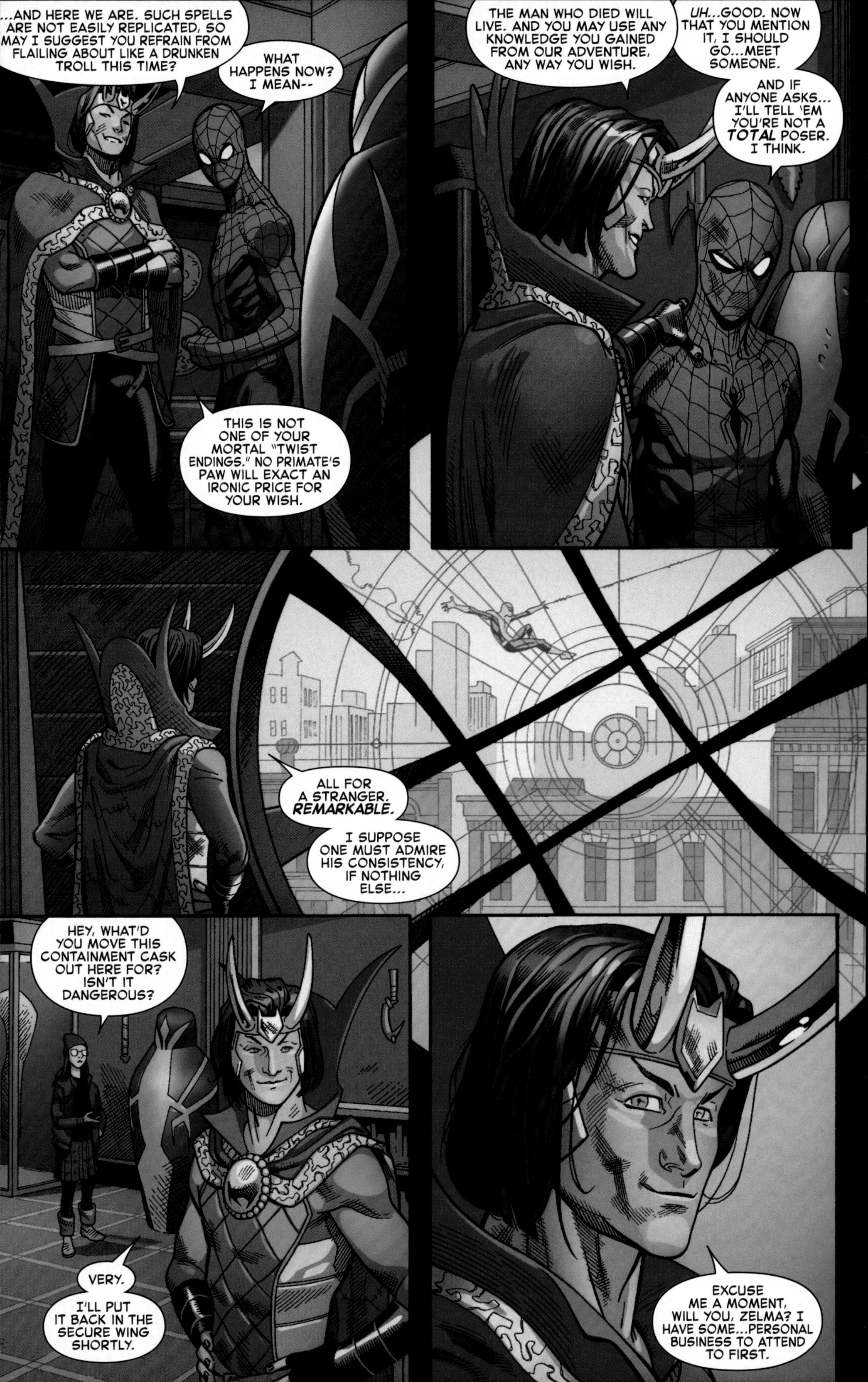
...AND HERE WE ARE. SUCH SPELLS ARE NOT EASILY REPLICATED, SO MAY I SUGGEST YOU REFRAIN FROM FLAILING ABOUT LIKE A DRUNKEN TROLL THIS TIME?
WHAT HAPPENS NOW? I MEAN--
THIS IS NOT ONE OF YOUR MORTAL "TWIST ENDINGS." NO PRIMATE'S PAW WILL EXACT AN IRONIC PRICE FOR YOUR WISH.
THE MAN WHO DIED WILL LIVE. AND YOU MAY USE ANY KNOWLEDGE YOU GAINED FROM OUR ADVENTURE, ANY WAY YOU WISH.
UH...GOOD. NOW THAT YOU MENTION IT, I SHOULD GO...MEET SOMEONE.
AND IF ANYONE ASKS... I'LL TELL 'EM YOU'RE NOT A TOTAL POSER. I THINK.
ALL FOR A STRANGER. REMARKABLE.
I SUPPOSE ONE MUST ADMIRE HIS CONSISTENCY, IF NOTHING ELSE...
HEY, WHAT'D YOU MOVE THIS CONTAINMENT CASK OUT HERE FOR? ISN'T IT DANGEROUS?
VERY.
I'LL PUT IT BACK IN THE SECURE WING SHORTLY.
EXCUSE ME A MOMENT, WILL YOU, ZELMA? I HAVE SOME...PERSONAL BUSINESS TO ATTEND TO FIRST.

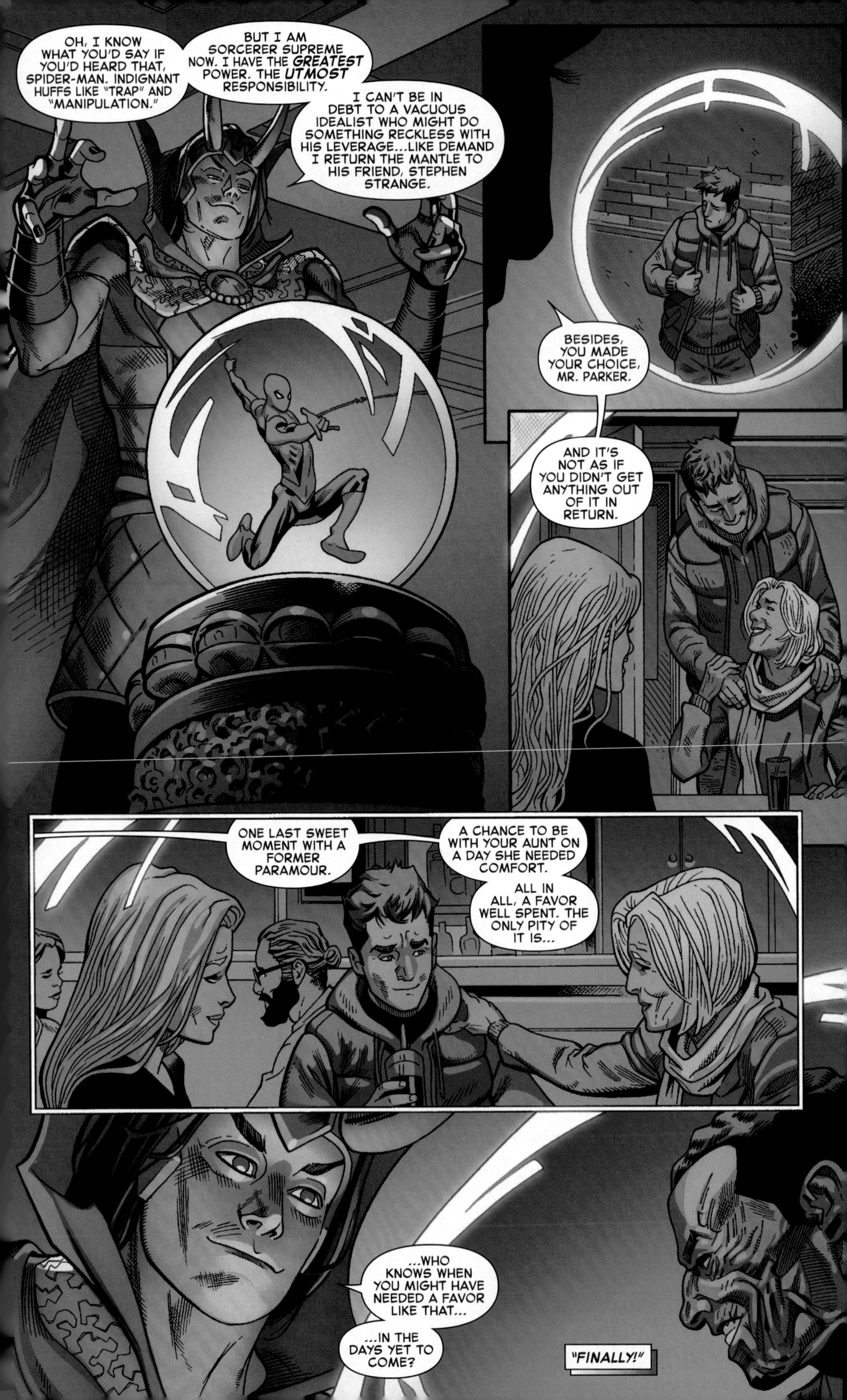
OH, I KNOW WHAT YOU'D SAY IF YOU'D HEARD THAT, SPIDER-MAN. INDIGNANT HUFFS LIKE "TRAP" AND "MANIPULATION."
BUT I AM SORCERER SUPREME NOW. I HAVE THE GREATEST POWER. THE UTMOST RESPONSIBILITY.
I CAN'T BE IN DEBT TO A VACUOUS IDEALIST WHO MIGHT DO SOMETHING RECKLESS WITH HIS LEVERAGE...LIKE DEMAND I RETURN THE MANTLE TO HIS FRIEND, STEPHEN STRANGE.
BESIDES, YOU MADE YOUR CHOICE, MR. PARKER.
AND IT'S NOT AS IF YOU DIDN'T GET ANYTHING OUT OF IT IN RETURN.
ONE LAST SWEET MOMENT WITH A FORMER PARAMOUR.
A CHANCE TO BE WITH YOUR AUNT ON A DAY SHE NEEDED COMFORT.
ALL IN ALL, A FAVOR WELL SPENT. THE ONLY PITY OF IT IS...
...WHO KNOWS WHEN YOU MIGHT HAVE NEEDED A FAVOR LIKE THAT...
...IN THE DAYS YET TO COME?
"FINALLY!"

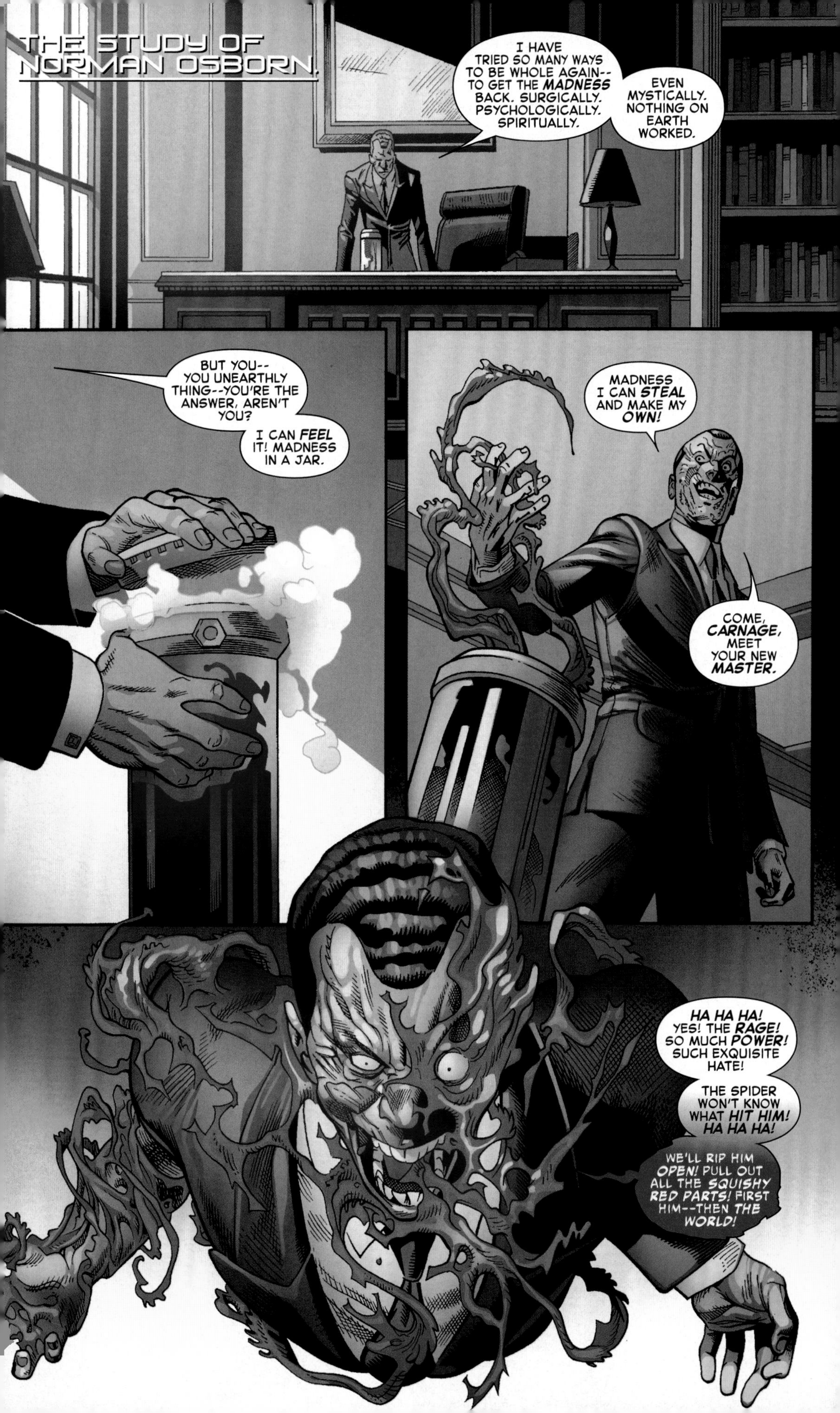
THE STUDY OF NORMAN OSBORN.
I HAVE TRIED SO MANY WAYS TO BE WHOLE AGAIN-- TO GET THE MADNESS BACK. SURGICALLY. PSYCHOLOGICALLY. SPIRITUALLY.
EVEN MYSTICALLY. NOTHING ON EARTH WORKED.
BUT YOU-- YOU UNEARTHLY THING--YOU'RE THE ANSWER, AREN'T YOU?
I CAN FEEL IT! MADNESS IN A JAR.
MADNESS I CAN STEAL AND MAKE MY OWN!
COME, CARNAGE, MEET YOUR NEW MASTER.
HA HA HA! YES! THE RAGE! SO MUCH POWER! SUCH EXQUISITE HATE!
THE SPIDER WON'T KNOW WHAT HIT HIM! HA HA HA!
WE'LL RIP HIM OPEN! PULL OUT ALL THE SQUISHY RED PARTS! FIRST HIM--THEN THE WORLD!

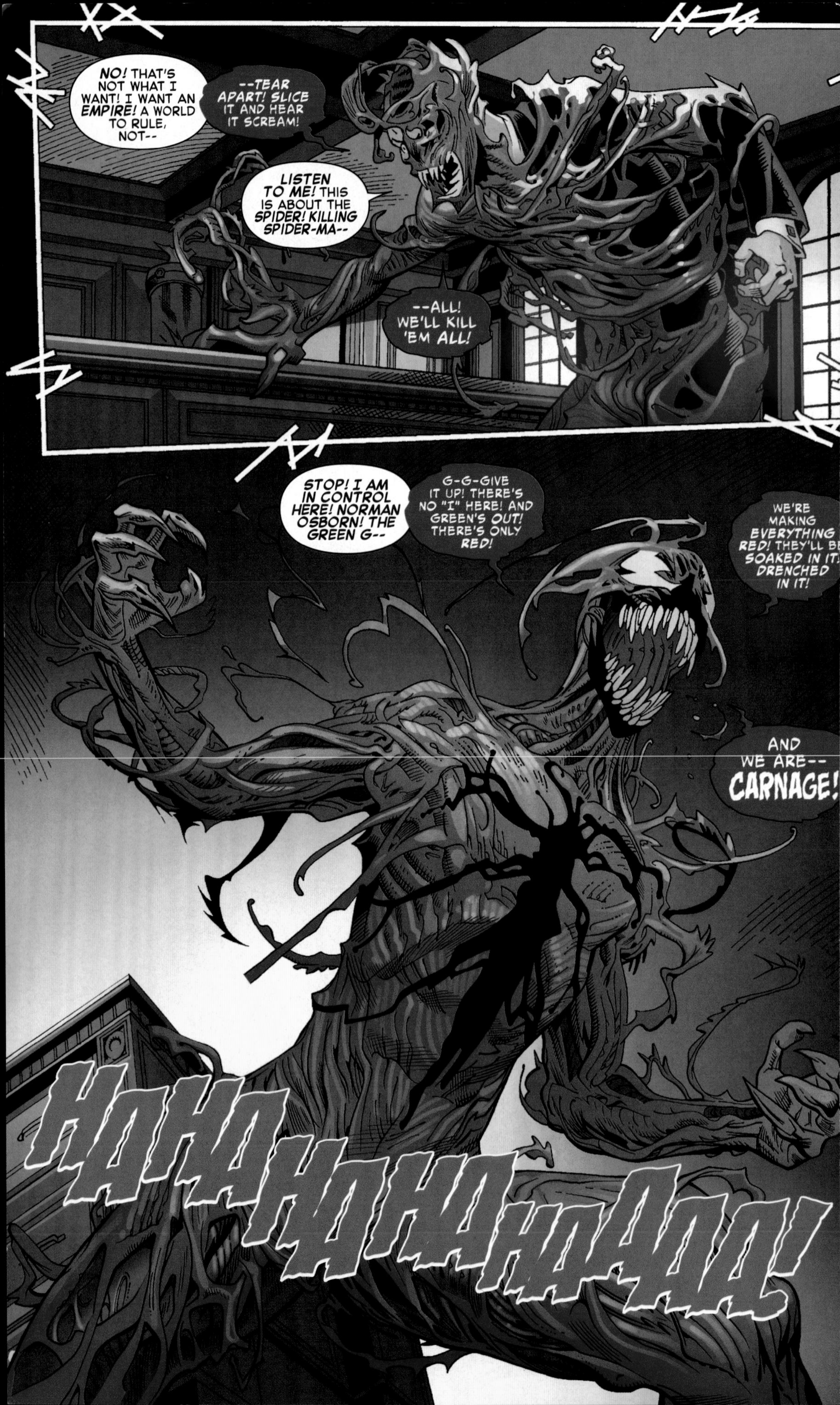
NO! THAT'S NOT WHAT I WANT! I WANT AN EMPIRE! A WORLD TO RULE, NOT--
--TEAR APART! SLICE IT AND HEAR IT SCREAM!
LISTEN TO ME! THIS IS ABOUT THE SPIDER! KILLING SPIDER-MA--
--ALL! WE'LL KILL 'EM ALL!
STOP! I AM IN CONTROL HERE! NORMAN OSBORN! THE GREEN G--
G-G-GIVE IT UP! THERE'S NO "I" HERE! AND GREEN'S OUT! THERE'S ONLY RED!
WE'RE MAKING EVERYTHING RED! THEY'LL BE SOAKED IN IT! DRENCHED IN IT!
AND WE ARE-- CARNAGE!

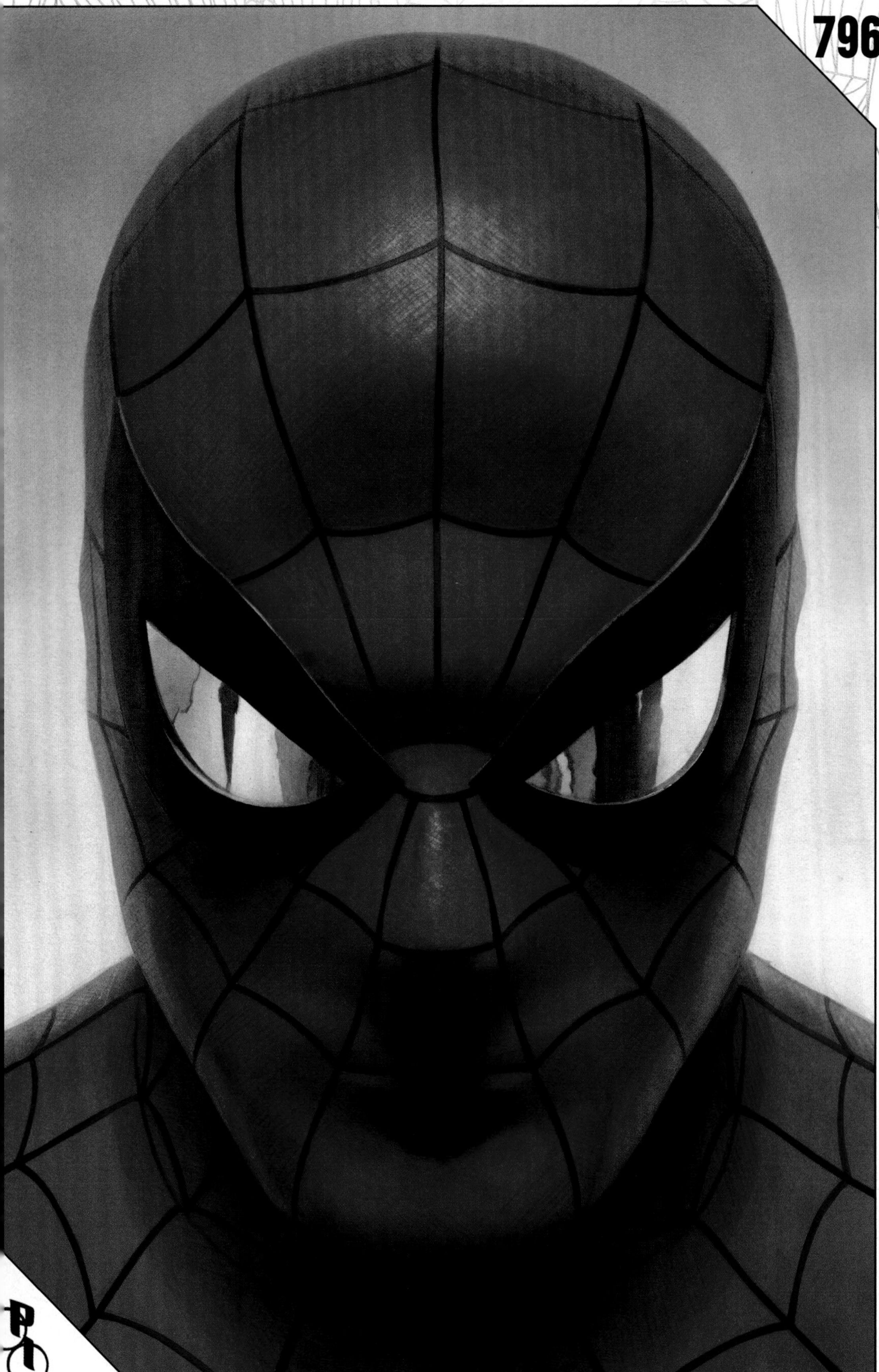
796

THREAT LEVEL: RED PART THREE "HIGHER PRIORITIES"

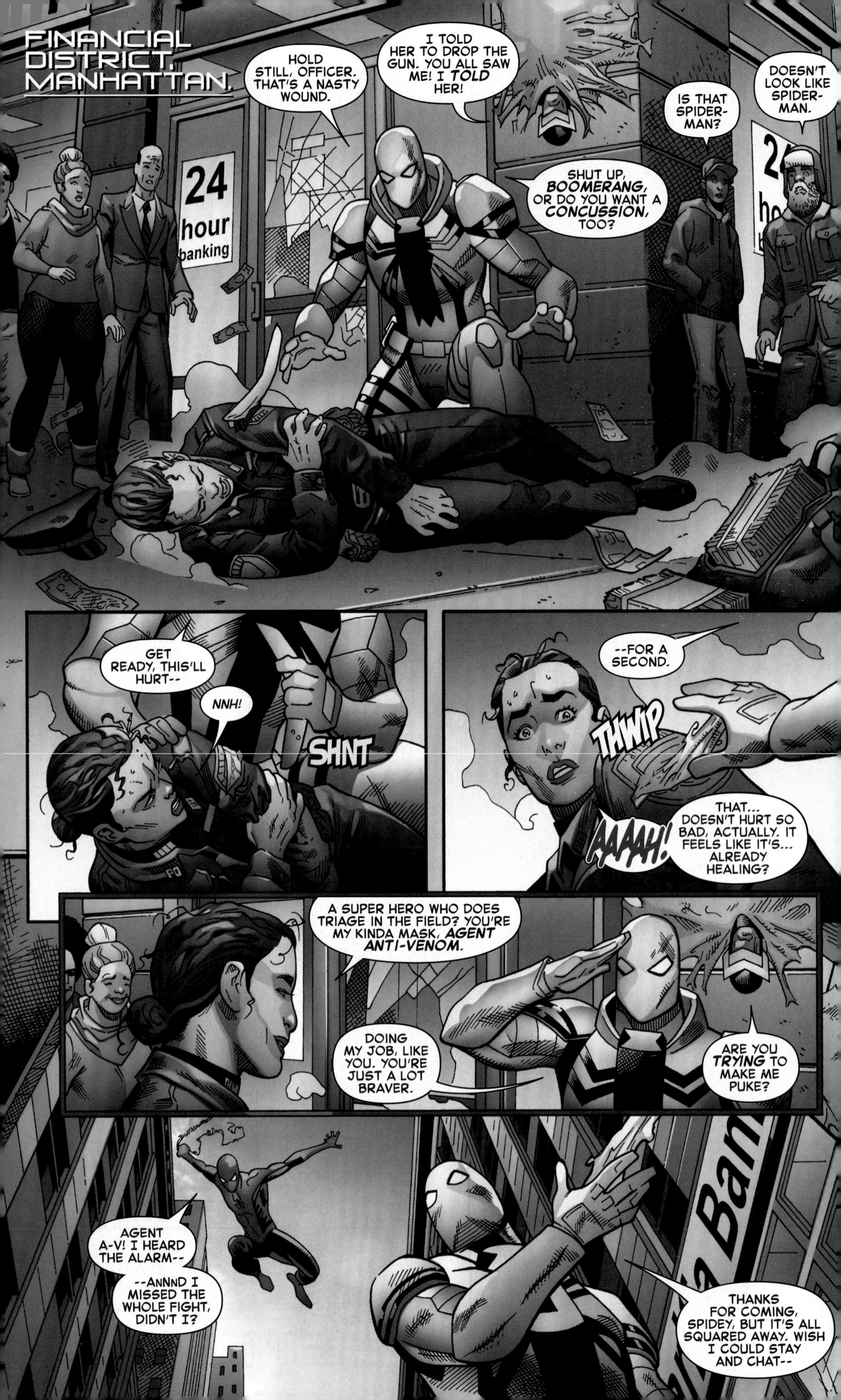

FINANCIAL DISTRICT, MANHATTAN.
HOLD STILL, OFFICER. THAT'S A NASTY WOUND.
I TOLD HER TO DROP THE GUN. YOU ALL SAW ME! I TOLD HER!
IS THAT SPIDER-MAN?
DOESN'T LOOK LIKE SPIDER-MAN.
SHUT UP, BOOMERANG, OR DO YOU WANT A CONCUSSION, TOO?
24 hour banking
GET READY, THIS'LL HURT--
NNH!
SHNT
--FOR A SECOND.
THWIP
AAAAH!
THAT... DOESN'T HURT SO BAD, ACTUALLY. IT FEELS LIKE IT'S... ALREADY HEALING?
A SUPER HERO WHO DOES TRIAGE IN THE FIELD? YOU'RE MY KINDA MASK, AGENT ANTI-VENOM.
DOING MY JOB, LIKE YOU. YOU'RE JUST A LOT BRAVER.
ARE YOU TRYING TO MAKE ME PUKE?
AGENT A-V! I HEARD THE ALARM--
--ANNND I MISSED THE WHOLE FIGHT, DIDN'T I?
THANKS FOR COMING, SPIDEY, BUT IT'S ALL SQUARED AWAY. WISH I COULD STAY AND CHAT--

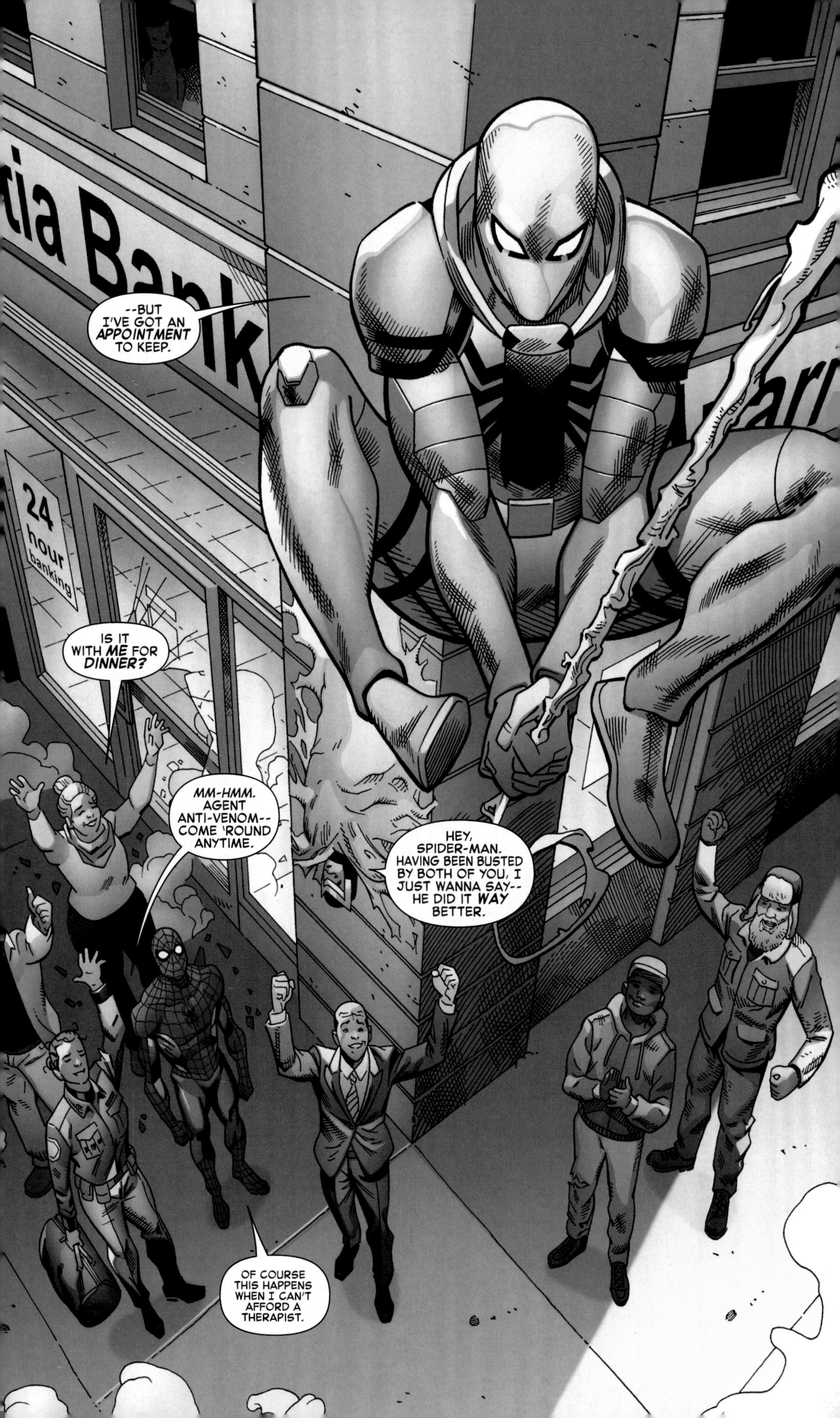
tia Bank
--BUT I'VE GOT AN APPOINTMENT TO KEEP.
24 hour banking
IS IT WITH ME FOR DINNER?
MM-HMM. AGENT ANTI-VENOM--COME 'ROUND ANYTIME.
HEY, SPIDER-MAN. HAVING BEEN BUSTED BY BOTH OF YOU, I JUST WANNA SAY--HE DID IT WAY BETTER.
OF COURSE THIS HAPPENS WHEN I CAN'T AFFORD A THERAPIST.

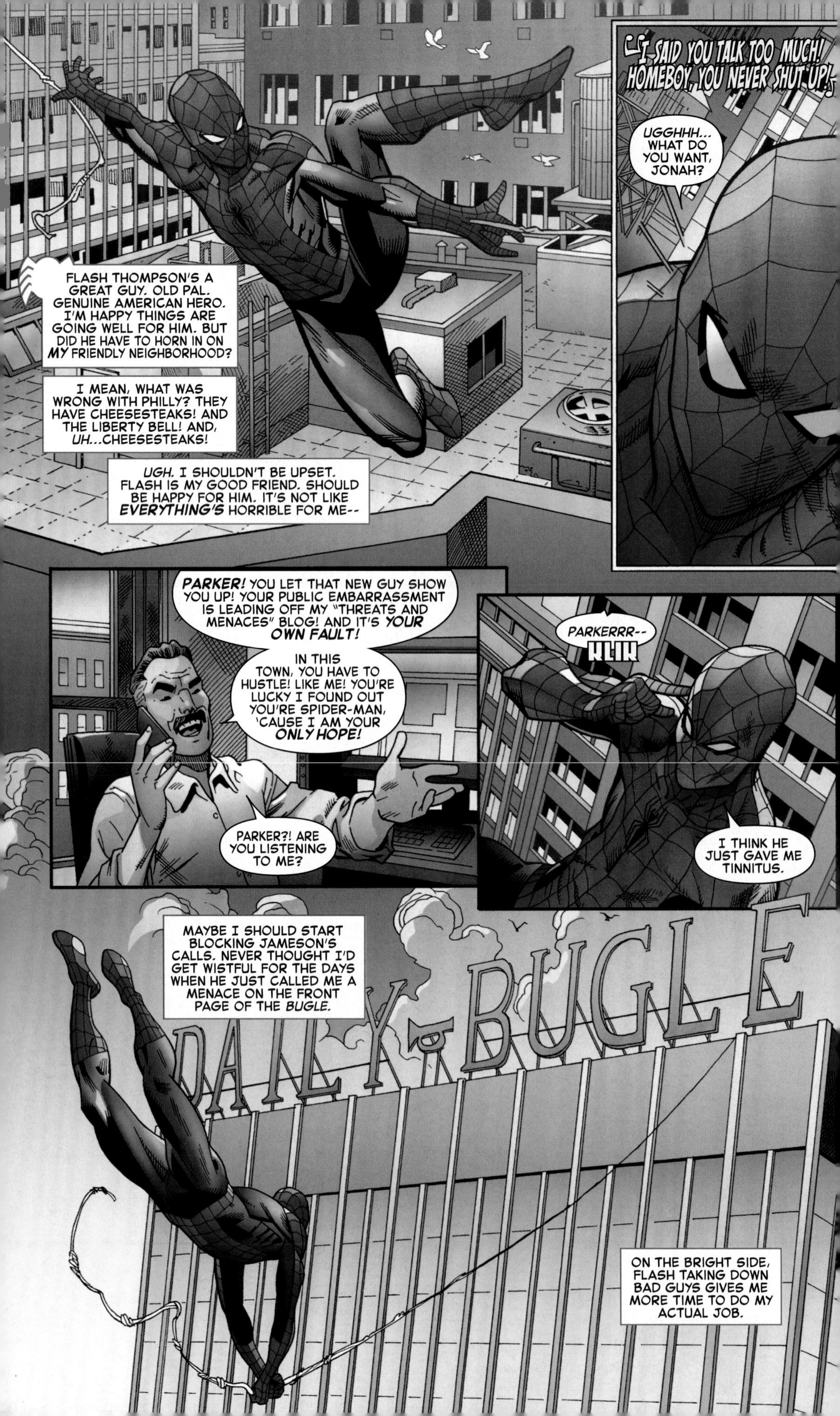
FLASH THOMPSON'S A GREAT GUY. OLD PAL. GENUINE AMERICAN HERO. I'M HAPPY THINGS ARE GOING WELL FOR HIM. BUT DID HE HAVE TO HORN IN ON *MY* FRIENDLY NEIGHBORHOOD?
I MEAN, WHAT WAS WRONG WITH PHILLY? THEY HAVE CHEESESTEAKS! AND THE LIBERTY BELL! AND, *UH*...CHEESESTEAKS!
UGH. I SHOULDN'T BE UPSET. FLASH IS MY GOOD FRIEND. SHOULD BE HAPPY FOR HIM. IT'S NOT LIKE ***EVERYTHING'S*** HORRIBLE FOR ME--
I SAID YOU TALK TOO MUCH! HOMEBOY, YOU NEVER SHUT UP!
UGGHHH... WHAT DO YOU WANT, JONAH?
PARKER! YOU LET THAT NEW GUY SHOW YOU UP! YOUR PUBLIC EMBARRASSMENT IS LEADING OFF MY "THREATS AND MENACES" BLOG! AND IT'S ***YOUR OWN FAULT!***
IN THIS TOWN, YOU HAVE TO HUSTLE! LIKE ME! YOU'RE LUCKY I FOUND OUT YOU'RE SPIDER-MAN, 'CAUSE I AM YOUR ***ONLY HOPE!***
PARKER?! ARE YOU LISTENING TO ME?
PARKERRR--
KLIK
I THINK HE JUST GAVE ME TINNITUS.
MAYBE I SHOULD START BLOCKING JAMESON'S CALLS. NEVER THOUGHT I'D GET WISTFUL FOR THE DAYS WHEN HE JUST CALLED ME A MENACE ON THE FRONT PAGE OF THE *BUGLE.*
DAILY BUGLE
ON THE BRIGHT SIDE, FLASH TAKING DOWN BAD GUYS GIVES ME MORE TIME TO DO MY ACTUAL JOB.

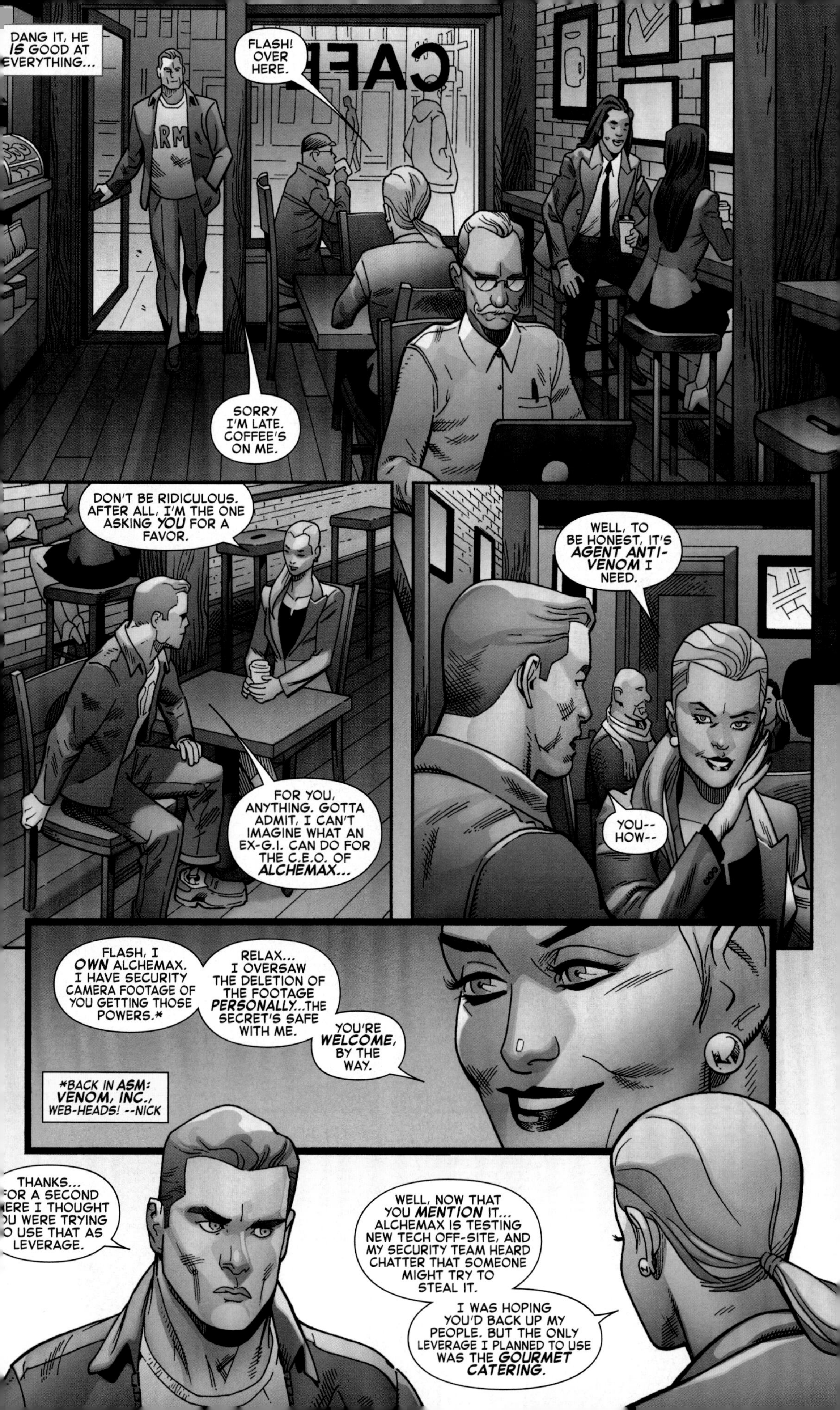

DANG IT, HE IS GOOD AT EVERYTHING...
FLASH! OVER HERE.
CAFE
SORRY I'M LATE. COFFEE'S ON ME.
DON'T BE RIDICULOUS. AFTER ALL, I'M THE ONE ASKING YOU FOR A FAVOR.
FOR YOU, ANYTHING. GOTTA ADMIT, I CAN'T IMAGINE WHAT AN EX-G.I. CAN DO FOR THE C.E.O. OF ALCHEMAX...
WELL, TO BE HONEST, IT'S AGENT ANTI-VENOM I NEED.
YOU-- HOW--
FLASH, I OWN ALCHEMAX. I HAVE SECURITY CAMERA FOOTAGE OF YOU GETTING THOSE POWERS.*
RELAX... I OVERSAW THE DELETION OF THE FOOTAGE PERSONALLY...THE SECRET'S SAFE WITH ME.
YOU'RE WELCOME, BY THE WAY.
*BACK IN ASM: VENOM, INC., WEB-HEADS! --NICK
THANKS... FOR A SECOND THERE I THOUGHT YOU WERE TRYING TO USE THAT AS LEVERAGE.
WELL, NOW THAT YOU MENTION IT... ALCHEMAX IS TESTING NEW TECH OFF-SITE, AND MY SECURITY TEAM HEARD CHATTER THAT SOMEONE MIGHT TRY TO STEAL IT.
I WAS HOPING YOU'D BACK UP MY PEOPLE. BUT THE ONLY LEVERAGE I PLANNED TO USE WAS THE GOURMET CATERING.

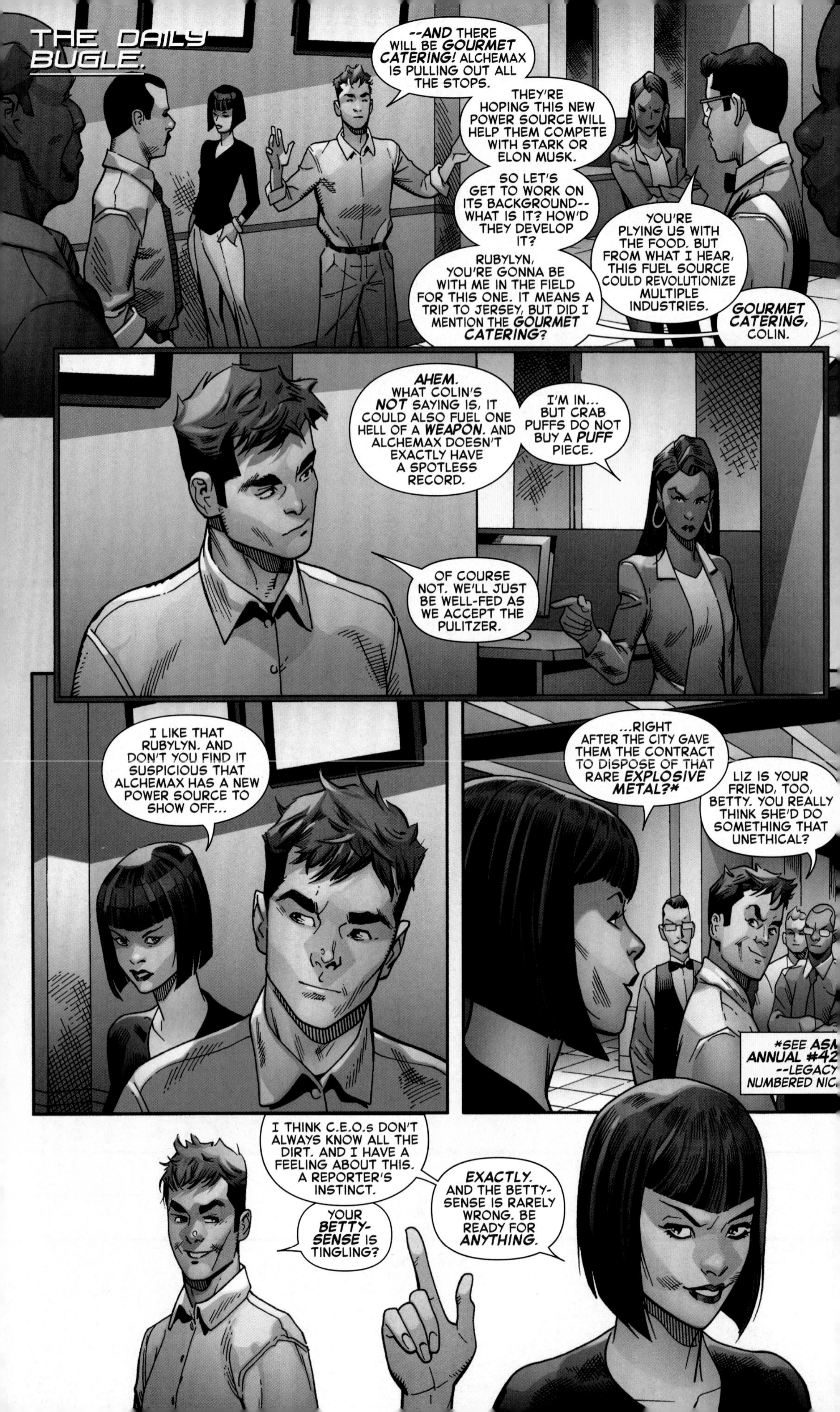
THE DAILY BUGLE.
--AND THERE WILL BE GOURMET CATERING! ALCHEMAX IS PULLING OUT ALL THE STOPS.
THEY'RE HOPING THIS NEW POWER SOURCE WILL HELP THEM COMPETE WITH STARK OR ELON MUSK.
SO LET'S GET TO WORK ON ITS BACKGROUND-- WHAT IS IT? HOW'D THEY DEVELOP IT?
RUBYLYN, YOU'RE GONNA BE WITH ME IN THE FIELD FOR THIS ONE. IT MEANS A TRIP TO JERSEY, BUT DID I MENTION THE GOURMET CATERING?
YOU'RE PLYING US WITH THE FOOD. BUT FROM WHAT I HEAR, THIS FUEL SOURCE COULD REVOLUTIONIZE MULTIPLE INDUSTRIES.
GOURMET CATERING, COLIN.
AHEM. WHAT COLIN'S NOT SAYING IS, IT COULD ALSO FUEL ONE HELL OF A WEAPON. AND ALCHEMAX DOESN'T EXACTLY HAVE A SPOTLESS RECORD.
I'M IN... BUT CRAB PUFFS DO NOT BUY A PUFF PIECE.
OF COURSE NOT. WE'LL JUST BE WELL-FED AS WE ACCEPT THE PULITZER.
I LIKE THAT RUBYLYN. AND DON'T YOU FIND IT SUSPICIOUS THAT ALCHEMAX HAS A NEW POWER SOURCE TO SHOW OFF...
...RIGHT AFTER THE CITY GAVE THEM THE CONTRACT TO DISPOSE OF THAT RARE EXPLOSIVE METAL?*
LIZ IS YOUR FRIEND, TOO, BETTY. YOU REALLY THINK SHE'D DO SOMETHING THAT UNETHICAL?
*SEE ASM ANNUAL #42 --LEGACY NUMBERED NIC
I THINK C.E.O.s DON'T ALWAYS KNOW ALL THE DIRT. AND I HAVE A FEELING ABOUT THIS. A REPORTER'S INSTINCT.
YOUR BETTY-SENSE IS TINGLING?
EXACTLY. AND THE BETTY-SENSE IS RARELY WRONG. BE READY FOR ANYTHING.

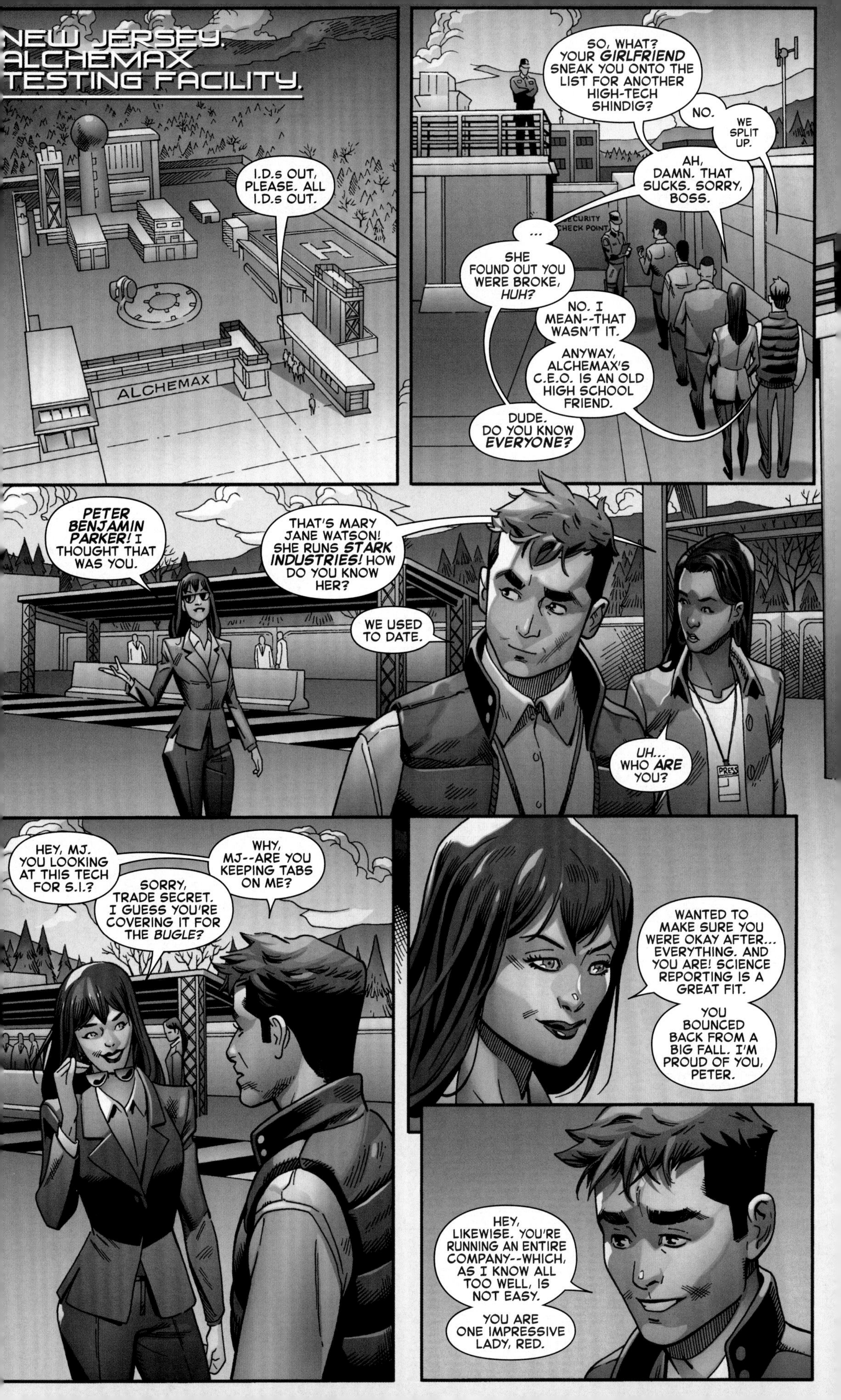
NEW JERSEY. ALCHEMAX TESTING FACILITY.
I.D.s OUT, PLEASE. ALL I.D.s OUT.
ALCHEMAX
SO, WHAT? YOUR GIRLFRIEND SNEAK YOU ONTO THE LIST FOR ANOTHER HIGH-TECH SHINDIG?
NO.
WE SPLIT UP.
AH, DAMN. THAT SUCKS. SORRY, BOSS.
SECURITY CHECK POINT
...
SHE FOUND OUT YOU WERE BROKE, HUH?
NO. I MEAN--THAT WASN'T IT.
ANYWAY, ALCHEMAX'S C.E.O. IS AN OLD HIGH SCHOOL FRIEND.
DUDE. DO YOU KNOW EVERYONE?
PETER BENJAMIN PARKER! I THOUGHT THAT WAS YOU.
THAT'S MARY JANE WATSON! SHE RUNS STARK INDUSTRIES! HOW DO YOU KNOW HER?
WE USED TO DATE.
UH... WHO ARE YOU?
PRESS
HEY, MJ. YOU LOOKING AT THIS TECH FOR S.I.?
SORRY, TRADE SECRET. I GUESS YOU'RE COVERING IT FOR THE BUGLE?
WHY, MJ--ARE YOU KEEPING TABS ON ME?
WANTED TO MAKE SURE YOU WERE OKAY AFTER... EVERYTHING. AND YOU ARE! SCIENCE REPORTING IS A GREAT FIT.
YOU BOUNCED BACK FROM A BIG FALL. I'M PROUD OF YOU, PETER.
HEY, LIKEWISE. YOU'RE RUNNING AN ENTIRE COMPANY--WHICH, AS I KNOW ALL TOO WELL, IS NOT EASY.
YOU ARE ONE IMPRESSIVE LADY, RED.

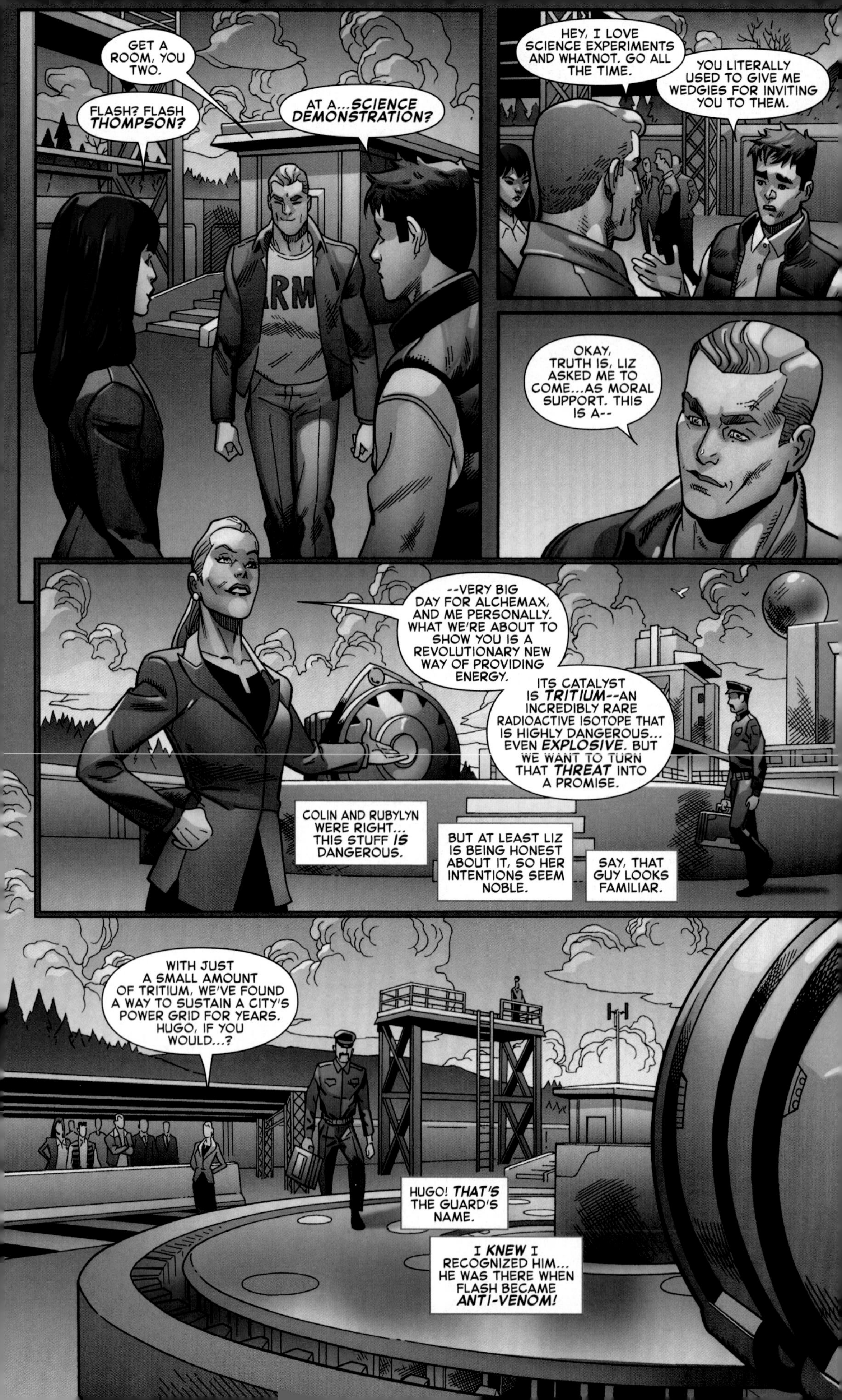
GET A ROOM, YOU TWO.
FLASH? FLASH THOMPSON?
AT A...SCIENCE DEMONSTRATION?
HEY, I LOVE SCIENCE EXPERIMENTS AND WHATNOT. GO ALL THE TIME.
YOU LITERALLY USED TO GIVE ME WEDGIES FOR INVITING YOU TO THEM.
OKAY, TRUTH IS, LIZ ASKED ME TO COME...AS MORAL SUPPORT. THIS IS A--
--VERY BIG DAY FOR ALCHEMAX, AND ME PERSONALLY. WHAT WE'RE ABOUT TO SHOW YOU IS A REVOLUTIONARY NEW WAY OF PROVIDING ENERGY.
ITS CATALYST IS TRITIUM--AN INCREDIBLY RARE RADIOACTIVE ISOTOPE THAT IS HIGHLY DANGEROUS... EVEN EXPLOSIVE. BUT WE WANT TO TURN THAT THREAT INTO A PROMISE.
COLIN AND RUBYLYN WERE RIGHT... THIS STUFF IS DANGEROUS.
BUT AT LEAST LIZ IS BEING HONEST ABOUT IT, SO HER INTENTIONS SEEM NOBLE.
SAY, THAT GUY LOOKS FAMILIAR.
WITH JUST A SMALL AMOUNT OF TRITIUM, WE'VE FOUND A WAY TO SUSTAIN A CITY'S POWER GRID FOR YEARS. HUGO, IF YOU WOULD...?
HUGO! THAT'S THE GUARD'S NAME.
I KNEW I RECOGNIZED HIM... HE WAS THERE WHEN FLASH BECAME ANTI-VENOM!

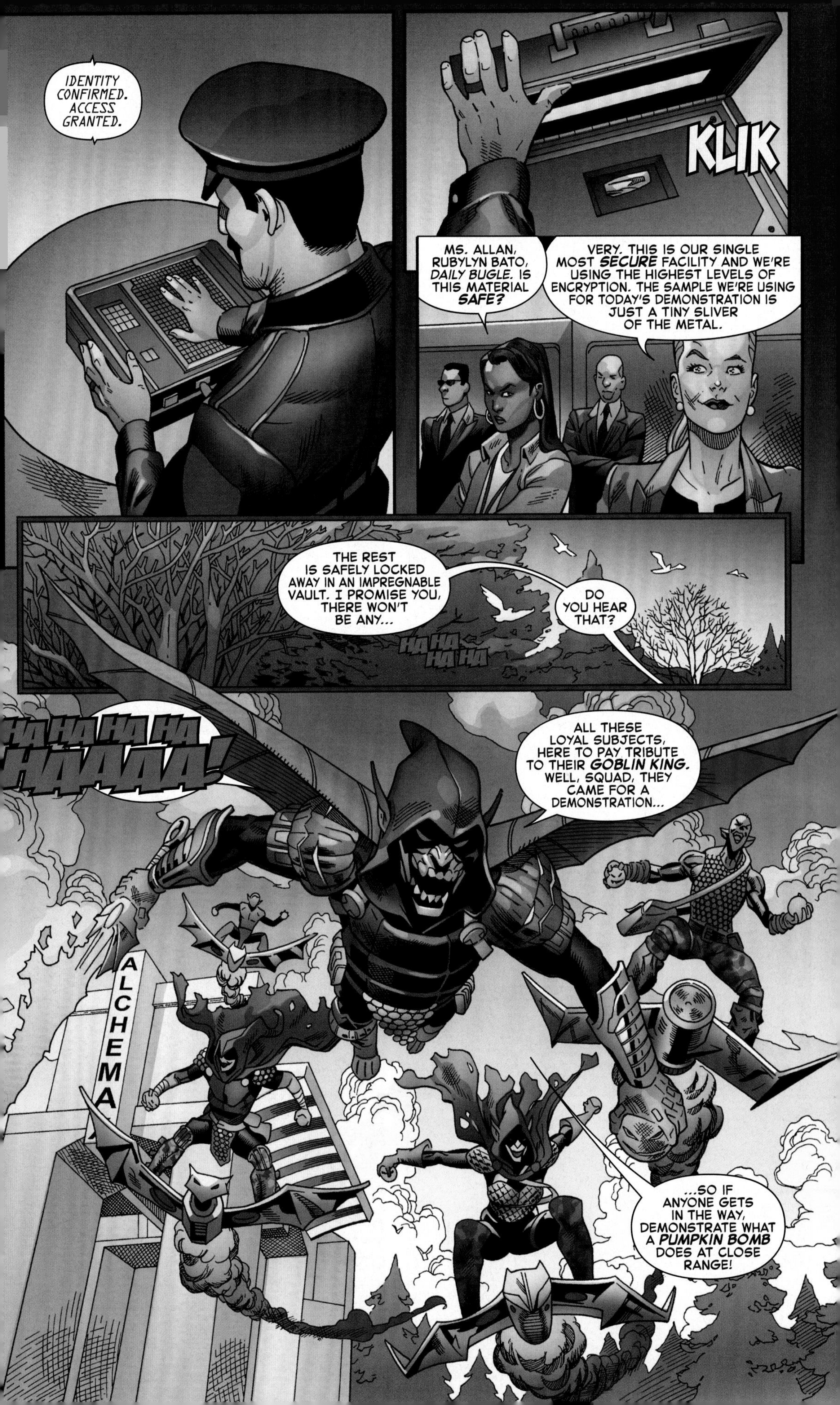

IDENTITY CONFIRMED. ACCESS GRANTED.
KLIK
MS. ALLAN, RUBYLYN BATO, DAILY BUGLE. IS THIS MATERIAL SAFE?
VERY. THIS IS OUR SINGLE MOST SECURE FACILITY AND WE'RE USING THE HIGHEST LEVELS OF ENCRYPTION. THE SAMPLE WE'RE USING FOR TODAY'S DEMONSTRATION IS JUST A TINY SLIVER OF THE METAL.
THE REST IS SAFELY LOCKED AWAY IN AN IMPREGNABLE VAULT. I PROMISE YOU, THERE WON'T BE ANY...
DO YOU HEAR THAT?
HA HA HA HA
HA HA HA HA HAAAAA!
ALL THESE LOYAL SUBJECTS, HERE TO PAY TRIBUTE TO THEIR GOBLIN KING. WELL, SQUAD, THEY CAME FOR A DEMONSTRATION...
ALCHEMA
...SO IF ANYONE GETS IN THE WAY, DEMONSTRATE WHAT A PUMPKIN BOMB DOES AT CLOSE RANGE!

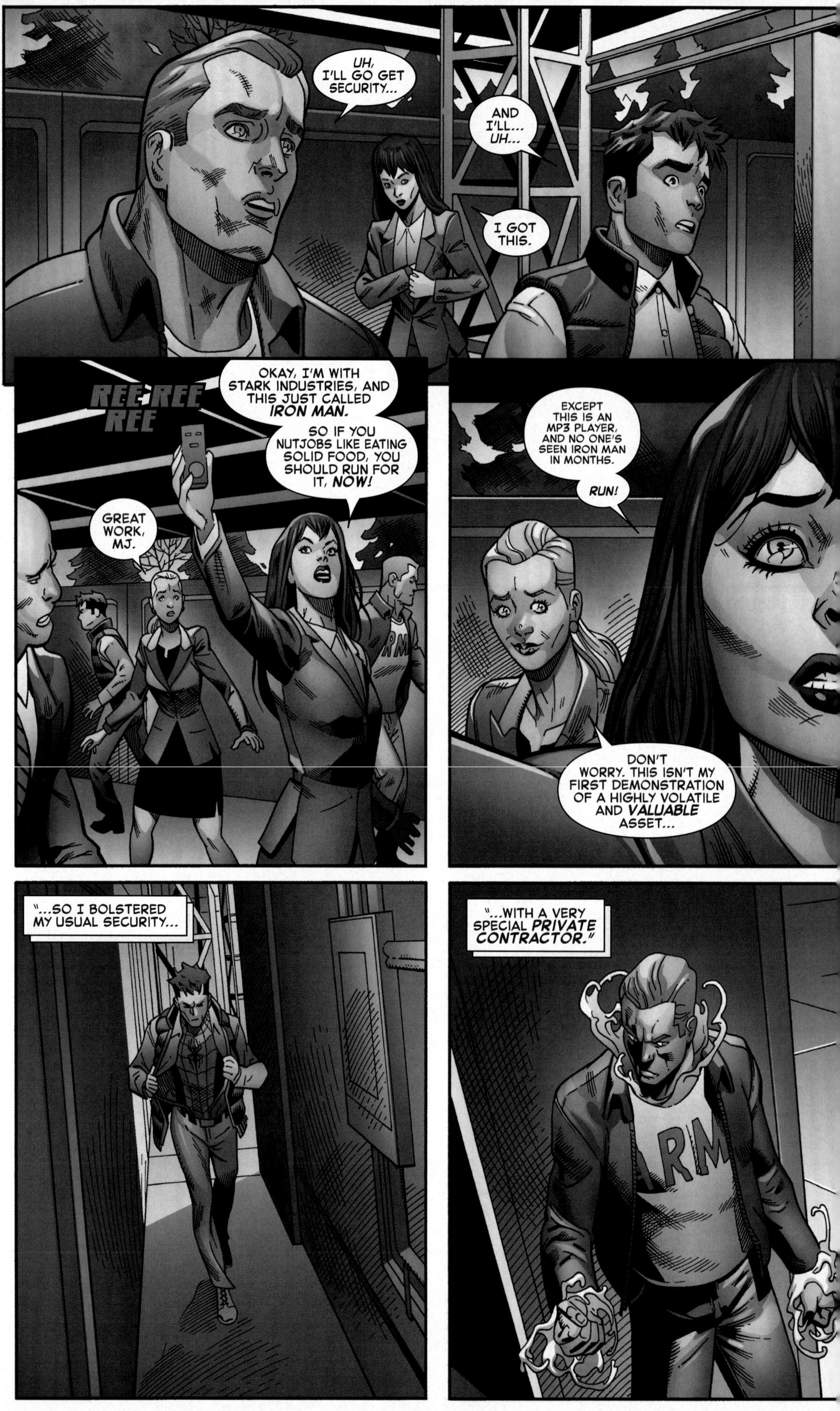
UH, I'LL GO GET SECURITY...
AND I'LL... UH...
I GOT THIS.
REE REE REE
OKAY, I'M WITH STARK INDUSTRIES, AND THIS JUST CALLED IRON MAN.
SO IF YOU NUTJOBS LIKE EATING SOLID FOOD, YOU SHOULD RUN FOR IT, NOW!
GREAT WORK, MJ.
EXCEPT THIS IS AN MP3 PLAYER, AND NO ONE'S SEEN IRON MAN IN MONTHS.
RUN!
DON'T WORRY. THIS ISN'T MY FIRST DEMONSTRATION OF A HIGHLY VOLATILE AND VALUABLE ASSET...
"...SO I BOLSTERED MY USUAL SECURITY...
"...WITH A VERY SPECIAL PRIVATE CONTRACTOR."

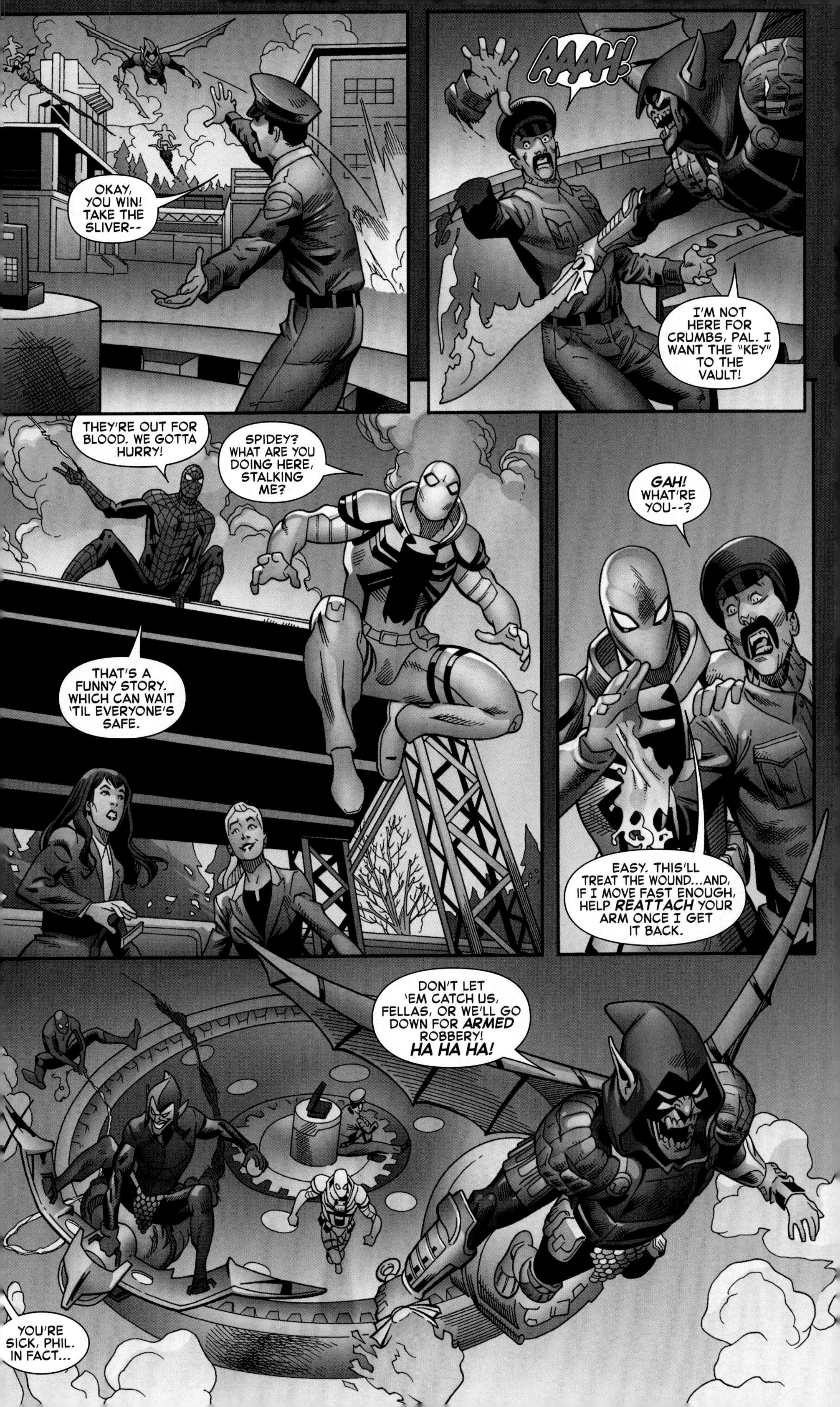

OKAY, YOU WIN! TAKE THE SLIVER--
AAAH!
I'M NOT HERE FOR CRUMBS, PAL. I WANT THE "KEY" TO THE VAULT!
THEY'RE OUT FOR BLOOD. WE GOTTA HURRY!
SPIDEY? WHAT ARE YOU DOING HERE, STALKING ME?
THAT'S A FUNNY STORY. WHICH CAN WAIT 'TIL EVERYONE'S SAFE.
GAH! WHAT'RE YOU--?
EASY. THIS'LL TREAT THE WOUND...AND, IF I MOVE FAST ENOUGH, HELP REATTACH YOUR ARM ONCE I GET IT BACK.
DON'T LET 'EM CATCH US, FELLAS, OR WE'LL GO DOWN FOR ARMED ROBBERY! HA HA HA!
YOU'RE SICK, PHIL. IN FACT...

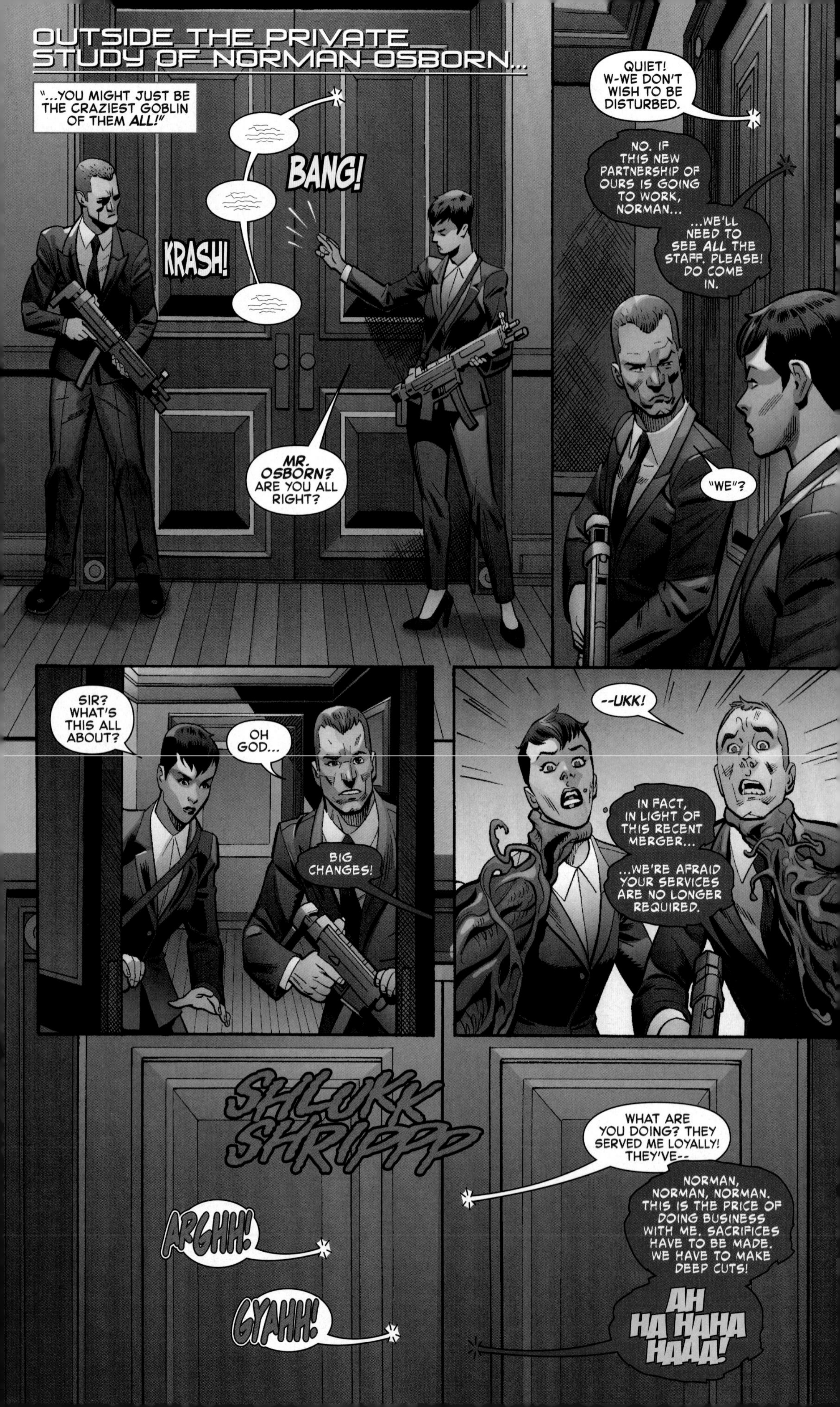
OUTSIDE THE PRIVATE STUDY OF NORMAN OSBORN...
"...YOU MIGHT JUST BE THE CRAZIEST GOBLIN OF THEM ALL!"
BANG!
KRASH!
MR. OSBORN? ARE YOU ALL RIGHT?
QUIET! W-WE DON'T WISH TO BE DISTURBED.
NO. IF THIS NEW PARTNERSHIP OF OURS IS GOING TO WORK, NORMAN...
...WE'LL NEED TO SEE ALL THE STAFF. PLEASE! DO COME IN.
"WE"?
SIR? WHAT'S THIS ALL ABOUT?
OH GOD...
BIG CHANGES!
--UKK!
IN FACT, IN LIGHT OF THIS RECENT MERGER...
...WE'RE AFRAID YOUR SERVICES ARE NO LONGER REQUIRED.
SHLUKK SHRIPPP
ARGHH!
GYAHH!
WHAT ARE YOU DOING? THEY SERVED ME LOYALLY! THEY'VE--
NORMAN, NORMAN, NORMAN. THIS IS THE PRICE OF DOING BUSINESS WITH ME. SACRIFICES HAVE TO BE MADE. WE HAVE TO MAKE DEEP CUTS!
AH HA HAHA HAAA!

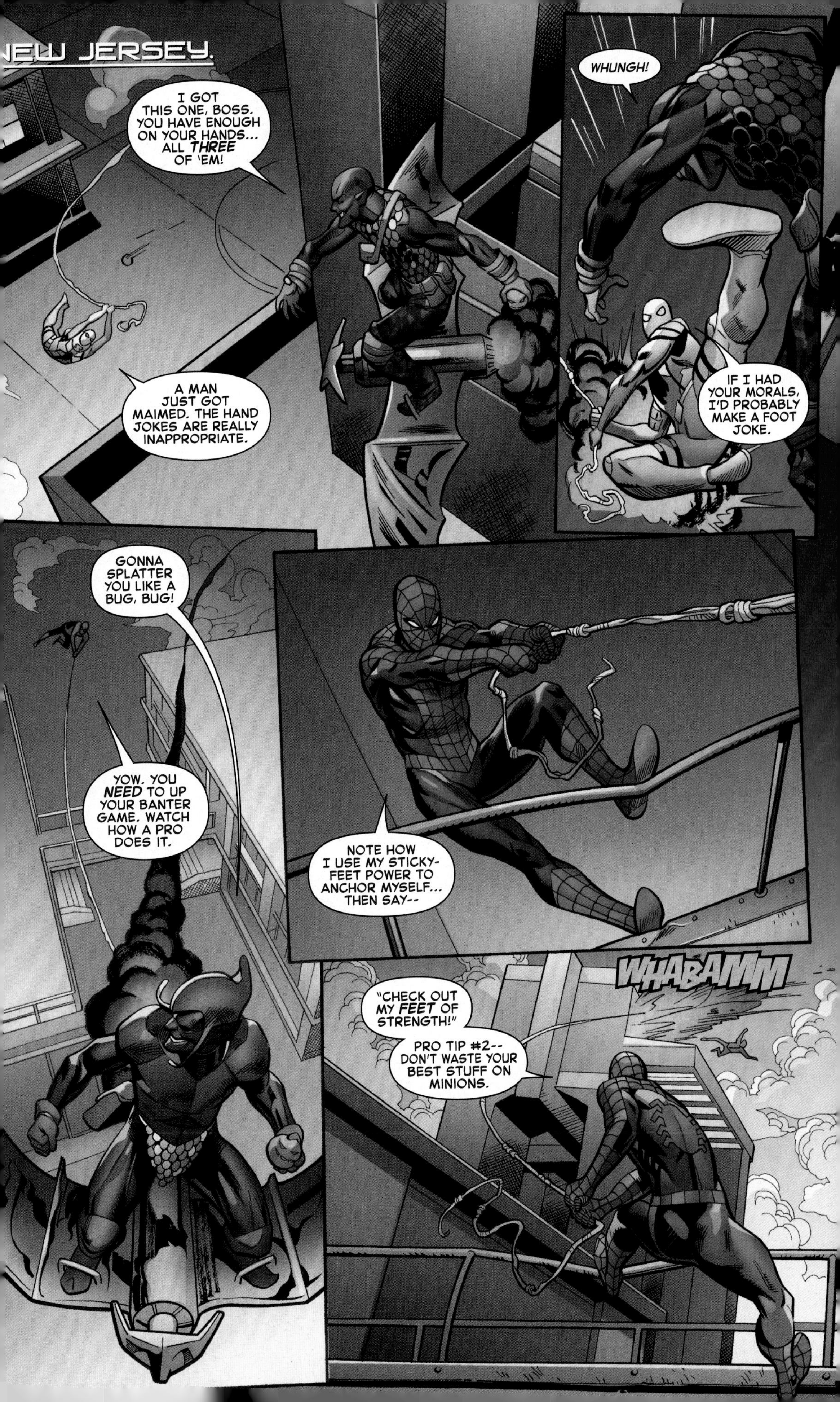
NEW JERSEY.
I GOT THIS ONE, BOSS. YOU HAVE ENOUGH ON YOUR HANDS... ALL THREE OF 'EM!
A MAN JUST GOT MAIMED. THE HAND JOKES ARE REALLY INAPPROPRIATE.
WHUNGH!
IF I HAD YOUR MORALS, I'D PROBABLY MAKE A FOOT JOKE.
GONNA SPLATTER YOU LIKE A BUG, BUG!
YOW. YOU NEED TO UP YOUR BANTER GAME. WATCH HOW A PRO DOES IT.
NOTE HOW I USE MY STICKY-FEET POWER TO ANCHOR MYSELF... THEN SAY--
WHABAMM
"CHECK OUT MY FEET OF STRENGTH!"
PRO TIP #2-- DON'T WASTE YOUR BEST STUFF ON MINIONS.

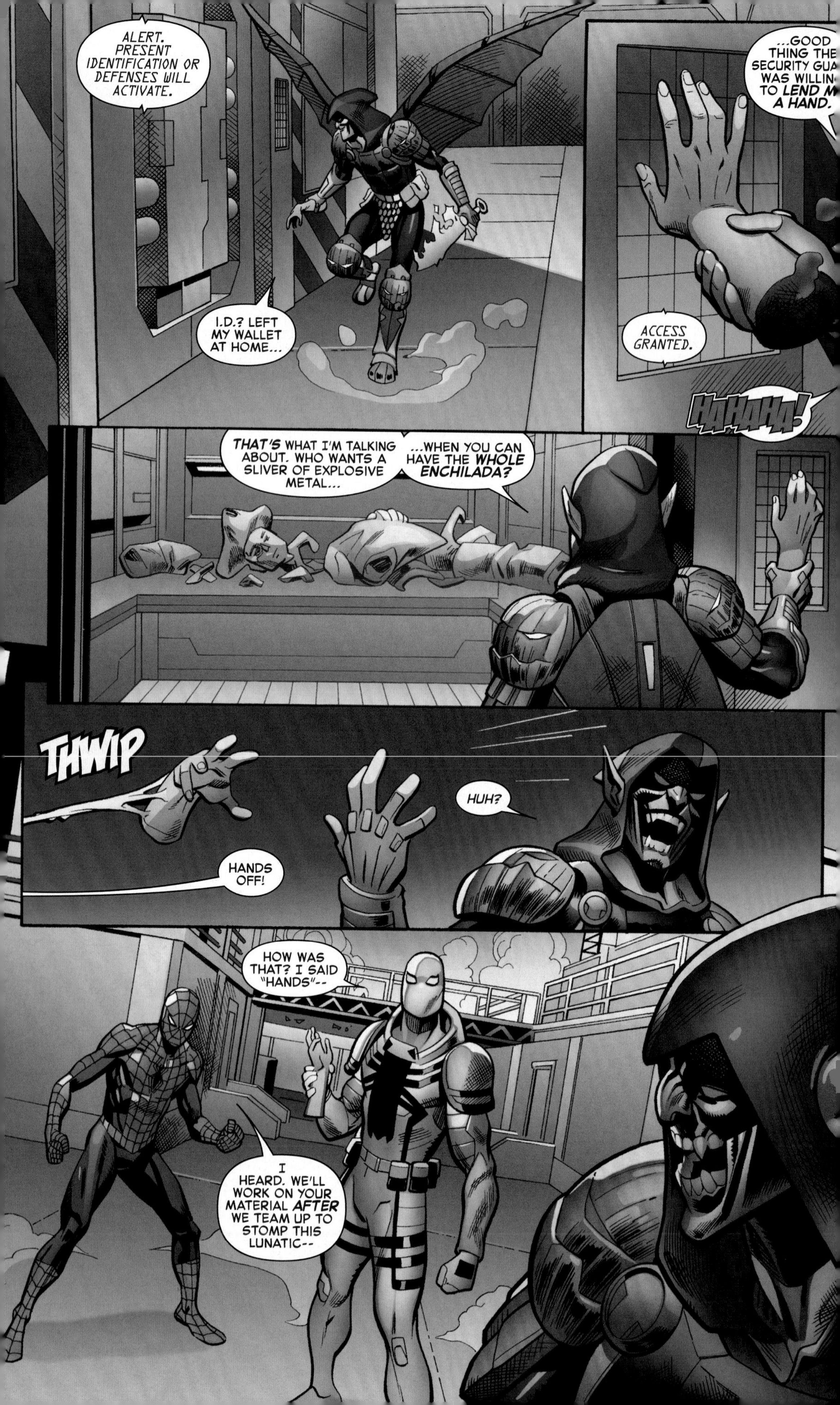

ALERT. PRESENT IDENTIFICATION OR DEFENSES WILL ACTIVATE.
I.D.? LEFT MY WALLET AT HOME...
...GOOD THING THE SECURITY GUA WAS WILLIN TO LEND M A HAND.
ACCESS GRANTED.
HAHAHA!
THAT'S WHAT I'M TALKING ABOUT. WHO WANTS A SLIVER OF EXPLOSIVE METAL...
...WHEN YOU CAN HAVE THE WHOLE ENCHILADA?
THWIP
HUH?
HANDS OFF!
HOW WAS THAT? I SAID "HANDS"--
I HEARD. WE'LL WORK ON YOUR MATERIAL AFTER WE TEAM UP TO STOMP THIS LUNATIC--

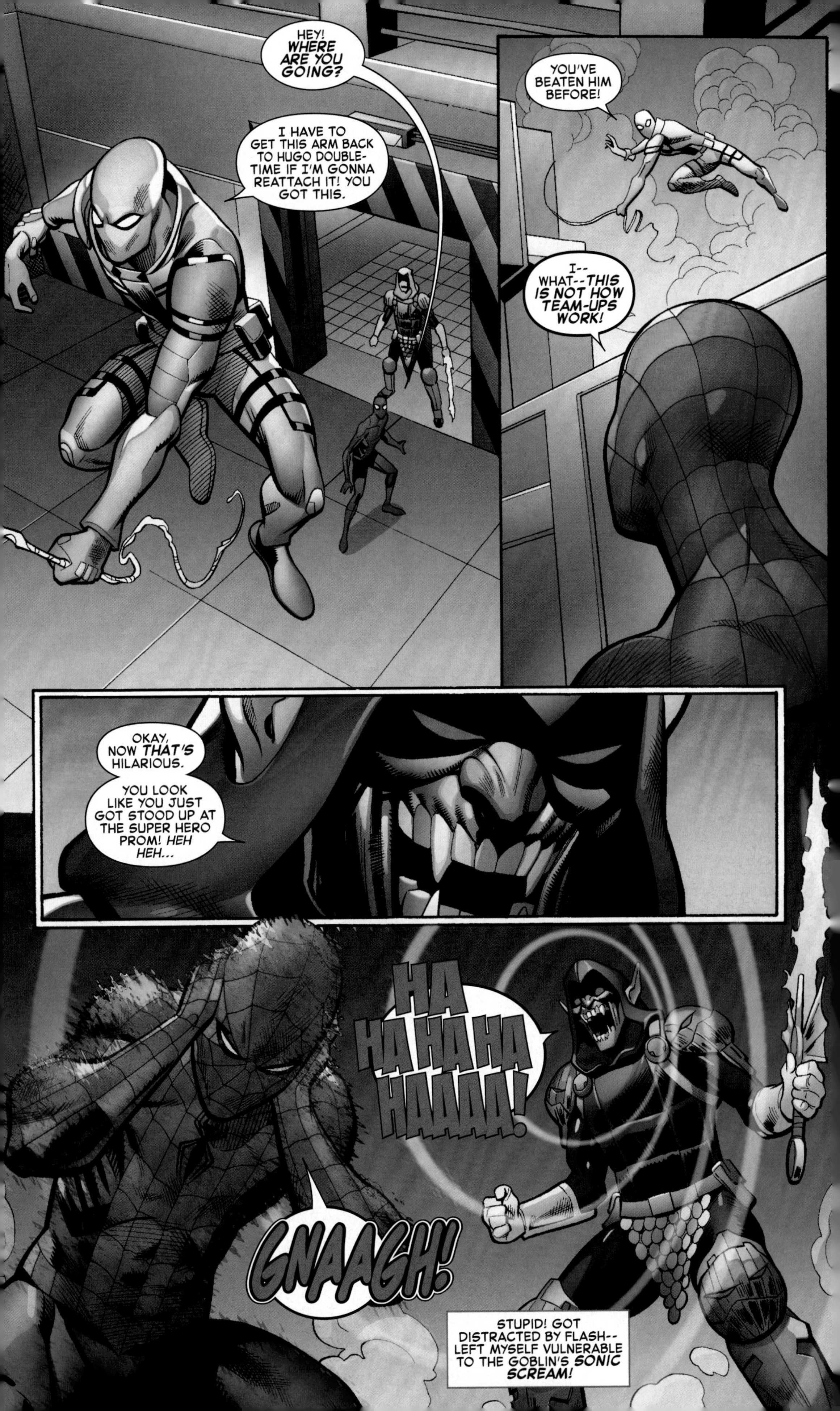
HEY! WHERE ARE YOU GOING?
I HAVE TO GET THIS ARM BACK TO HUGO DOUBLE-TIME IF I'M GONNA REATTACH IT! YOU GOT THIS.
YOU'VE BEATEN HIM BEFORE!
I-- WHAT--THIS IS NOT HOW TEAM-UPS WORK!
OKAY, NOW THAT'S HILARIOUS.
YOU LOOK LIKE YOU JUST GOT STOOD UP AT THE SUPER HERO PROM! HEH HEH...
HA HA HA HA HAAAA!
GNAAGH!
STUPID! GOT DISTRACTED BY FLASH--LEFT MYSELF VULNERABLE TO THE GOBLIN'S SONIC SCREAM!

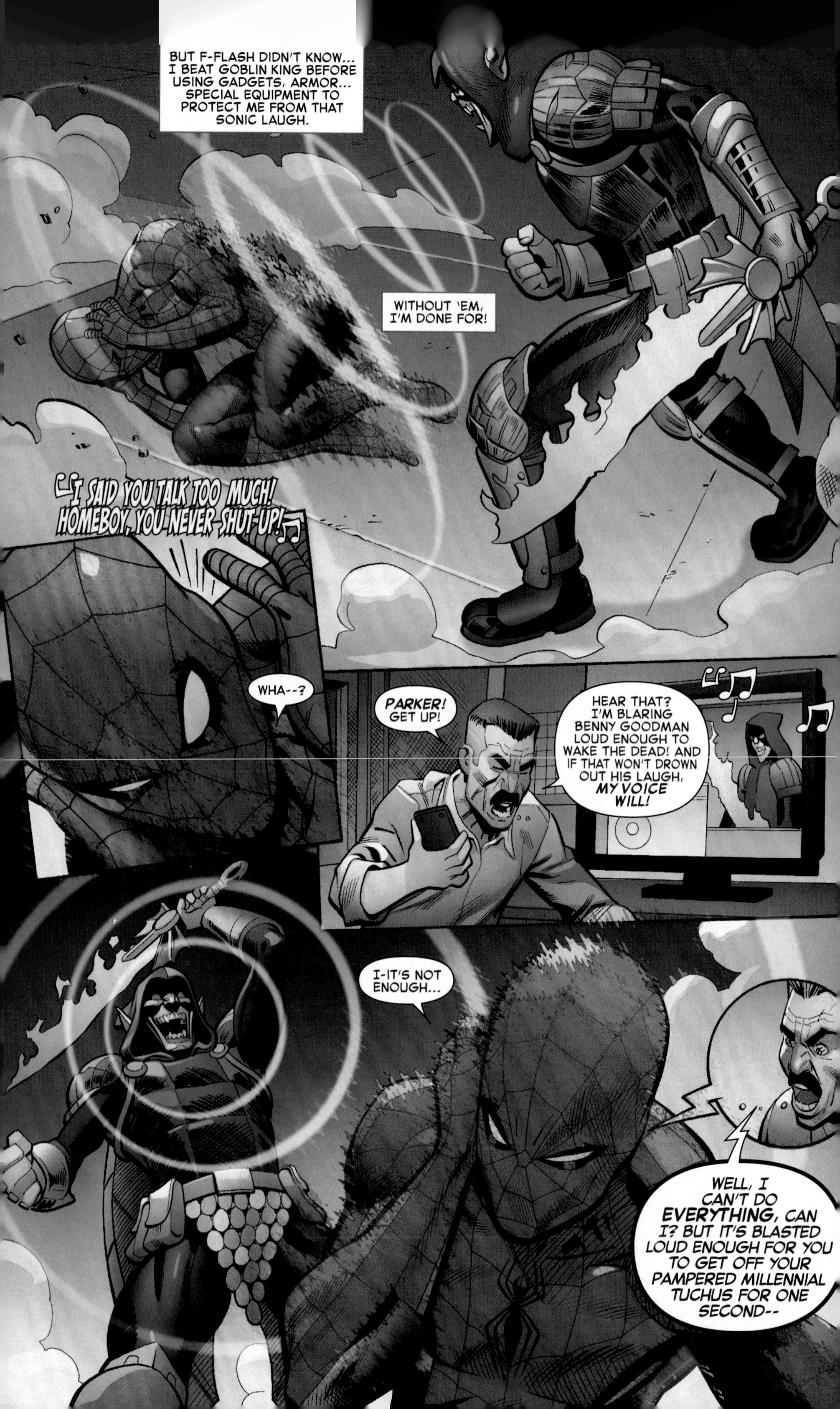

BUT F-FLASH DIDN'T KNOW... I BEAT GOBLIN KING BEFORE USING GADGETS, ARMOR... SPECIAL EQUIPMENT TO PROTECT ME FROM THAT SONIC LAUGH.
WITHOUT 'EM, I'M DONE FOR!
I SAID YOU TALK TOO MUCH! HOMEBOY, YOU NEVER SHUT-UP!
WHA--?
PARKER! GET UP!
HEAR THAT? I'M BLARING BENNY GOODMAN LOUD ENOUGH TO WAKE THE DEAD! AND IF THAT WON'T DROWN OUT HIS LAUGH, MY VOICE WILL!
I-IT'S NOT ENOUGH...
WELL, I CAN'T DO EVERYTHING, CAN I? BUT IT'S BLASTED LOUD ENOUGH FOR YOU TO GET OFF YOUR PAMPERED MILLENNIAL TUCHUS FOR ONE SECOND--

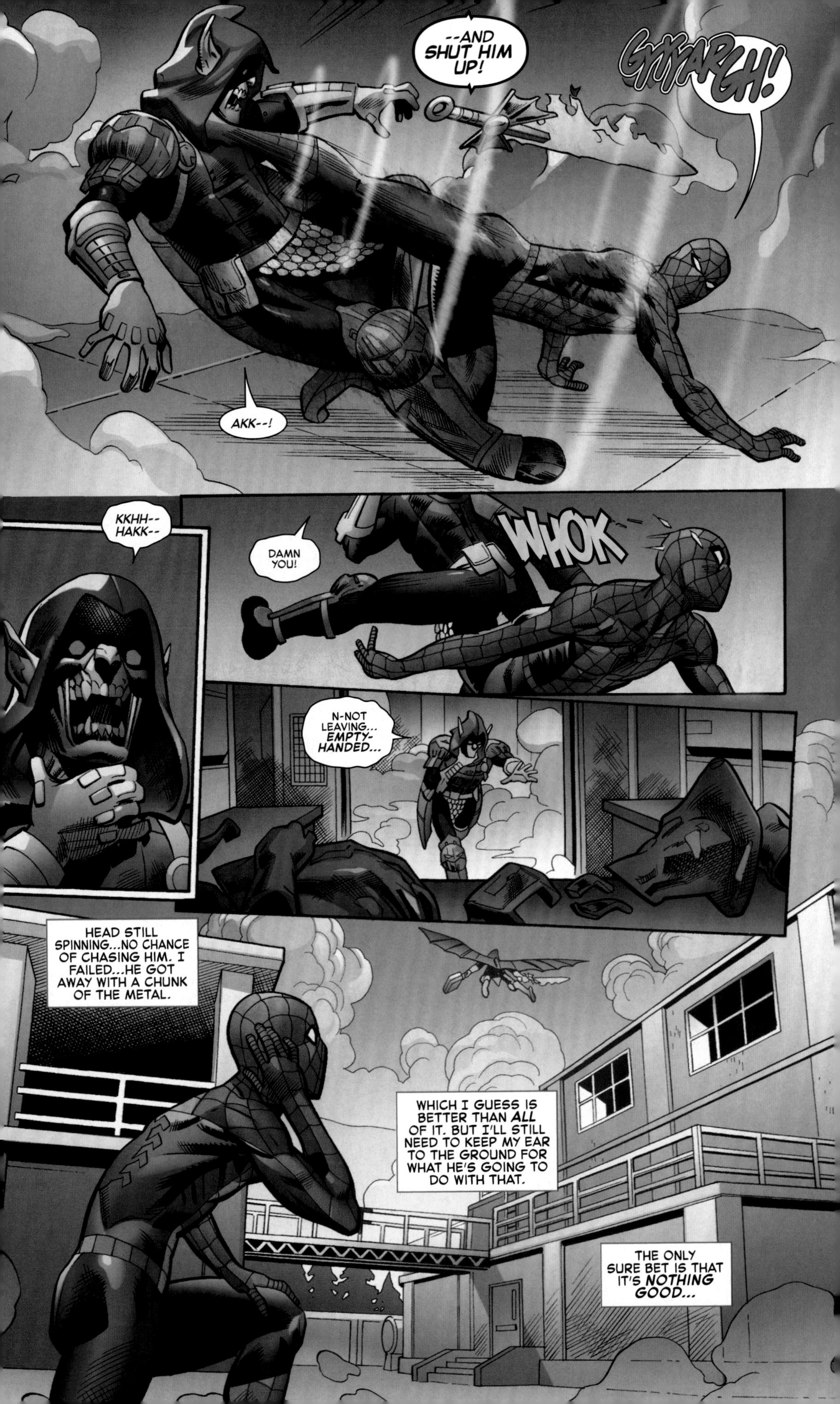
--AND SHUT HIM UP!
GYYYARGH!
AKK--!
KKHH--HAKK--
DAMN YOU!
WHOK
N-NOT LEAVING... EMPTY-HANDED...
HEAD STILL SPINNING...NO CHANCE OF CHASING HIM. I FAILED...HE GOT AWAY WITH A CHUNK OF THE METAL.
WHICH I GUESS IS BETTER THAN ALL OF IT. BUT I'LL STILL NEED TO KEEP MY EAR TO THE GROUND FOR WHAT HE'S GOING TO DO WITH THAT.
THE ONLY SURE BET IS THAT IT'S NOTHING GOOD...

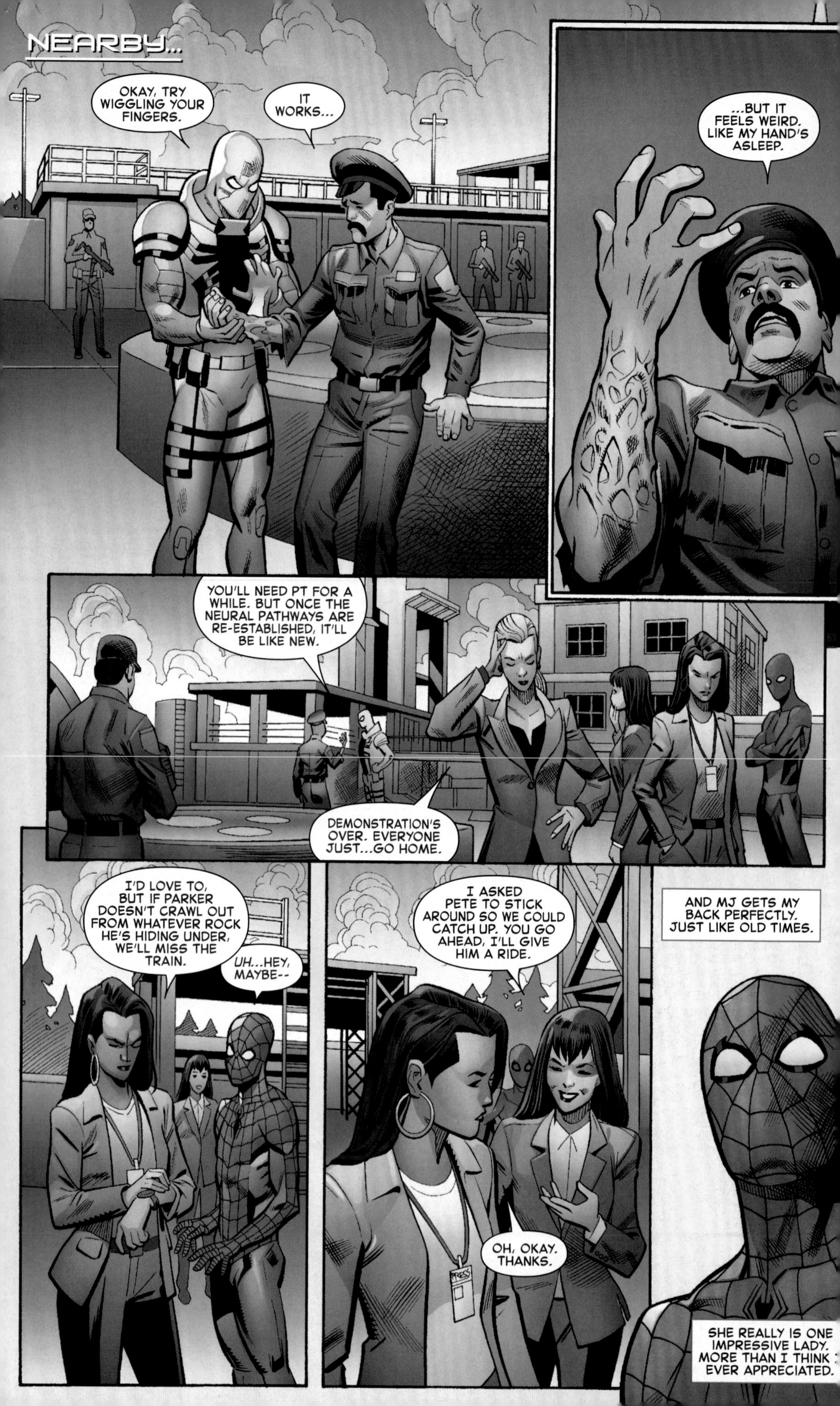
NEARBY...
OKAY, TRY WIGGLING YOUR FINGERS.
IT WORKS...
...BUT IT FEELS WEIRD. LIKE MY HAND'S ASLEEP.
YOU'LL NEED PT FOR A WHILE. BUT ONCE THE NEURAL PATHWAYS ARE RE-ESTABLISHED, IT'LL BE LIKE NEW.
DEMONSTRATION'S OVER. EVERYONE JUST...GO HOME.
I'D LOVE TO, BUT IF PARKER DOESN'T CRAWL OUT FROM WHATEVER ROCK HE'S HIDING UNDER, WE'LL MISS THE TRAIN.
UH...HEY, MAYBE--
I ASKED PETE TO STICK AROUND SO WE COULD CATCH UP. YOU GO AHEAD, I'LL GIVE HIM A RIDE.
OH, OKAY. THANKS.
PRESS
AND MJ GETS MY BACK PERFECTLY. JUST LIKE OLD TIMES.
SHE REALLY IS ONE IMPRESSIVE LADY. MORE THAN I THINK I EVER APPRECIATED.

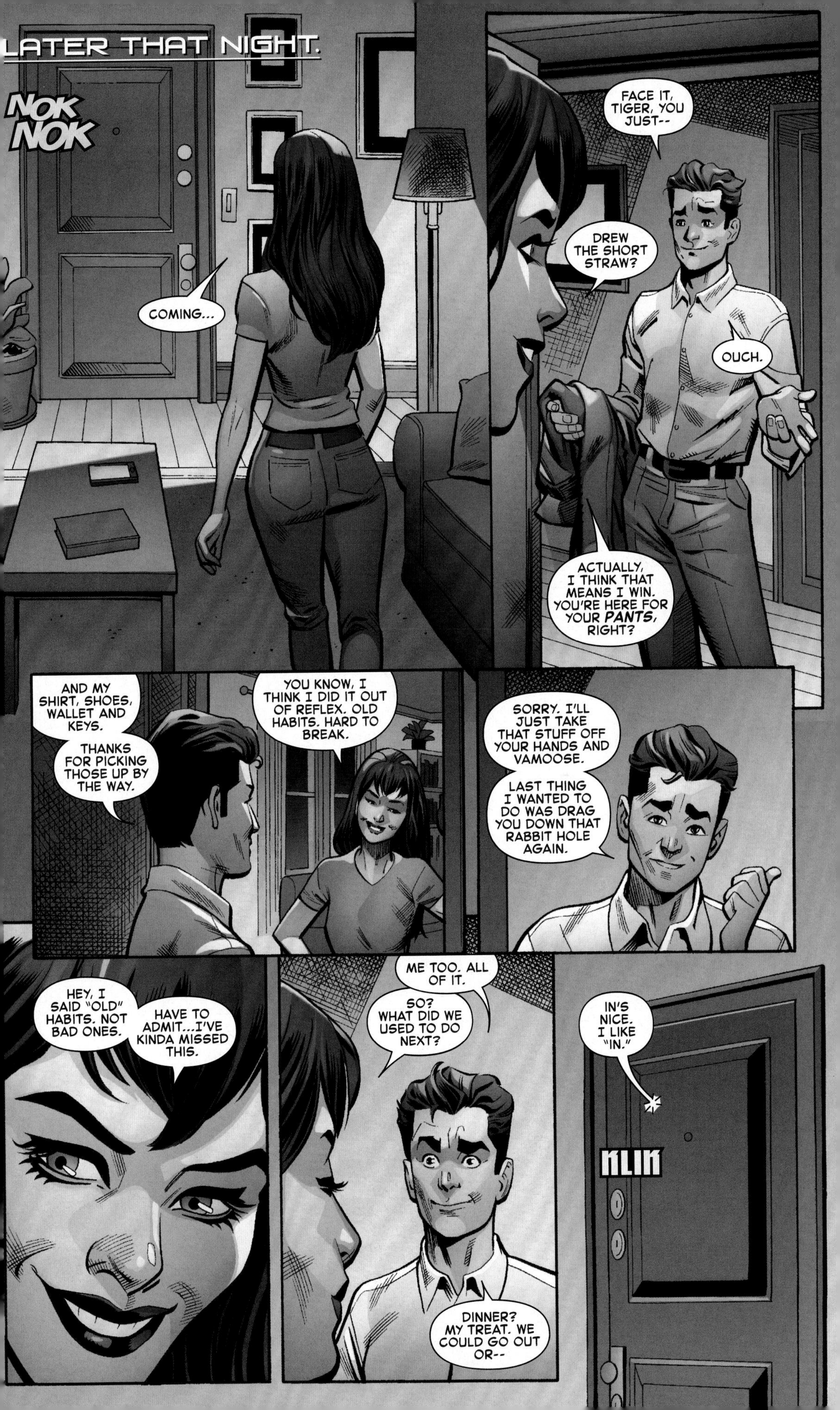
LATER THAT NIGHT.
NOK NOK
COMING...
FACE IT, TIGER, YOU JUST--
DREW THE SHORT STRAW?
OUCH.
ACTUALLY, I THINK THAT MEANS I WIN. YOU'RE HERE FOR YOUR PANTS, RIGHT?
AND MY SHIRT, SHOES, WALLET AND KEYS.
THANKS FOR PICKING THOSE UP BY THE WAY.
YOU KNOW, I THINK I DID IT OUT OF REFLEX. OLD HABITS. HARD TO BREAK.
SORRY. I'LL JUST TAKE THAT STUFF OFF YOUR HANDS AND VAMOOSE.
LAST THING I WANTED TO DO WAS DRAG YOU DOWN THAT RABBIT HOLE AGAIN.
HEY, I SAID "OLD" HABITS. NOT BAD ONES.
HAVE TO ADMIT...I'VE KINDA MISSED THIS.
ME TOO. ALL OF IT.
SO? WHAT DID WE USED TO DO NEXT?
DINNER? MY TREAT. WE COULD GO OUT OR--
IN'S NICE. I LIKE "IN."
KLIK

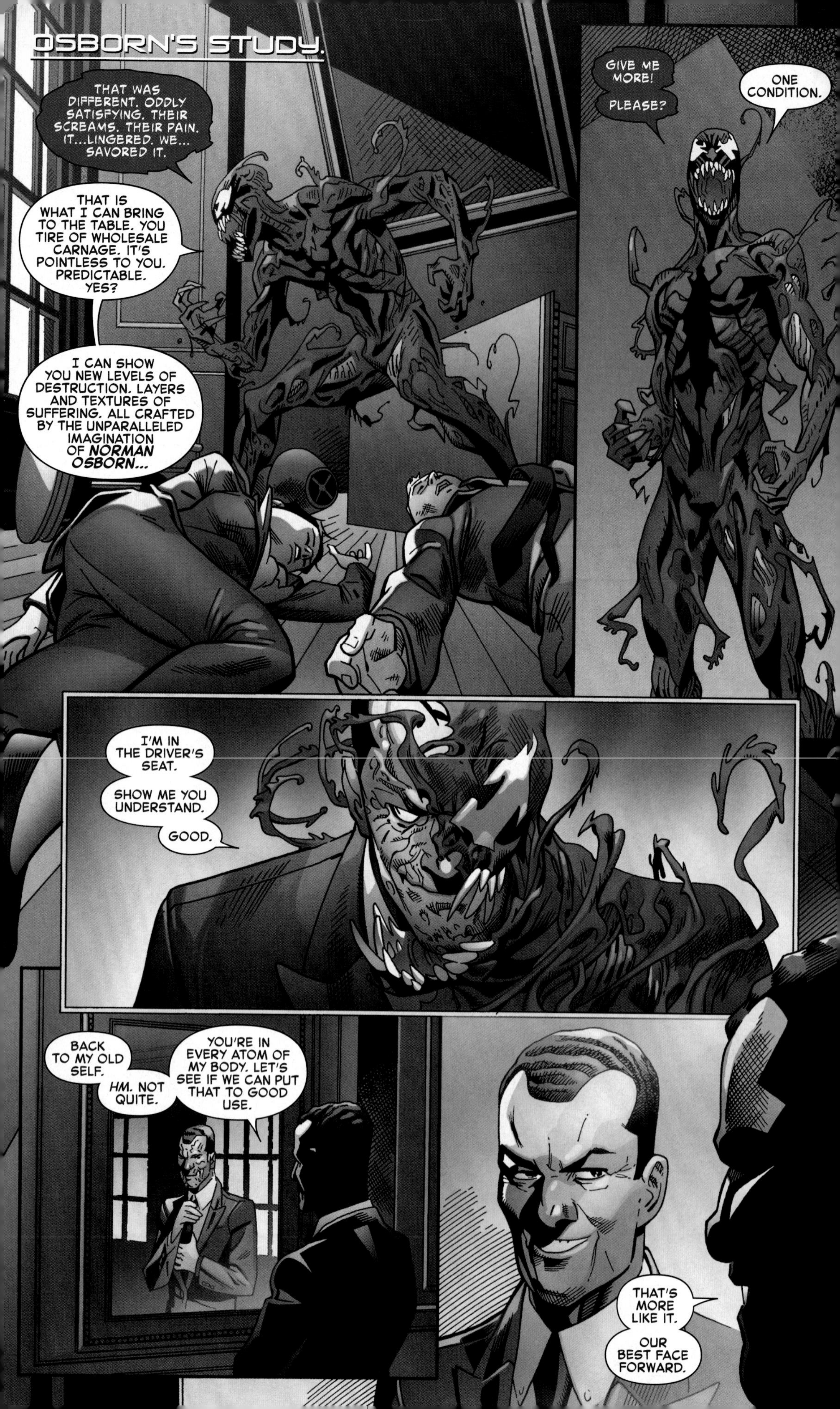

OSBORN'S STUDY.
THAT WAS DIFFERENT. ODDLY SATISFYING. THEIR SCREAMS. THEIR PAIN. IT...LINGERED. WE... SAVORED IT.
THAT IS WHAT I CAN BRING TO THE TABLE. YOU TIRE OF WHOLESALE CARNAGE. IT'S POINTLESS TO YOU. PREDICTABLE. YES?
I CAN SHOW YOU NEW LEVELS OF DESTRUCTION. LAYERS AND TEXTURES OF SUFFERING. ALL CRAFTED BY THE UNPARALLELED IMAGINATION OF NORMAN OSBORN...
GIVE ME MORE!
PLEASE?
ONE CONDITION.
I'M IN THE DRIVER'S SEAT.
SHOW ME YOU UNDERSTAND.
GOOD.
BACK TO MY OLD SELF.
HM. NOT QUITE.
YOU'RE IN EVERY ATOM OF MY BODY. LET'S SEE IF WE CAN PUT THAT TO GOOD USE.
THAT'S MORE LIKE IT.
OUR BEST FACE FORWARD.

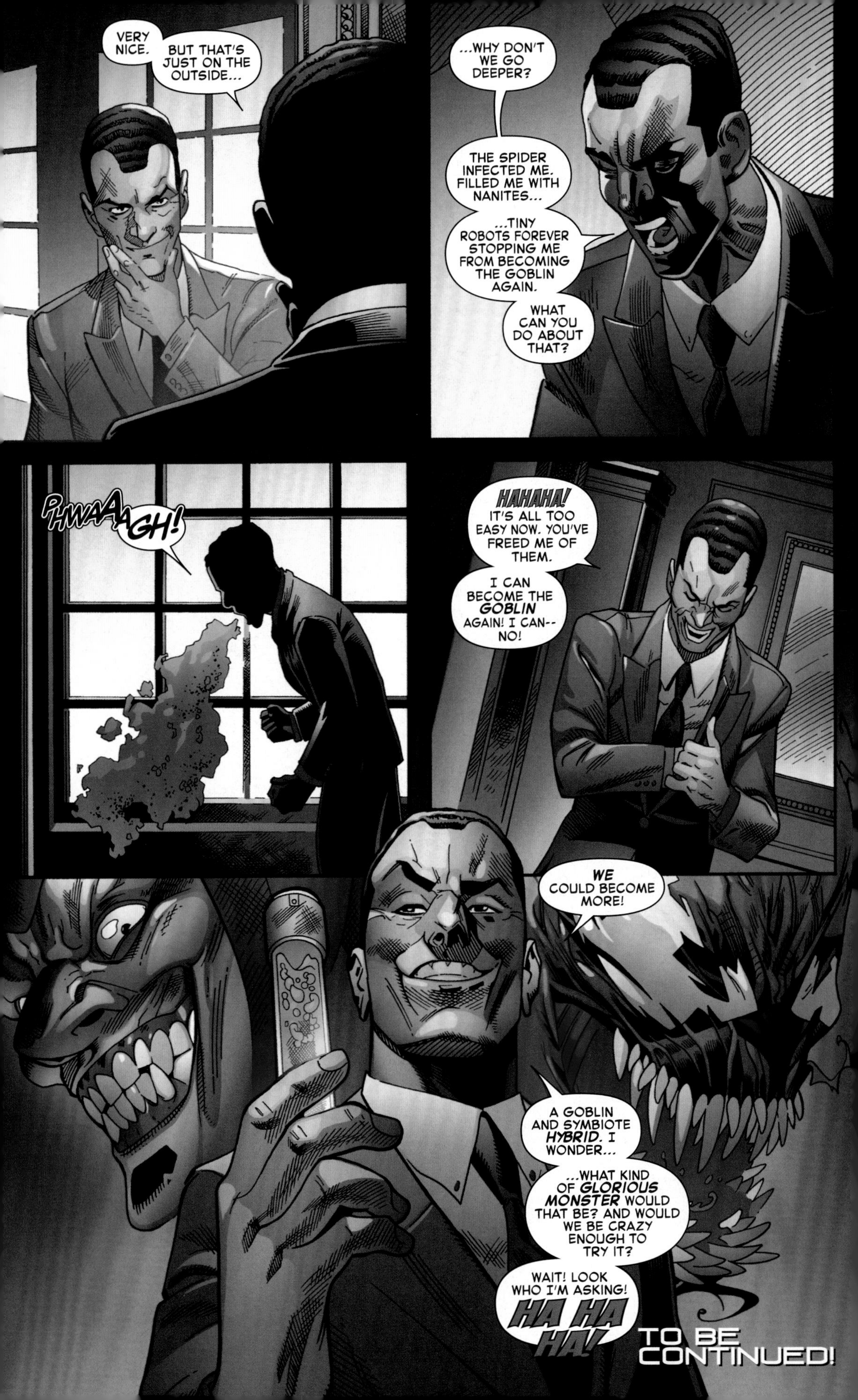
VERY NICE.
BUT THAT'S JUST ON THE OUTSIDE...
...WHY DON'T WE GO DEEPER?
THE SPIDER INFECTED ME. FILLED ME WITH NANITES...
...TINY ROBOTS FOREVER STOPPING ME FROM BECOMING THE GOBLIN AGAIN.
WHAT CAN YOU DO ABOUT THAT?
PHWAAAAGH!
HAHAHA! IT'S ALL TOO EASY NOW. YOU'VE FREED ME OF THEM.
I CAN BECOME THE GOBLIN AGAIN! I CAN-- NO!
WE COULD BECOME MORE!
A GOBLIN AND SYMBIOTE HYBRID. I WONDER...
...WHAT KIND OF GLORIOUS MONSTER WOULD THAT BE? AND WOULD WE BE CRAZY ENOUGH TO TRY IT?
WAIT! LOOK WHO I'M ASKING! HA HA HA!
TO BE CONTINUED!

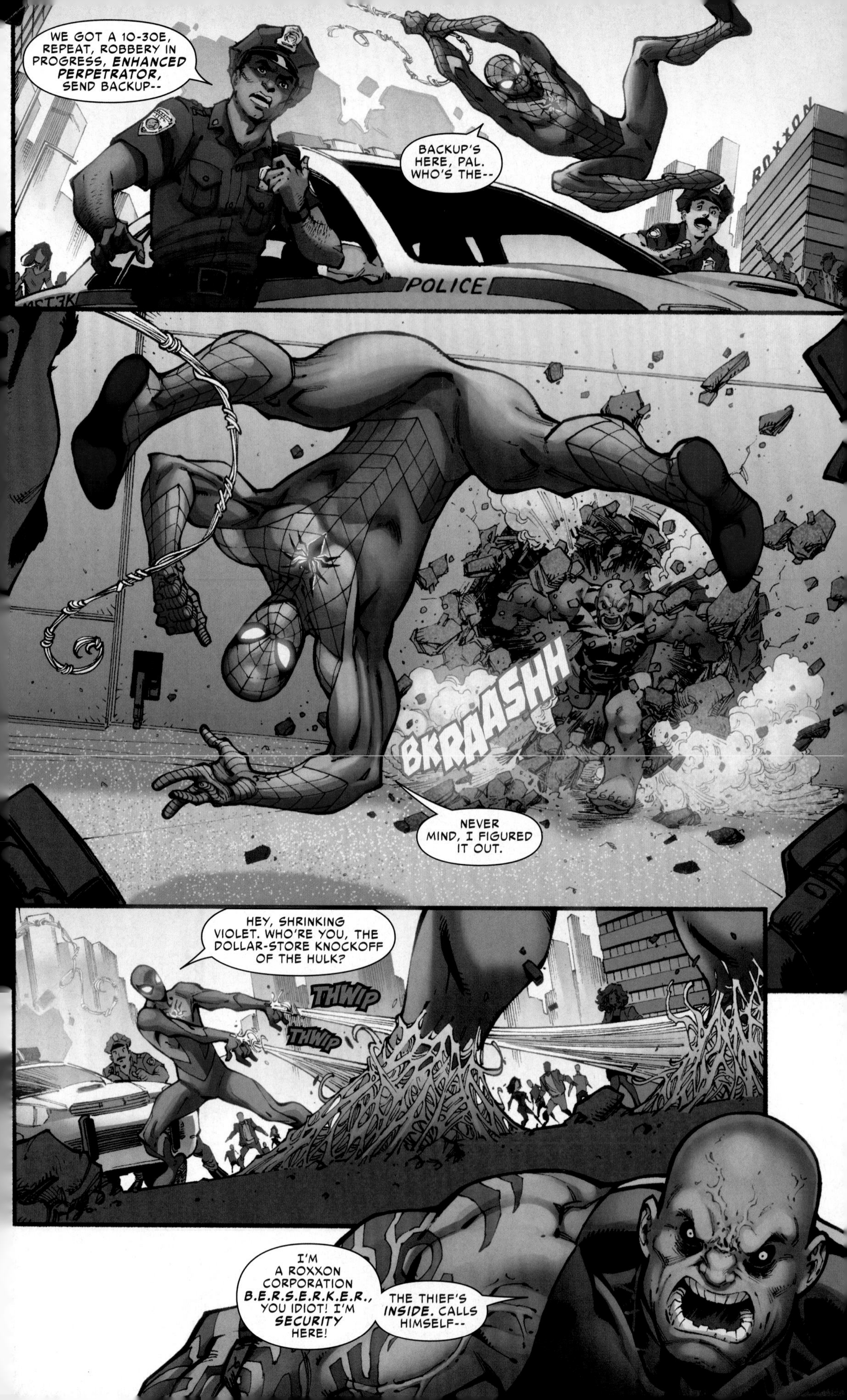

WE GOT A 10-30E, REPEAT, ROBBERY IN PROGRESS, ENHANCED PERPETRATOR, SEND BACKUP--
BACKUP'S HERE, PAL. WHO'S THE--
ROXXON
POLICE
BKRAASHH
NEVER MIND, I FIGURED IT OUT.
HEY, SHRINKING VIOLET. WHO'RE YOU, THE DOLLAR-STORE KNOCKOFF OF THE HULK?
THWIP
THWIP
I'M A ROXXON CORPORATION B.E.R.S.E.R.K.E.R., YOU IDIOT! I'M SECURITY HERE!
THE THIEF'S INSIDE. CALLS HIMSELF--

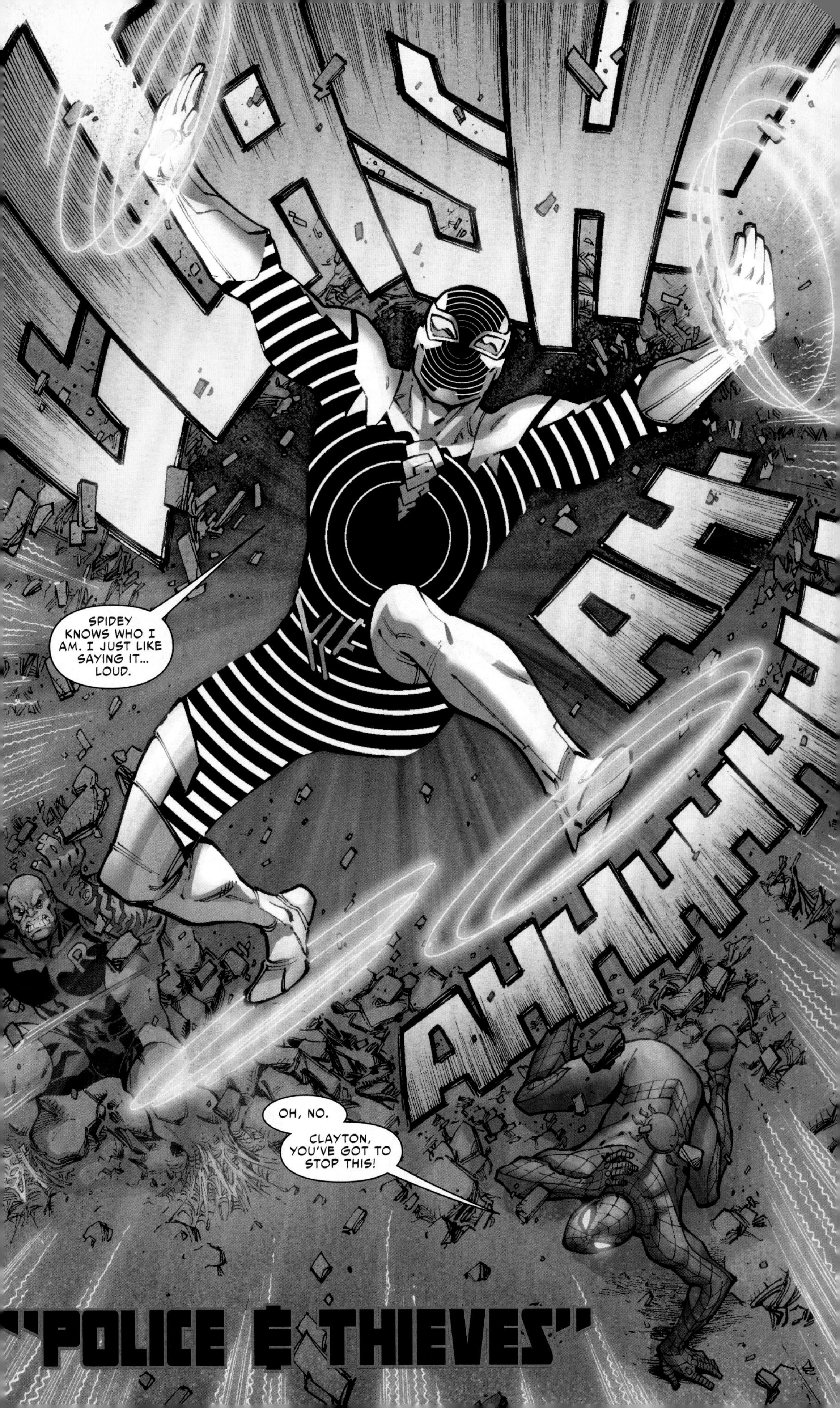

SPIDEY KNOWS WHO I AM. I JUST LIKE SAYING IT... LOUD.
OH, NO.
CLAYTON, YOU'VE GOT TO STOP THIS!
"POLICE & THIEVES"

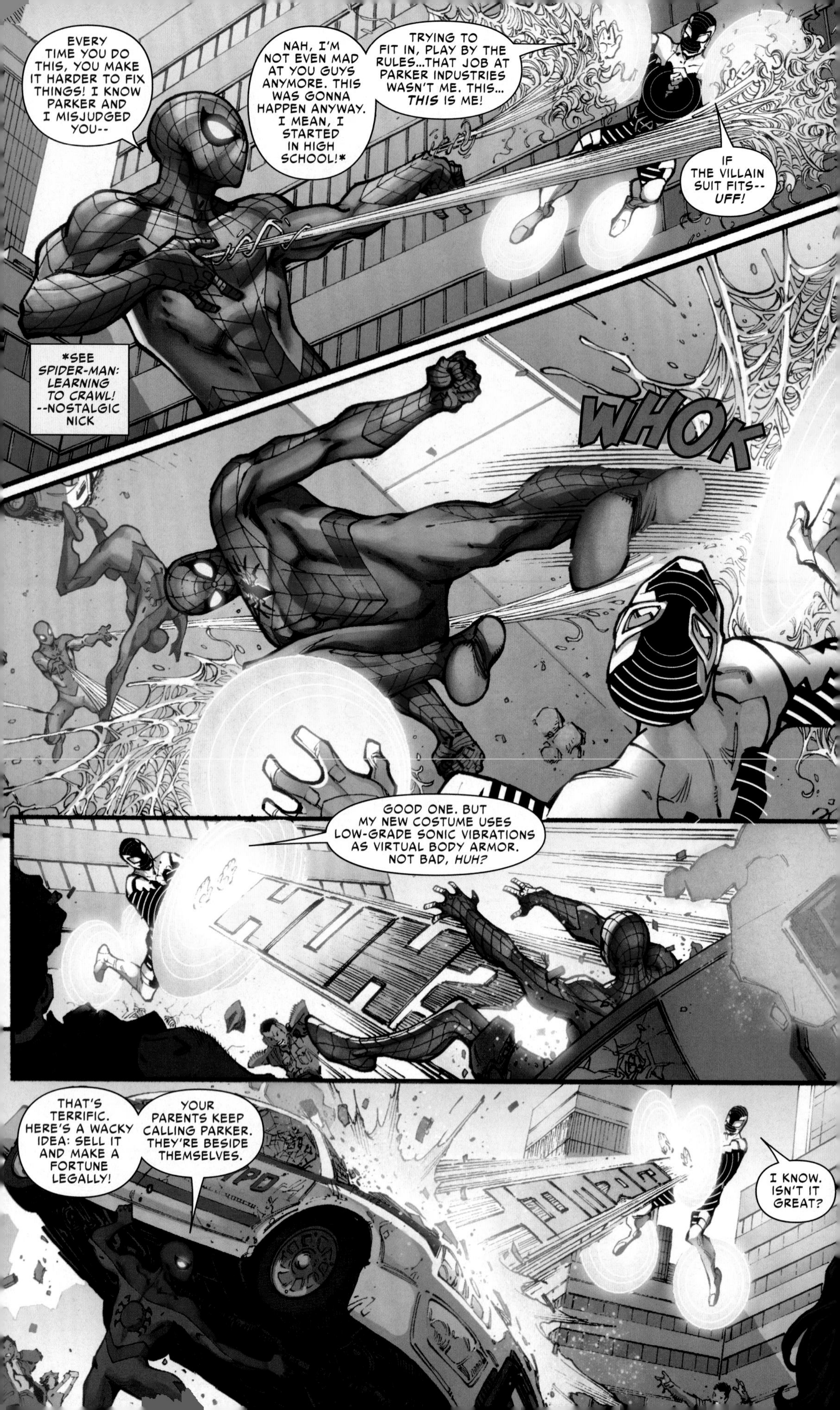
EVERY TIME YOU DO THIS, YOU MAKE IT HARDER TO FIX THINGS! I KNOW PARKER AND I MISJUDGED YOU--
NAH, I'M NOT EVEN MAD AT YOU GUYS ANYMORE. THIS WAS GONNA HAPPEN ANYWAY. I MEAN, I STARTED IN HIGH SCHOOL!*
TRYING TO FIT IN, PLAY BY THE RULES...THAT JOB AT PARKER INDUSTRIES WASN'T ME. THIS... THIS IS ME!
IF THE VILLAIN SUIT FITS-- UFF!
*SEE SPIDER-MAN: LEARNING TO CRAWL! --NOSTALGIC NICK
WHOK
GOOD ONE. BUT MY NEW COSTUME USES LOW-GRADE SONIC VIBRATIONS AS VIRTUAL BODY ARMOR. NOT BAD, HUH?
THAT'S TERRIFIC. HERE'S A WACKY IDEA: SELL IT AND MAKE A FORTUNE LEGALLY!
YOUR PARENTS KEEP CALLING PARKER. THEY'RE BESIDE THEMSELVES.
I KNOW. ISN'T IT GREAT?

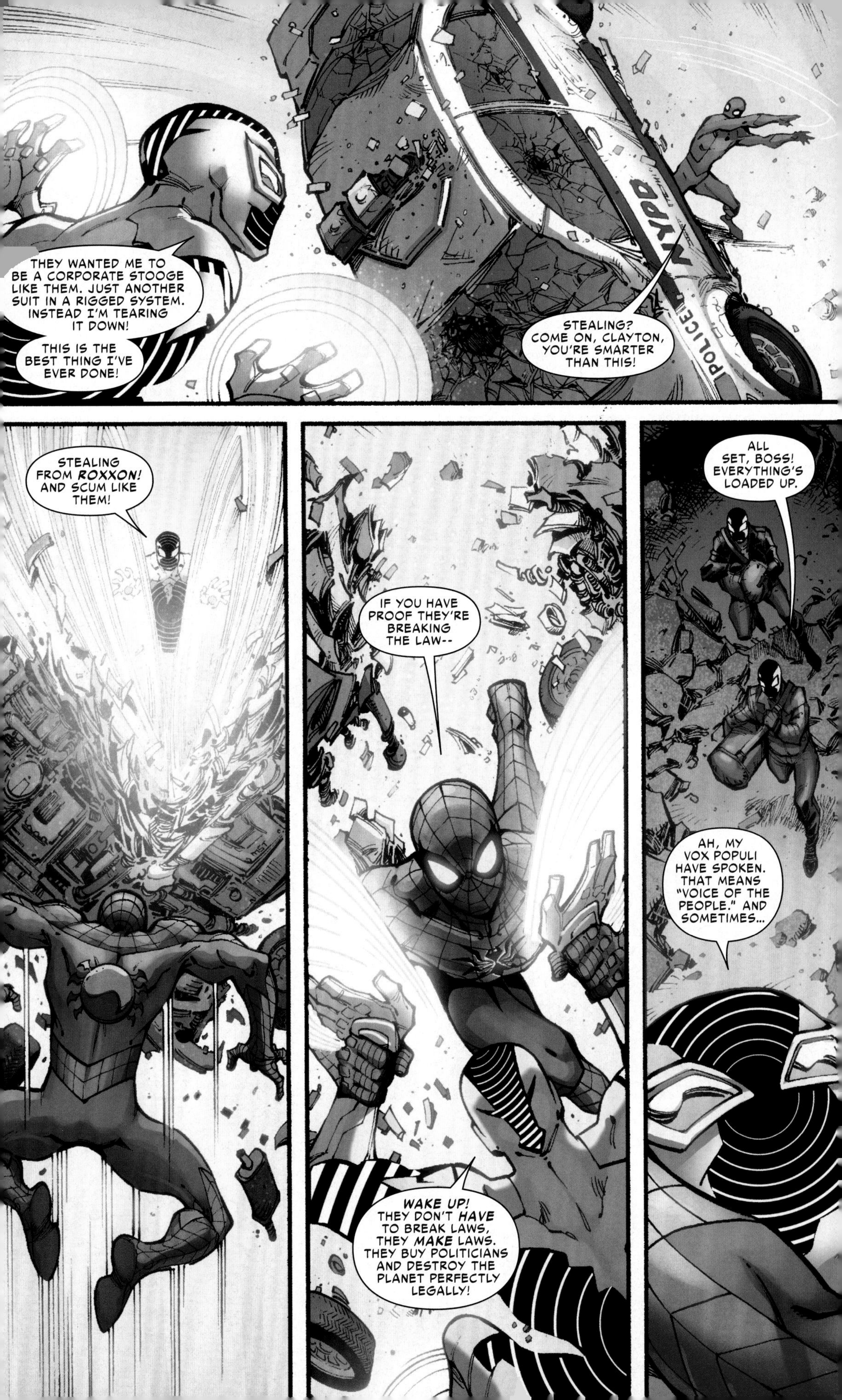
THEY WANTED ME TO BE A CORPORATE STOOGE LIKE THEM. JUST ANOTHER SUIT IN A RIGGED SYSTEM. INSTEAD I'M TEARING IT DOWN!
THIS IS THE BEST THING I'VE EVER DONE!
NYPD
POLICE
STEALING? COME ON, CLAYTON, YOU'RE SMARTER THAN THIS!
STEALING FROM ROXXON! AND SCUM LIKE THEM!
IF YOU HAVE PROOF THEY'RE BREAKING THE LAW--
WAKE UP! THEY DON'T HAVE TO BREAK LAWS, THEY MAKE LAWS. THEY BUY POLITICIANS AND DESTROY THE PLANET PERFECTLY LEGALLY!
ALL SET, BOSS! EVERYTHING'S LOADED UP.
AH, MY VOX POPULI HAVE SPOKEN. THAT MEANS "VOICE OF THE PEOPLE." AND SOMETIMES...

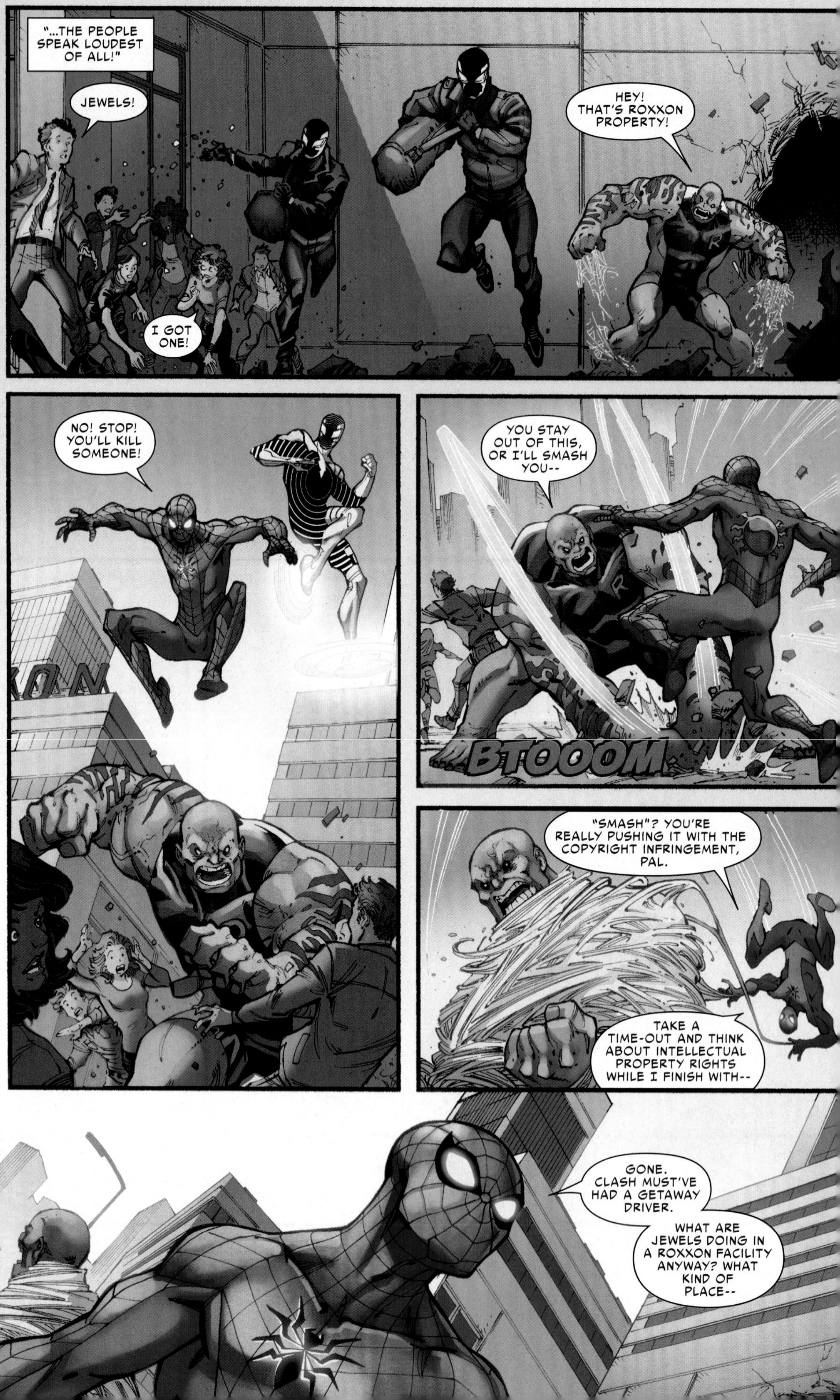
"...THE PEOPLE SPEAK LOUDEST OF ALL!"
JEWELS!
I GOT ONE!
HEY! THAT'S ROXXON PROPERTY!
NO! STOP! YOU'LL KILL SOMEONE!
YOU STAY OUT OF THIS, OR I'LL SMASH YOU--
BTOOOM
"SMASH"? YOU'RE REALLY PUSHING IT WITH THE COPYRIGHT INFRINGEMENT, PAL.
TAKE A TIME-OUT AND THINK ABOUT INTELLECTUAL PROPERTY RIGHTS WHILE I FINISH WITH--
GONE. CLASH MUST'VE HAD A GETAWAY DRIVER.
WHAT ARE JEWELS DOING IN A ROXXON FACILITY ANYWAY? WHAT KIND OF PLACE--

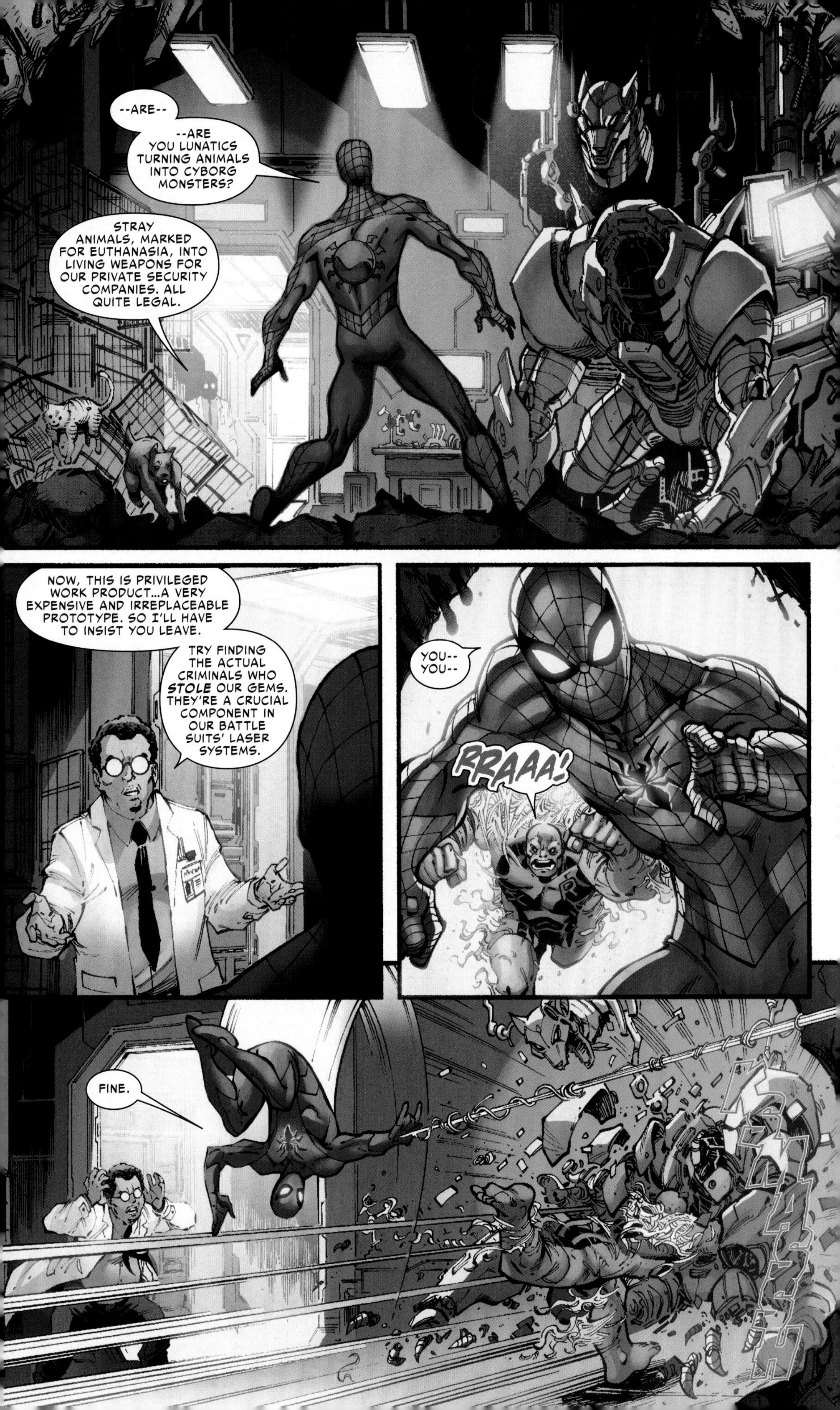

--ARE--
--ARE YOU LUNATICS TURNING ANIMALS INTO CYBORG MONSTERS?
STRAY ANIMALS, MARKED FOR EUTHANASIA, INTO LIVING WEAPONS FOR OUR PRIVATE SECURITY COMPANIES. ALL QUITE LEGAL.
NOW, THIS IS PRIVILEGED WORK PRODUCT...A VERY EXPENSIVE AND IRREPLACEABLE PROTOTYPE. SO I'LL HAVE TO INSIST YOU LEAVE.
TRY FINDING THE ACTUAL CRIMINALS WHO STOLE OUR GEMS. THEY'RE A CRUCIAL COMPONENT IN OUR BATTLE SUITS' LASER SYSTEMS.
YOU-- YOU--
RRAAA!
FINE.

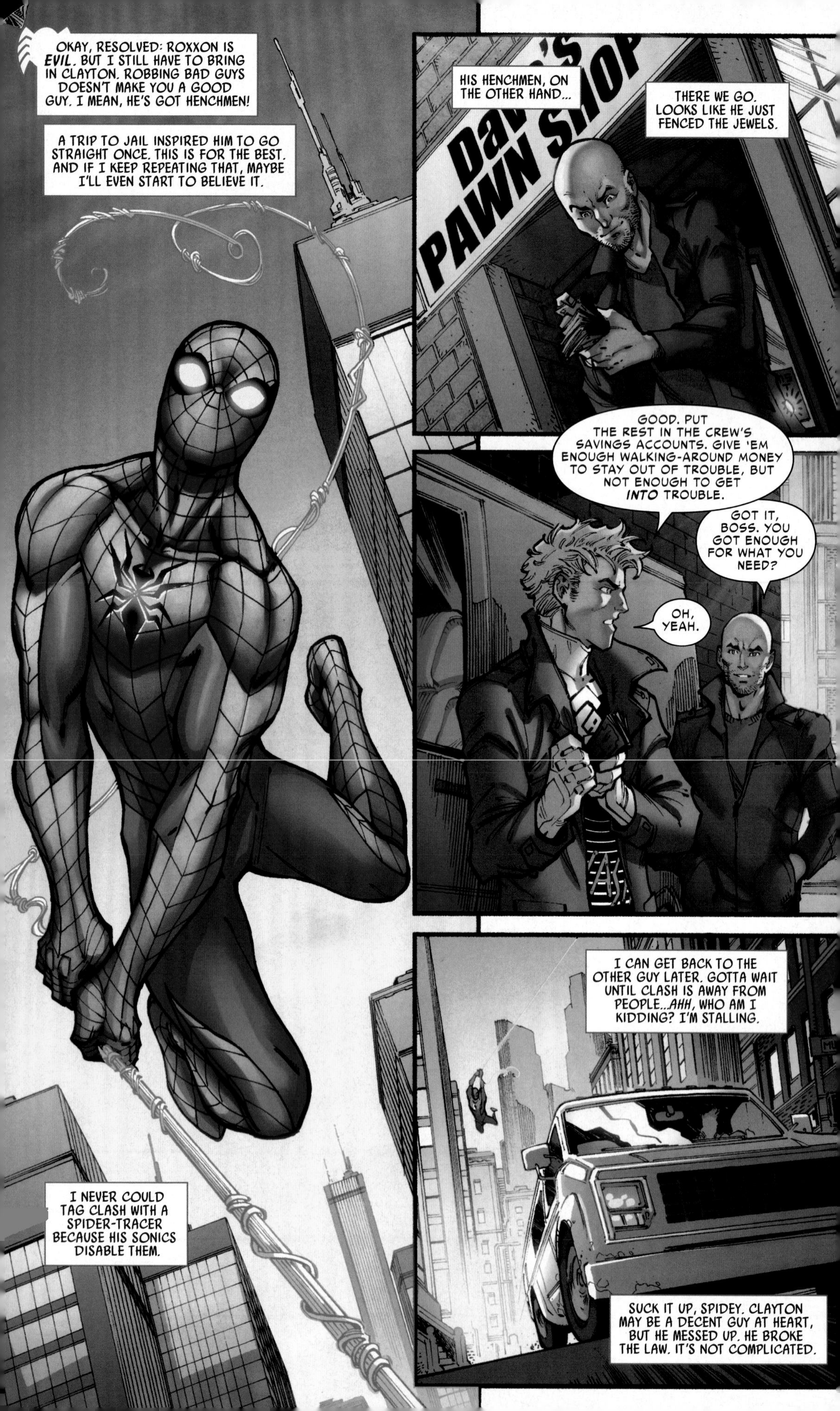
OKAY, RESOLVED: ROXXON IS EVIL. BUT I STILL HAVE TO BRING IN CLAYTON. ROBBING BAD GUYS DOESN'T MAKE YOU A GOOD GUY. I MEAN, HE'S GOT HENCHMEN!
A TRIP TO JAIL INSPIRED HIM TO GO STRAIGHT ONCE. THIS IS FOR THE BEST. AND IF I KEEP REPEATING THAT, MAYBE I'LL EVEN START TO BELIEVE IT.
I NEVER COULD TAG CLASH WITH A SPIDER-TRACER BECAUSE HIS SONICS DISABLE THEM.
HIS HENCHMEN, ON THE OTHER HAND...
THERE WE GO. LOOKS LIKE HE JUST FENCED THE JEWELS.
PAWN SHOP
GOOD. PUT THE REST IN THE CREW'S SAVINGS ACCOUNTS. GIVE 'EM ENOUGH WALKING-AROUND MONEY TO STAY OUT OF TROUBLE, BUT NOT ENOUGH TO GET INTO TROUBLE.
GOT IT, BOSS. YOU GOT ENOUGH FOR WHAT YOU NEED?
OH, YEAH.
I CAN GET BACK TO THE OTHER GUY LATER. GOTTA WAIT UNTIL CLASH IS AWAY FROM PEOPLE...AHH, WHO AM I KIDDING? I'M STALLING.
SUCK IT UP, SPIDEY. CLAYTON MAY BE A DECENT GUY AT HEART, BUT HE MESSED UP. HE BROKE THE LAW. IT'S NOT COMPLICATED.

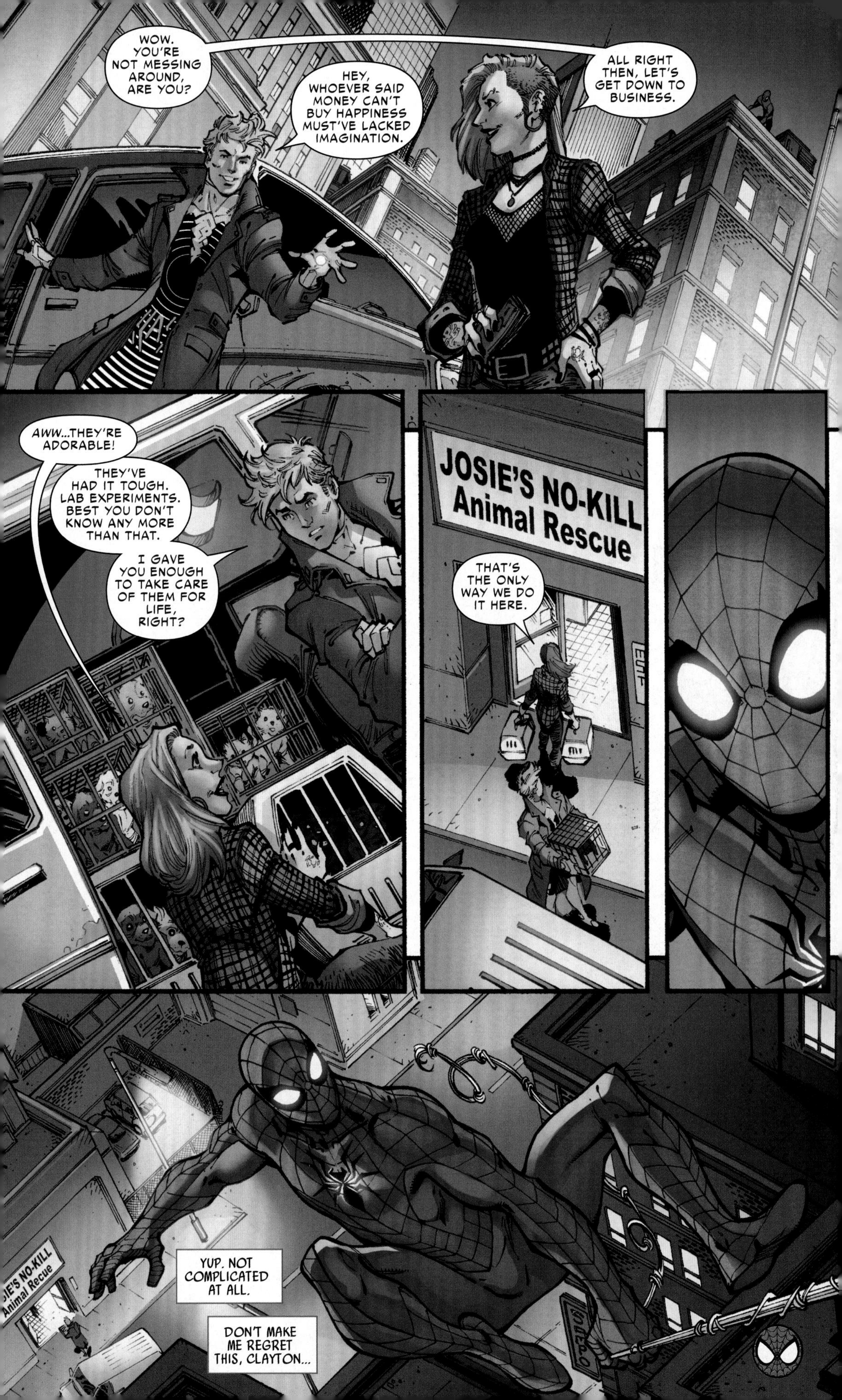
WOW. YOU'RE NOT MESSING AROUND, ARE YOU?
HEY, WHOEVER SAID MONEY CAN'T BUY HAPPINESS MUST'VE LACKED IMAGINATION.
ALL RIGHT THEN, LET'S GET DOWN TO BUSINESS.
AWW...THEY'RE ADORABLE!
THEY'VE HAD IT TOUGH. LAB EXPERIMENTS. BEST YOU DON'T KNOW ANY MORE THAN THAT.
I GAVE YOU ENOUGH TO TAKE CARE OF THEM FOR LIFE, RIGHT?
JOSIE'S NO-KILL Animal Rescue
THAT'S THE ONLY WAY WE DO IT HERE.
YUP. NOT COMPLICATED AT ALL.
DON'T MAKE ME REGRET THIS, CLAYTON...

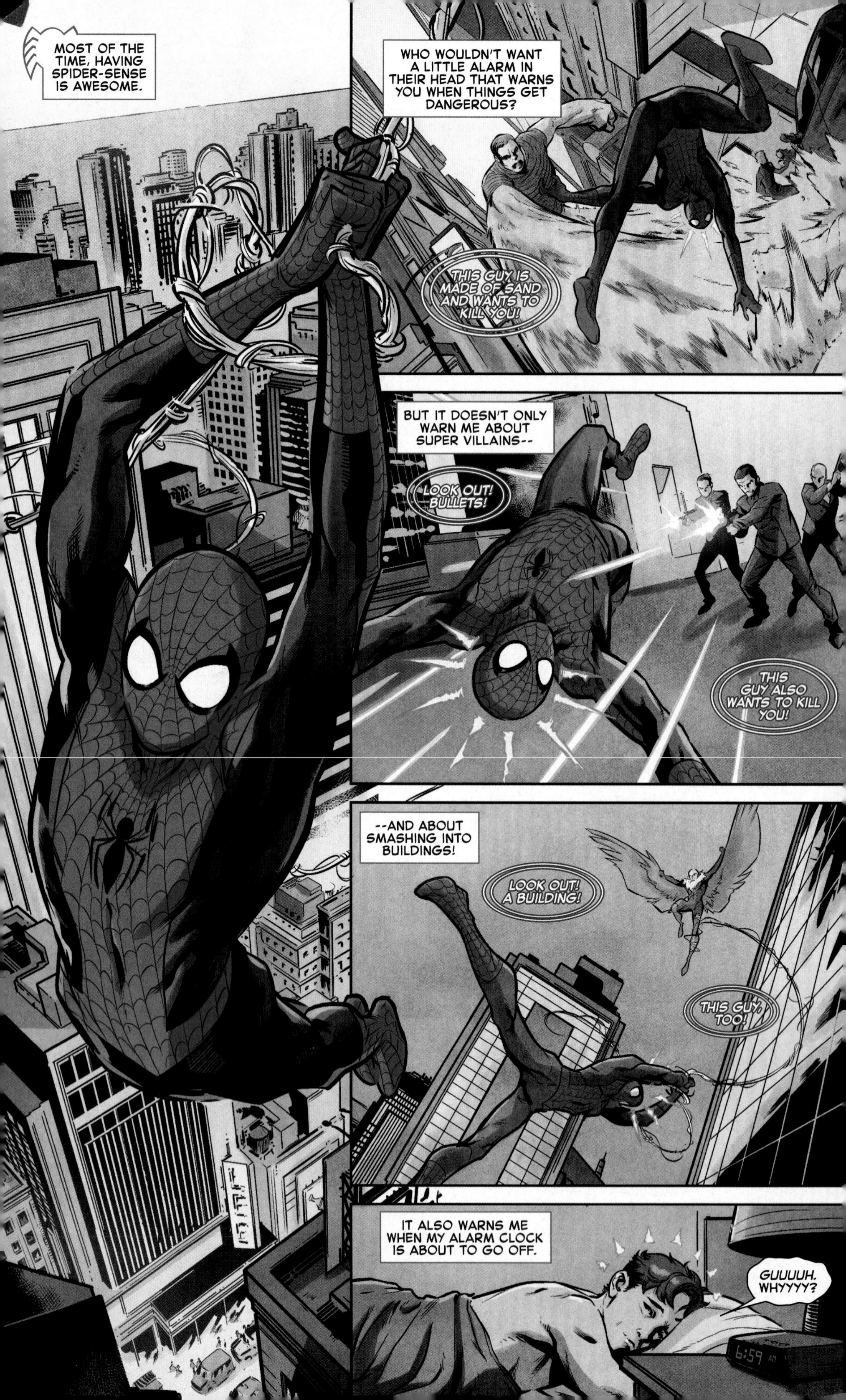
MOST OF THE TIME, HAVING SPIDER-SENSE IS AWESOME.
WHO WOULDN'T WANT A LITTLE ALARM IN THEIR HEAD THAT WARNS YOU WHEN THINGS GET DANGEROUS?
THIS GUY IS MADE OF SAND AND WANTS TO KILL YOU!
BUT IT DOESN'T ONLY WARN ME ABOUT SUPER VILLAINS--
LOOK OUT! BULLETS!
THIS GUY ALSO WANTS TO KILL YOU!
--AND ABOUT SMASHING INTO BUILDINGS!
LOOK OUT! A BUILDING!
THIS GUY, TOO!
IT ALSO WARNS ME WHEN MY ALARM CLOCK IS ABOUT TO GO OFF.
GUUUUH. WHYYYY?
6:59 AM

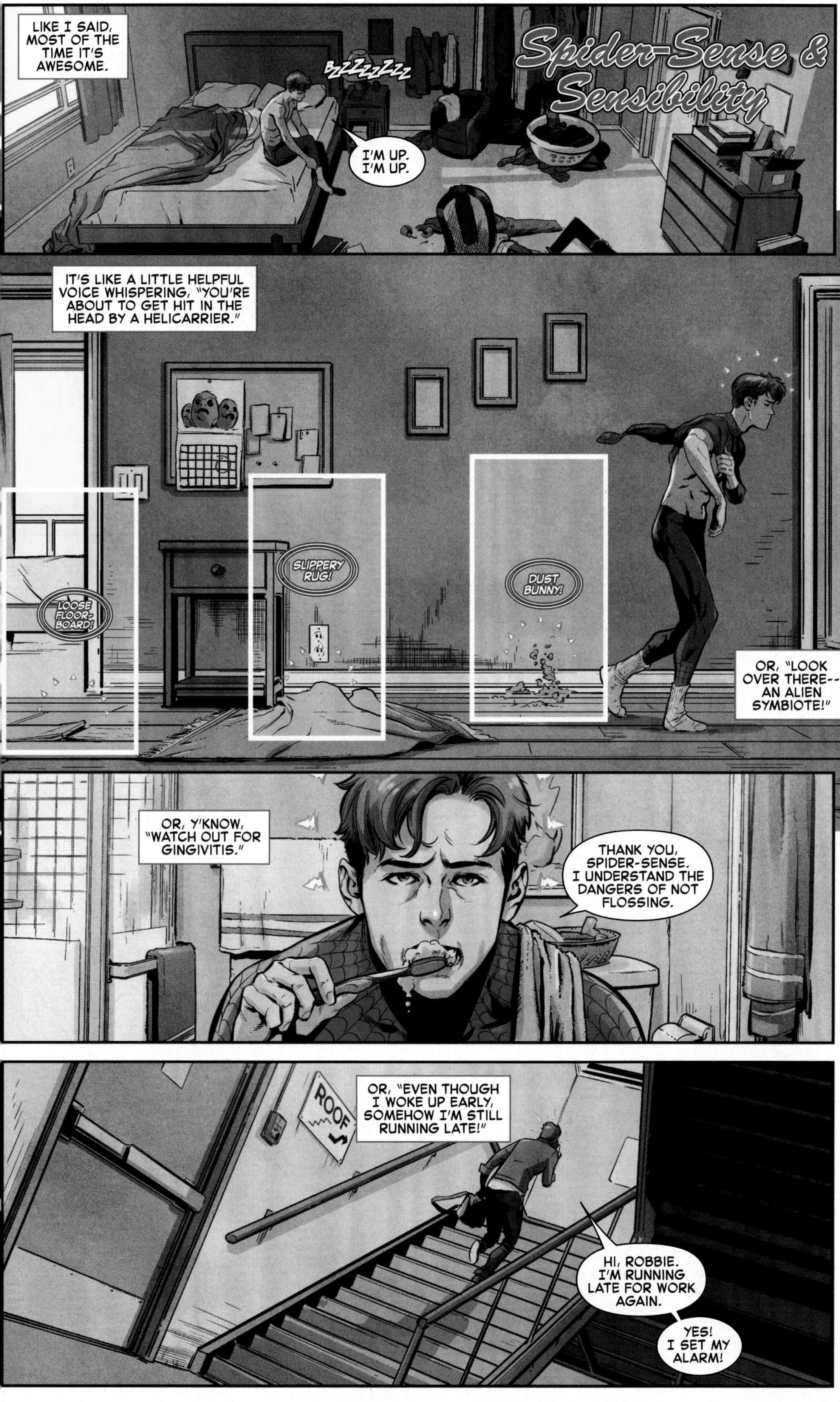

LIKE I SAID, MOST OF THE TIME IT'S AWESOME.
BZZZZZZZZ
Spider-Sense & Sensibility
I'M UP. I'M UP.
IT'S LIKE A LITTLE HELPFUL VOICE WHISPERING, "YOU'RE ABOUT TO GET HIT IN THE HEAD BY A HELICARRIER."
LOOSE FLOOR-BOARD!
SLIPPERY RUG!
DUST BUNNY!
OR, "LOOK OVER THERE--AN ALIEN SYMBIOTE!"
OR, Y'KNOW, "WATCH OUT FOR GINGIVITIS."
THANK YOU, SPIDER-SENSE. I UNDERSTAND THE DANGERS OF NOT FLOSSING.
ROOF
OR, "EVEN THOUGH I WOKE UP EARLY, SOMEHOW I'M STILL RUNNING LATE!"
HI, ROBBIE. I'M RUNNING LATE FOR WORK AGAIN.
YES! I SET MY ALARM!

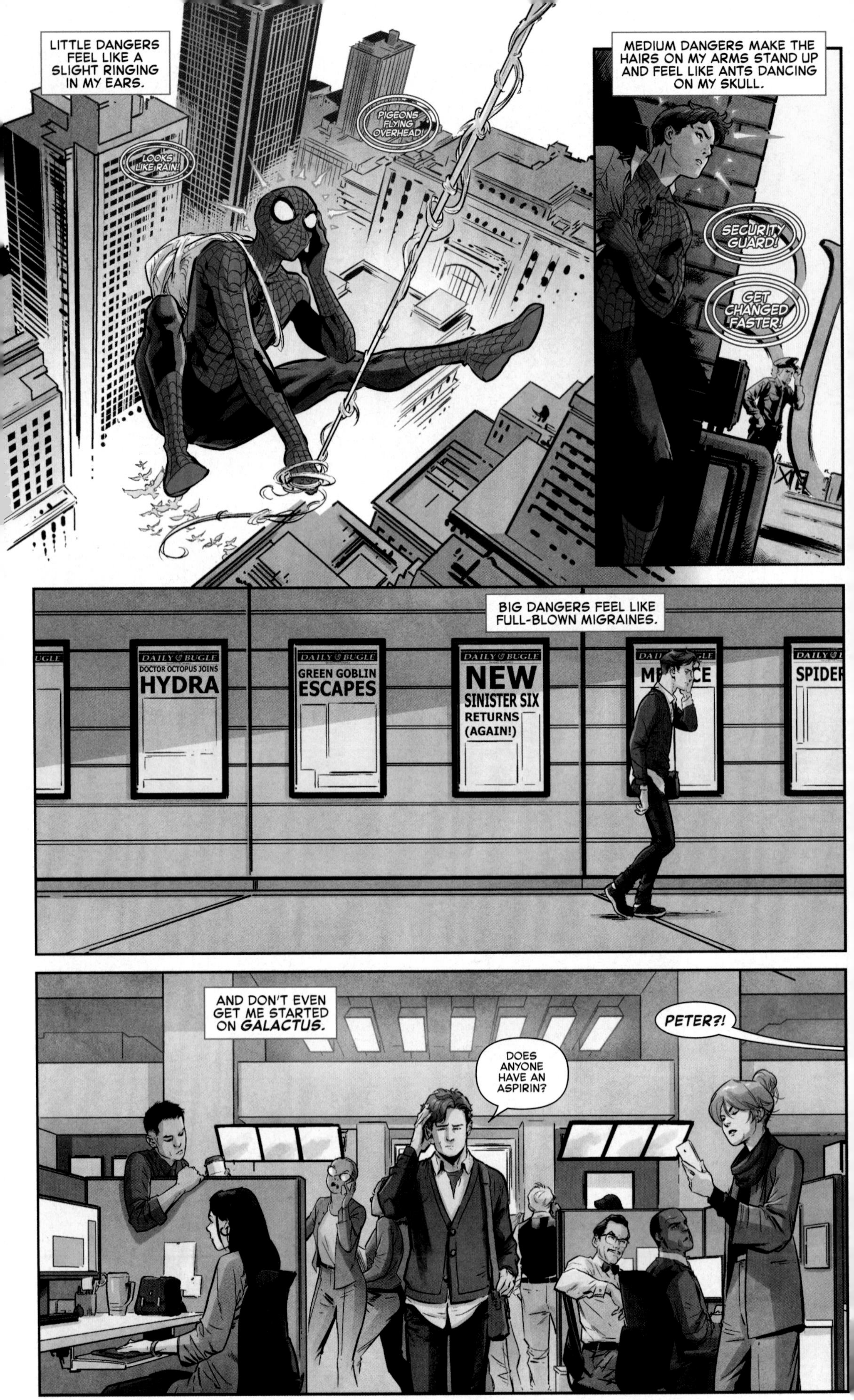
LITTLE DANGERS FEEL LIKE A SLIGHT RINGING IN MY EARS.
LOOKS LIKE RAIN!
PIGEONS FLYING OVERHEAD!
MEDIUM DANGERS MAKE THE HAIRS ON MY ARMS STAND UP AND FEEL LIKE ANTS DANCING ON MY SKULL.
SECURITY GUARD!
GET CHANGED FASTER!
BIG DANGERS FEEL LIKE FULL-BLOWN MIGRAINES.
DAILY BUGLE
DOCTOR OCTOPUS JOINS HYDRA
DAILY BUGLE
GREEN GOBLIN ESCAPES
DAILY BUGLE
NEW SINISTER SIX RETURNS (AGAIN!)
SPIDER
AND DON'T EVEN GET ME STARTED ON *GALACTUS*.
PETER?!
DOES ANYONE HAVE AN ASPIRIN?

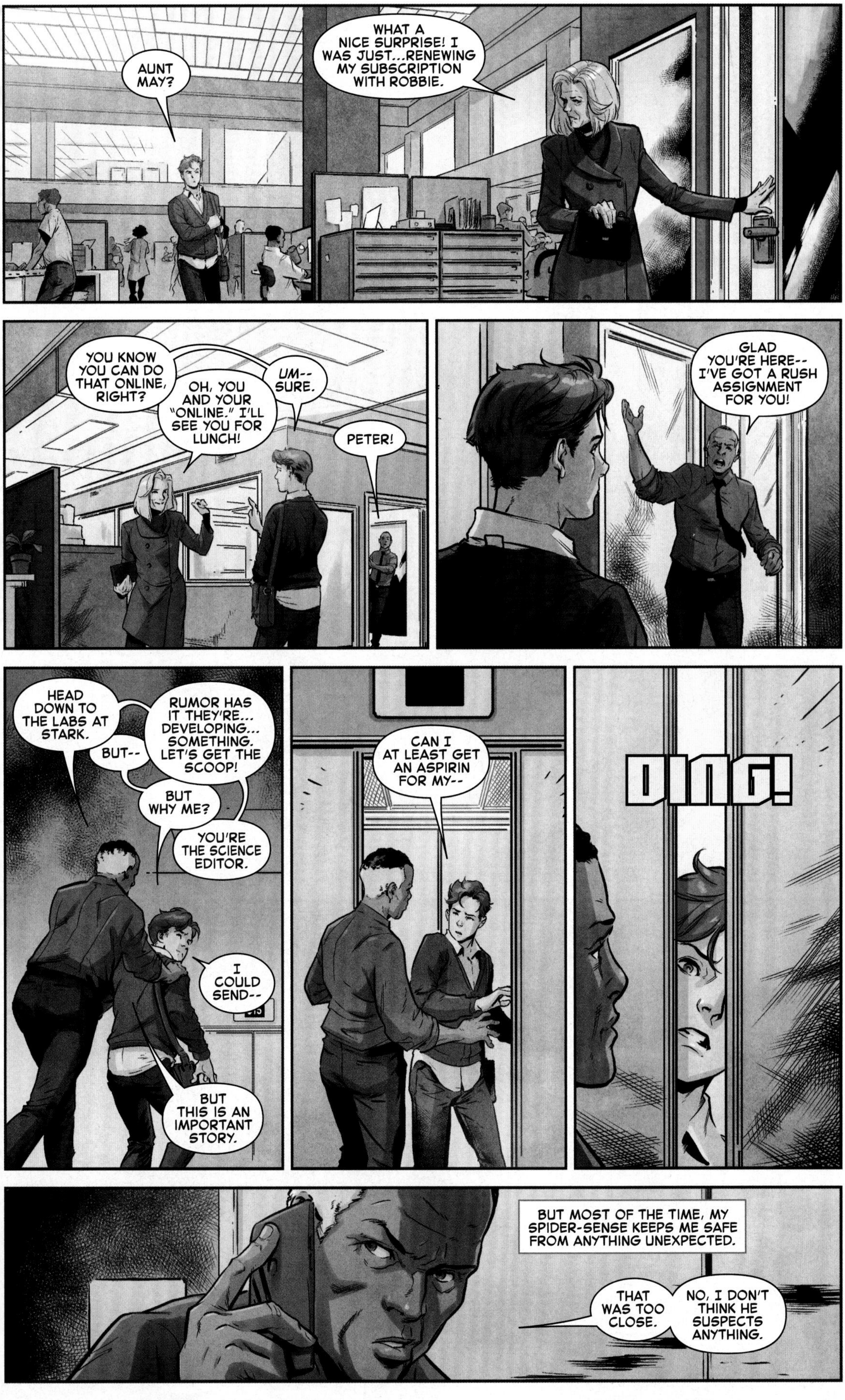
AUNT MAY?
WHAT A NICE SURPRISE! I WAS JUST...RENEWING MY SUBSCRIPTION WITH ROBBIE.
YOU KNOW YOU CAN DO THAT ONLINE, RIGHT?
UM-- SURE.
OH, YOU AND YOUR "ONLINE." I'LL SEE YOU FOR LUNCH!
PETER!
GLAD YOU'RE HERE-- I'VE GOT A RUSH ASSIGNMENT FOR YOU!
HEAD DOWN TO THE LABS AT STARK.
BUT--
RUMOR HAS IT THEY'RE... DEVELOPING... SOMETHING. LET'S GET THE SCOOP!
BUT WHY ME?
YOU'RE THE SCIENCE EDITOR.
I COULD SEND--
BUT THIS IS AN IMPORTANT STORY.
CAN I AT LEAST GET AN ASPIRIN FOR MY--
DING!
BUT MOST OF THE TIME, MY SPIDER-SENSE KEEPS ME SAFE FROM ANYTHING UNEXPECTED.
THAT WAS TOO CLOSE.
NO, I DON'T THINK HE SUSPECTS ANYTHING.

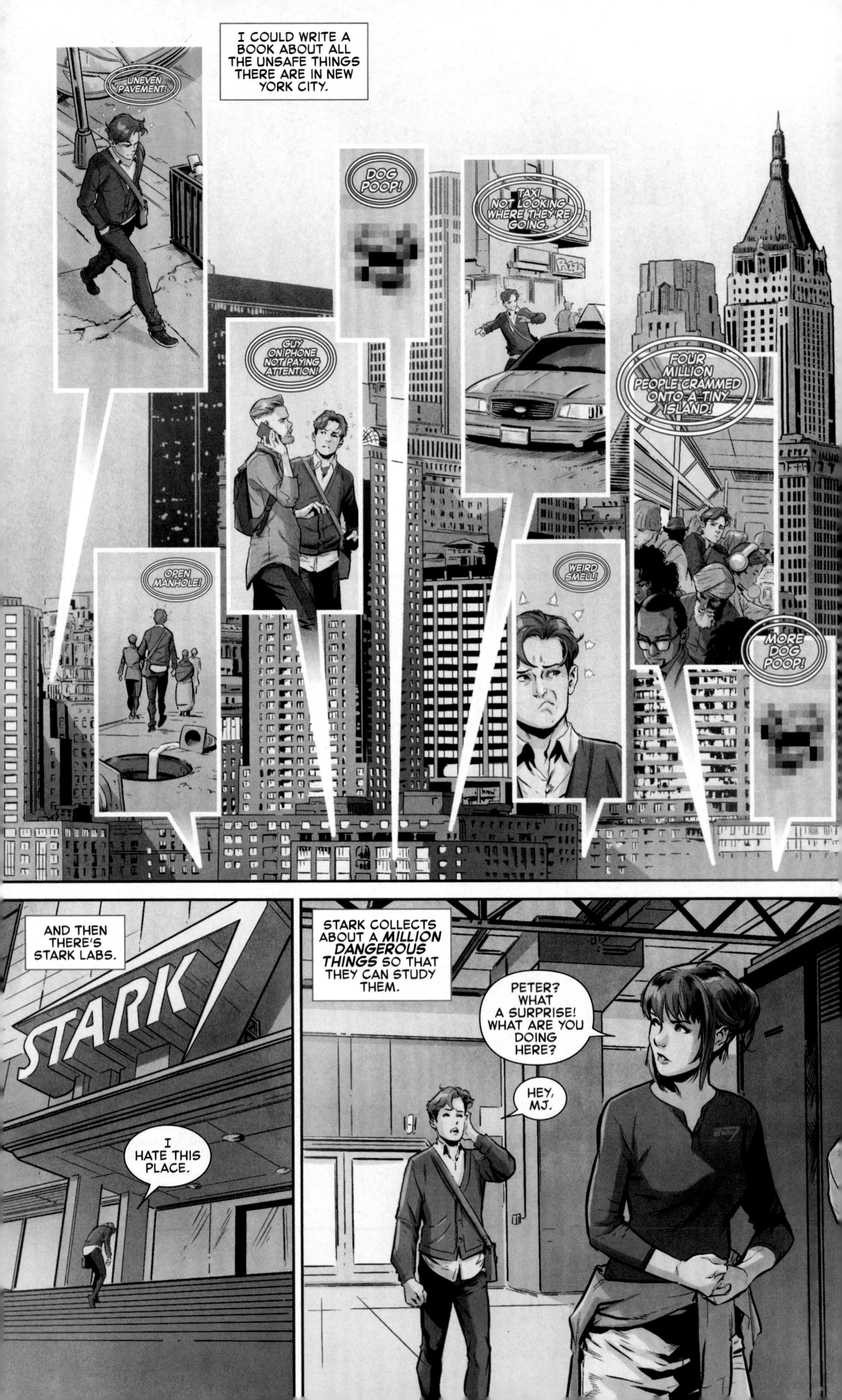

I COULD WRITE A BOOK ABOUT ALL THE UNSAFE THINGS THERE ARE IN NEW YORK CITY.
UNEVEN PAVEMENT!
OPEN MANHOLE!
GUY ON PHONE NOT PAYING ATTENTION!
DOG POOP!
TAXI NOT LOOKING WHERE THEY'RE GOING.
WEIRD SMELL!
FOUR MILLION PEOPLE CRAMMED ONTO A TINY ISLAND!
MORE DOG POOP!
AND THEN THERE'S STARK LABS.
STARK
I HATE THIS PLACE.
STARK COLLECTS ABOUT A MILLION DANGEROUS THINGS SO THAT THEY CAN STUDY THEM.
PETER? WHAT A SURPRISE! WHAT ARE YOU DOING HERE?
HEY, MJ.

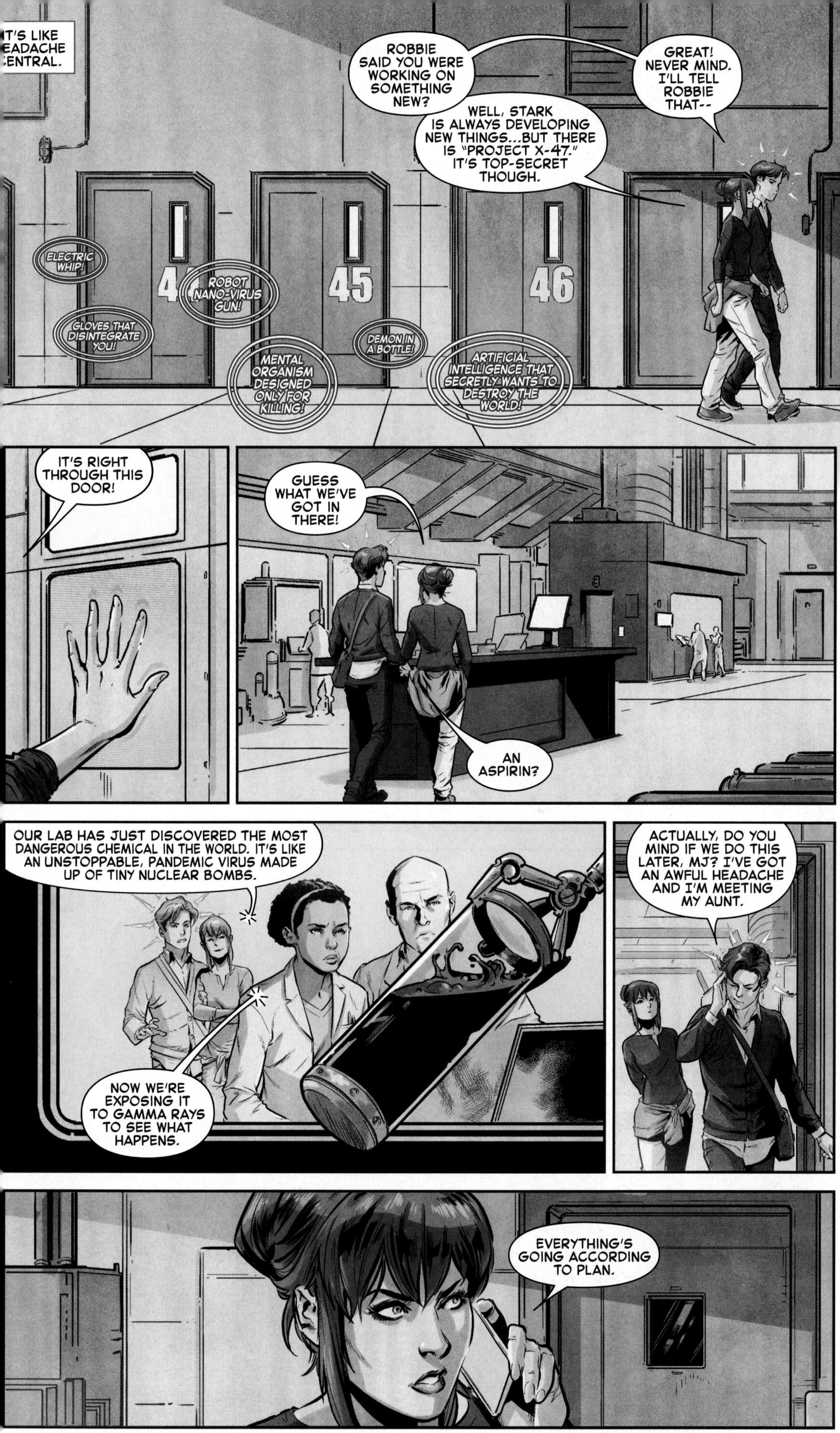

IT'S LIKE
HEADACHE
CENTRAL.
ROBBIE SAID YOU WERE WORKING ON SOMETHING NEW?
GREAT! NEVER MIND. I'LL TELL ROBBIE THAT--
WELL, STARK IS ALWAYS DEVELOPING NEW THINGS...BUT THERE IS "PROJECT X-47." IT'S TOP-SECRET THOUGH.
ELECTRIC WHIP!
GLOVES THAT DISINTEGRATE YOU!
ROBOT NANO-VIRUS GUN!
MENTAL ORGANISM DESIGNED ONLY FOR KILLING!
DEMON IN A BOTTLE!
ARTIFICIAL INTELLIGENCE THAT SECRETLY WANTS TO DESTROY THE WORLD!
45
46
IT'S RIGHT THROUGH THIS DOOR!
GUESS WHAT WE'VE GOT IN THERE!
AN ASPIRIN?
OUR LAB HAS JUST DISCOVERED THE MOST DANGEROUS CHEMICAL IN THE WORLD. IT'S LIKE AN UNSTOPPABLE, PANDEMIC VIRUS MADE UP OF TINY NUCLEAR BOMBS.
NOW WE'RE EXPOSING IT TO GAMMA RAYS TO SEE WHAT HAPPENS.
ACTUALLY, DO YOU MIND IF WE DO THIS LATER, MJ? I'VE GOT AN AWFUL HEADACHE AND I'M MEETING MY AUNT.
EVERYTHING'S GOING ACCORDING TO PLAN.

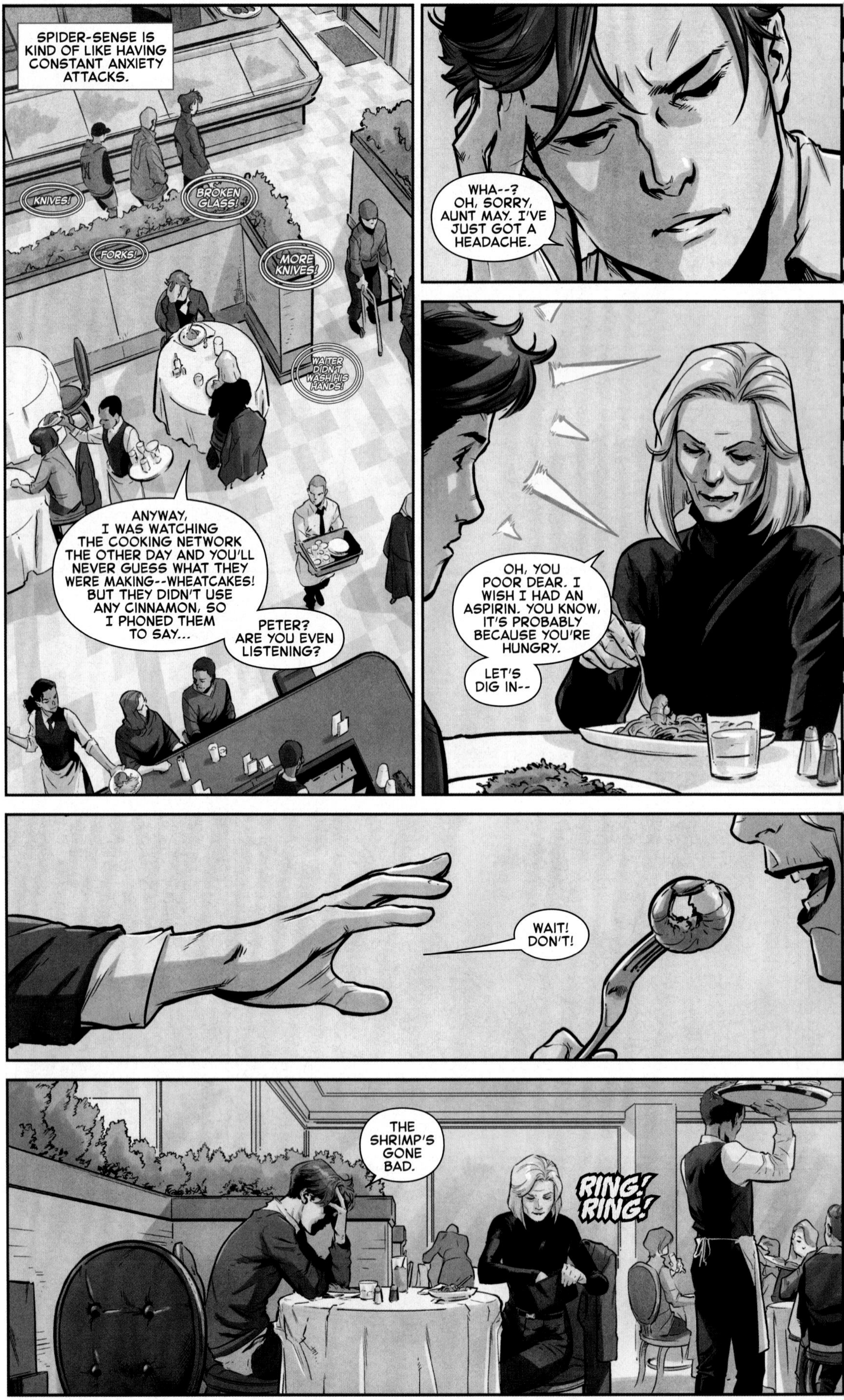
SPIDER-SENSE IS KIND OF LIKE HAVING CONSTANT ANXIETY ATTACKS.
KNIVES!
BROKEN GLASS!
FORKS!
MORE KNIVES!
WAITER DIDN'T WASH HIS HANDS!
ANYWAY, I WAS WATCHING THE COOKING NETWORK THE OTHER DAY AND YOU'LL NEVER GUESS WHAT THEY WERE MAKING--WHEATCAKES! BUT THEY DIDN'T USE ANY CINNAMON, SO I PHONED THEM TO SAY...
PETER? ARE YOU EVEN LISTENING?
WHA--? OH, SORRY, AUNT MAY. I'VE JUST GOT A HEADACHE.
OH, YOU POOR DEAR. I WISH I HAD AN ASPIRIN. YOU KNOW, IT'S PROBABLY BECAUSE YOU'RE HUNGRY.
LET'S DIG IN--
WAIT! DON'T!
THE SHRIMP'S GONE BAD.
RING! RING!

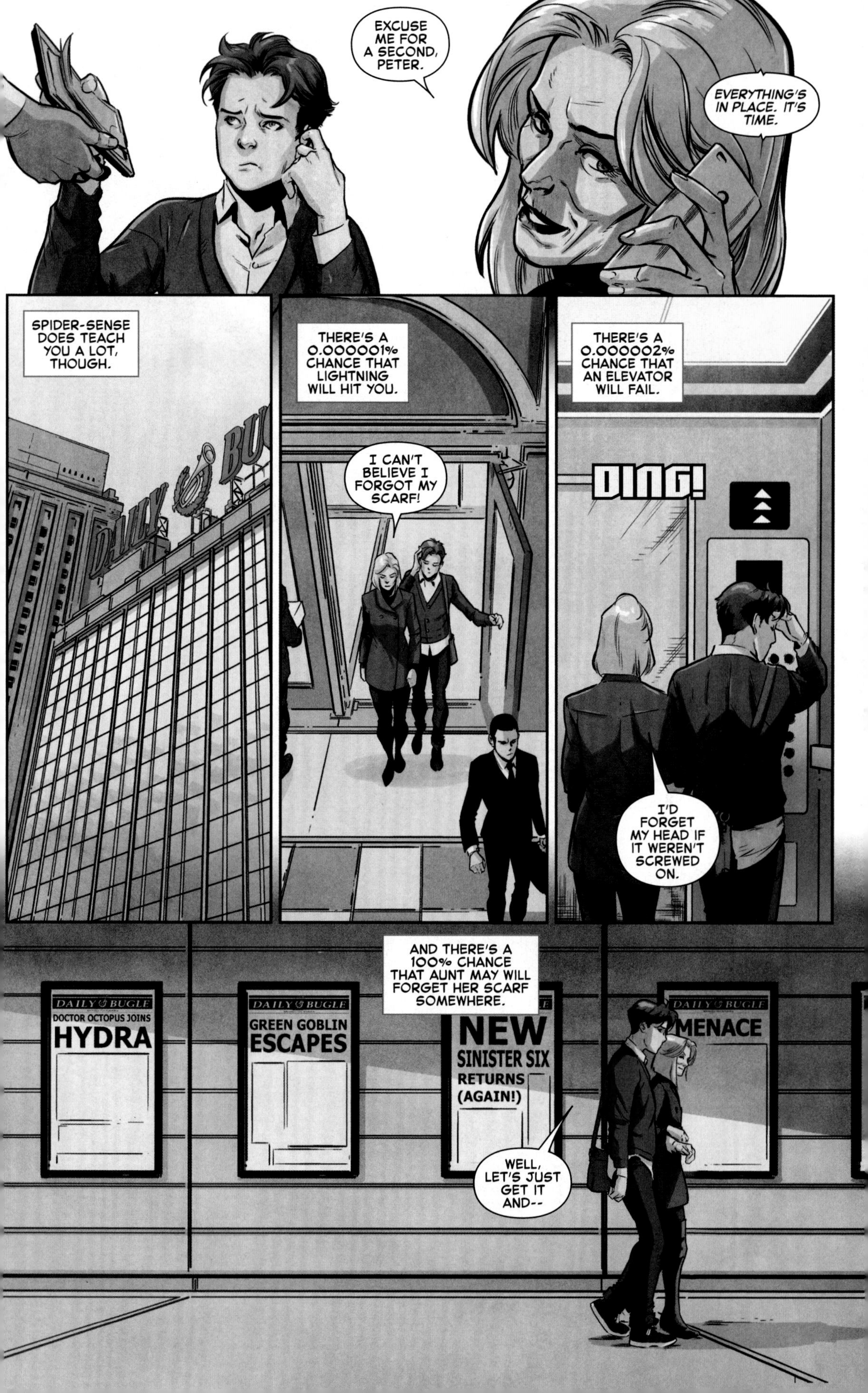

EXCUSE ME FOR A SECOND, PETER.
EVERYTHING'S IN PLACE. IT'S TIME.
SPIDER-SENSE DOES TEACH YOU A LOT, THOUGH.
DAILY BUGLE
THERE'S A 0.000001% CHANCE THAT LIGHTNING WILL HIT YOU.
I CAN'T BELIEVE I FORGOT MY SCARF!
THERE'S A 0.000002% CHANCE THAT AN ELEVATOR WILL FAIL.
DING!
I'D FORGET MY HEAD IF IT WEREN'T SCREWED ON.
AND THERE'S A 100% CHANCE THAT AUNT MAY WILL FORGET HER SCARF SOMEWHERE.
DAILY BUGLE
DOCTOR OCTOPUS JOINS HYDRA
DAILY BUGLE
GREEN GOBLIN ESCAPES
NEW SINISTER SIX RETURNS (AGAIN!)
DAILY BUGLE
MENACE
WELL, LET'S JUST GET IT AND--

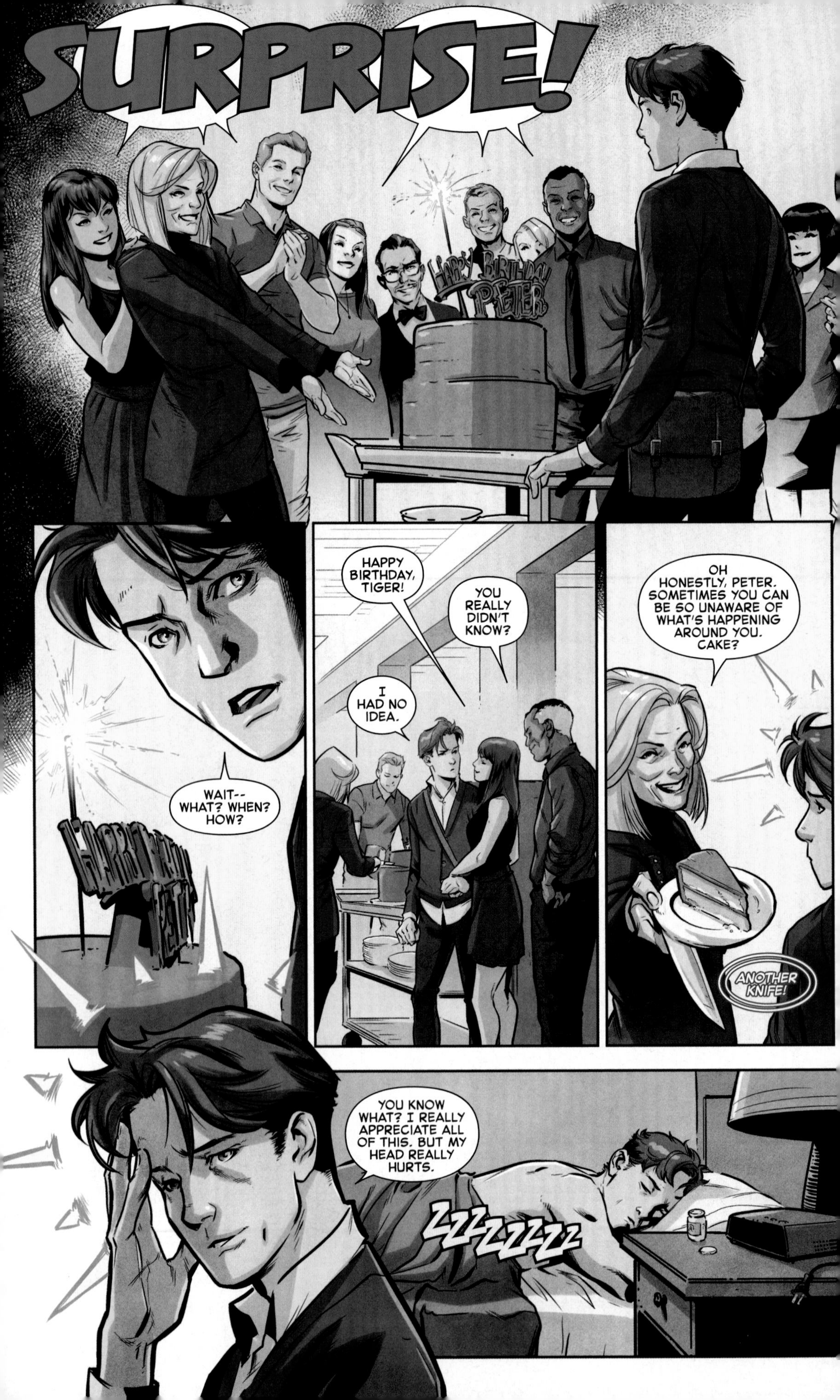
SURPRISE!
HAPPY BIRTHDAY PETER
WAIT-- WHAT? WHEN? HOW?
HAPPY BIRTHDAY, TIGER!
YOU REALLY DIDN'T KNOW?
I HAD NO IDEA.
OH HONESTLY, PETER. SOMETIMES YOU CAN BE SO UNAWARE OF WHAT'S HAPPENING AROUND YOU. CAKE?
ANOTHER KNIFE!
YOU KNOW WHAT? I REALLY APPRECIATE ALL OF THIS. BUT MY HEAD REALLY HURTS.
ZZZZZZZZ

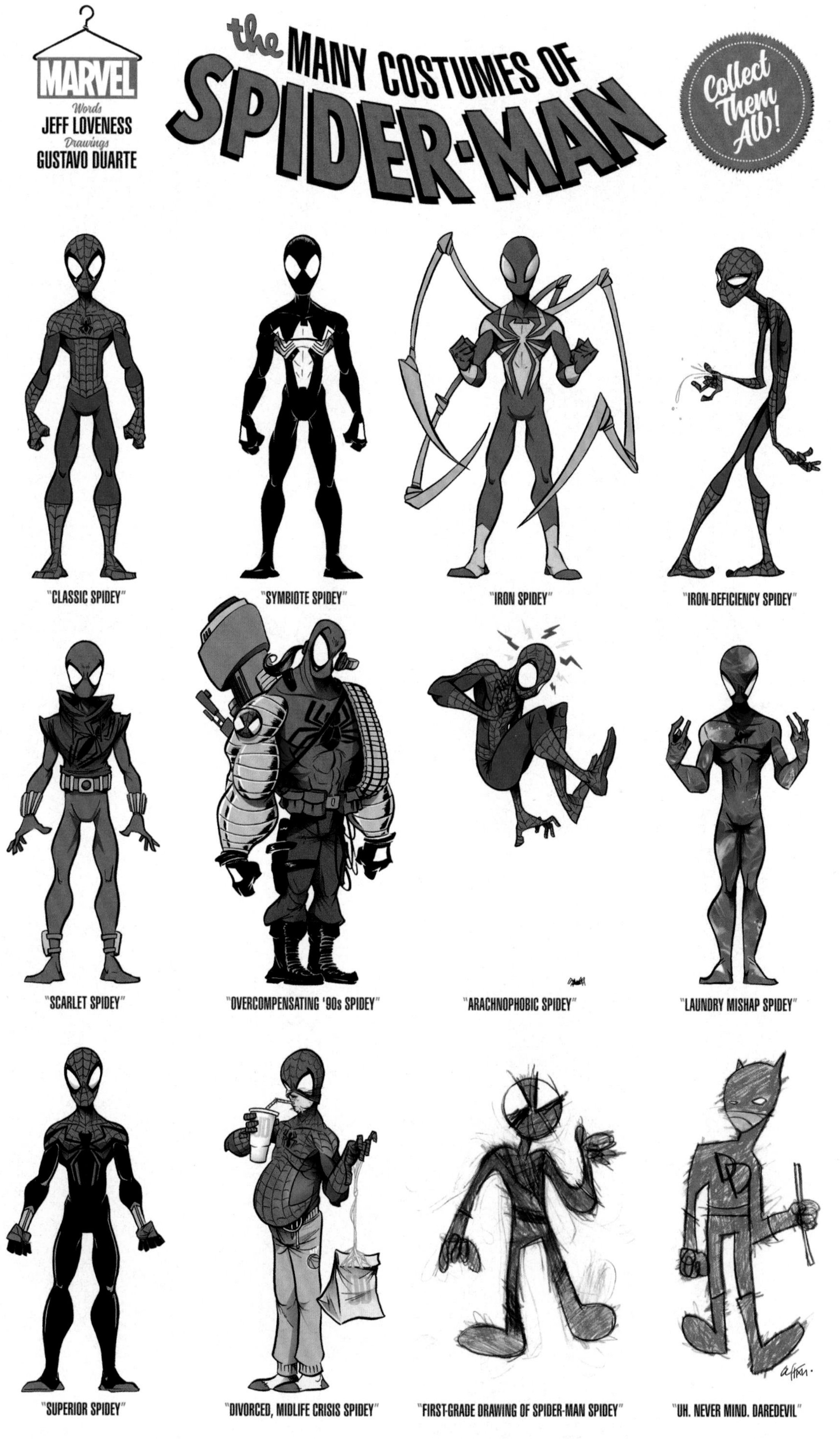

MARVEL
Words
JEFF LOVENESS
Drawings
GUSTAVO DUARTE
the MANY COSTUMES OF
SPIDER-MAN
Collect Them All!
"CLASSIC SPIDEY"
"SYMBIOTE SPIDEY"
"IRON SPIDEY"
"IRON-DEFICIENCY SPIDEY"
"SCARLET SPIDEY"
"OVERCOMPENSATING '90s SPIDEY"
"ARACHNOPHOBIC SPIDEY"
"LAUNDRY MISHAP SPIDEY"
"SUPERIOR SPIDEY"
"DIVORCED, MIDLIFE CRISIS SPIDEY"
"FIRST-GRADE DRAWING OF SPIDER-MAN SPIDEY"
"UH. NEVER MIND. DAREDEVIL"

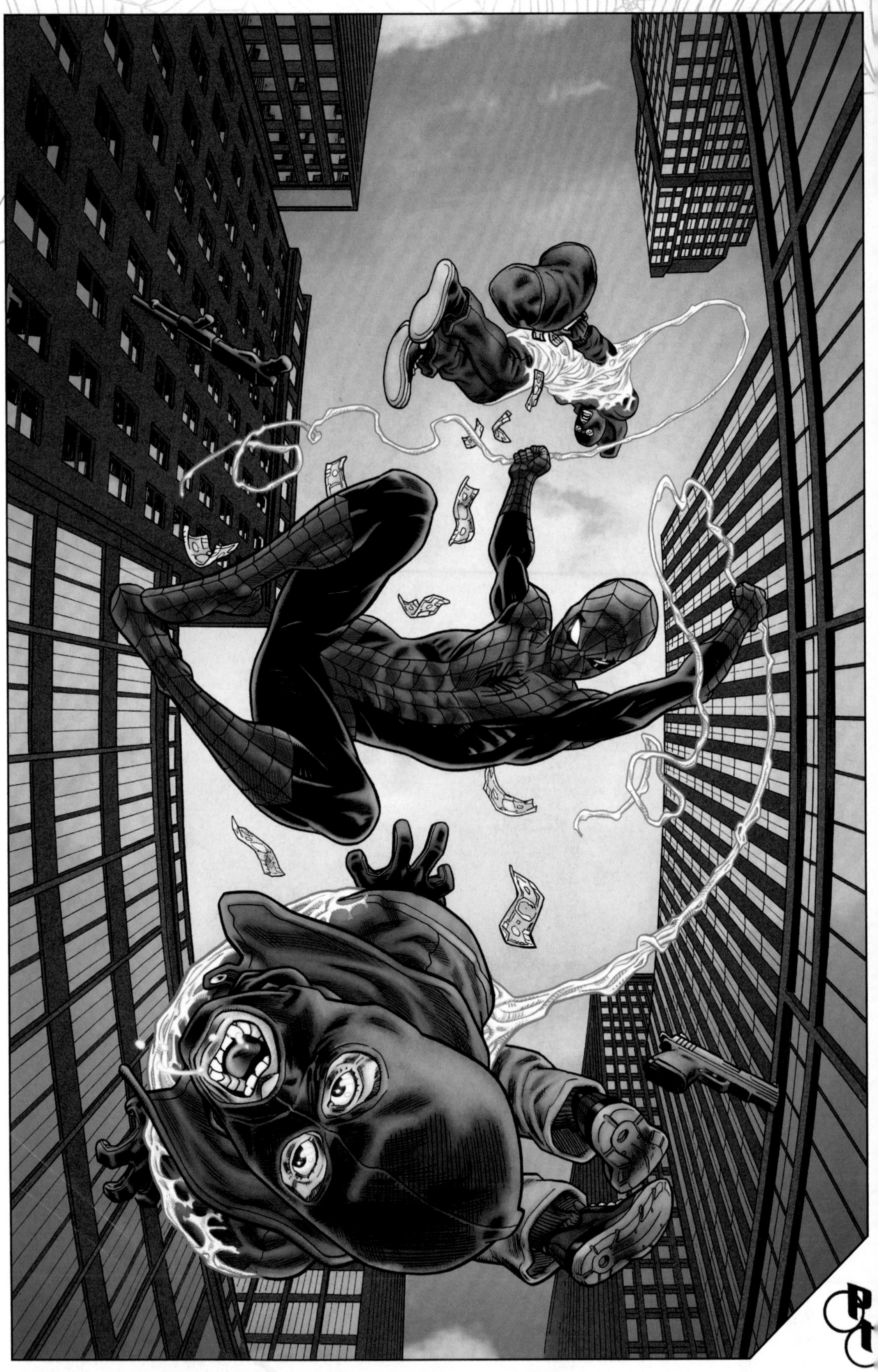

ANNUAL #42 VARIANT BY **MIKE HAWTHORNE & MORRY HOLLOWELL**